Buffalo

Buffalo

EDITED BY JOHN E. FOSTER, DICK HARRISON, I.S. MacLaren

ALBERTA NATURE AND CULTURE SERIES

John E. Foster and Dick Harrison
General Editors

THE UNIVERSITY OF ALBERTA PRESS

The University of Alberta Press
Athabasca Hall
Edmonton, Alberta
Canada T6G 2E8

Copyright © The University of Alberta Press 1992

ISBN 0-88864-237-7

The essays in this volume appeared simultaneously in *Alberta: Studies in the Arts and Sciences* 3:1.

Canadian Cataloguing in Publication Data

Main entry under title:
  Buffalo

  (Alberta nature and culture series)
  ISBN 0-88864-237-7

  1. Bison, American. I. Foster, John Elgin.
II. Harrison, Dick, 1937–   III. MacLaren, I.S.,
1951–   V. Series.
QL737.U53B83 1992   599.73'58   C92-091174-9

ACKNOWLEDGEMENTS
Our gratitude to the University of Alberta and the Historical Resources Division of the Alberta Department of Culture and Multiculturalism for their financial support and to the University/Community Special Projects Fund of the University of Alberta for a grant to enhance this project. The Alberta Foundation for the Arts provided funds towards publication. For permission to use the photographs in this book, the editors wish to thank the Amon Carter Museum (Texas), Archaeological Survey of Alberta, Bruce Peel Special Collections Library (Javitch Collection), Clarence Tillenius, Johnny Hart and Creators Syndicate, Inc., Manitoba Museum of Man and Nature, Mr and Mrs Friesen, Mr and Mrs Henderson, National Archives of Canada, National Gallery of Canada, North American Life Assurance Company, Penny Morris Photo, Provincial Archives of Manitoba, Robert R. Taylor Photo, Robert Stacey, Royal Ontario Museum, Stark Museum of Art (Texas), University of Alberta Archives, and Wood Bison Recovery Team.

Cover illustration
Clarence Tillenius, *Before the White Man Came*. Oil on canvas. (Courtesy the artist)

Title page illustration
W. Rowan, Buffalo Head, 1925? Graphite on paper. (Courtesy University of Alberta Archives 69–16)

Typeset by The Typeworks, Vancouver, British Columbia, Canada
Printed by D.W. Friesen & Sons Ltd., Altona, Manitoba, Canada ∞

CONTENTS

Alberta Nature and Culture Series offers informed commentary on Alberta and its people, past and present, and on related national and international issues. It brings together specialists from a range of disciplines in the Arts, Humanities, Social and Natural Sciences with writers and researchers from the wider community. Other titles to appear in the series will include *The Tyrrell Museum of Palaeontology* and *Women in Alberta*.

INTRODUCTION

As the Yellowhead highway curves through Elk Island National Park travellers frequently view buffalo in their several modes. Most often it is a solitary bull, grazing contently by the buffalo-proof fence or reclining splendidly on a shaded hillside, methodically ruminating in the presence of passing traffic. On other occasions gamboling, lighter-hued calves break the inexorable movement of the darker wave of grazing cows as the herds drift purposefully to new pasture. In the absence of the animals themselves, open meadows and park-like woods attest to their presence. Travellers who pause for a few hours to visit a buffalo paddock or to sample the cross-country trails of the park will probably encounter animals at fairly close quarters. It is the bulking size of the animal that initially captures attention. The massive head and hump denote strength and endurance; the size belies the quickness that in an instant can become readily apparent, and on occasion threatening, should an incautious visitor break with buffalo determined decorum. It is in these instances that the animal ceases to be a momentary curiosity, an artifact from our past, and becomes a facet of the world that we inhabit. Its image of strength and endurance coupled with quickness is appropriate in a land that far more frequently challenges its inhabitants with extremes rather than lulls them with moderate alternatives. It is an image of a past (not yet a history for most Albertans) in which the buffalo are juxtaposed with trekking bands of hunters in a series of timeless points of contact which suggest eternal but ill-defined verities. Little more than a century ago the world of the buffalo and the hunter ended. Still the image of the buffalo endures as an icon of the spiritual qualities which many feel the land evokes in its residents. It is fitting that we should celebrate the animal and the icon we have fashioned of it. It is equally appropriate that current threats to the animal's well-being should evoke concerned debate about how to ensure its future. Few will fail to appreciate how intimately the buffalo's fate may mirror our own.

Michael Wilson's article sets the stage for our volume with a history of the animal from the age of continental glaciers to the time of the species' recent past. With a broad awareness of the recent writing in his field, Wilson integrates his history with interpretive debate. In guiding the reader through this maze Wilson clearly and insightfully indicates his own assessment and suggests the emergence of a consensus which may well bear on the current question of whether woods and plains buffalo constitute separate subspecies or are merely regional variants of the same species.

Jack Brink examines the history of the Head-Smashed-In-Buffalo Jump project in terms of its significance to particular interests. The United Nations has declared HSI to be a world cultural site, a location of cultural importance to all heritages. Yet it is equally apparent that the Peigan Indians of the Blackfoot Confederacy have a particular interest in, and relevance to, the site. The process of working out a project and program that would acknowledge the importance and contribution of the museum tradition of the majority community with the religio-cultural traditions of the Peigan was a significant challenge for both parties. The results speak well for the character and intelligence of those involved. For the visitor to the site the results provide an experience that not only relates to the animal but, equally important, relates to the different human perspectives on the animal in the context of the HSI buffalo jump.

Ed Sponholz provides details on the programs and displays at the HSI Interpretive Centre. Critically important in the success of HSI is the extent to which the use of the site permits the expression of the museum interest and the religio-cultural interest. The architecture of the building as well as the surrounding pathways have structured site displays to emphasize both traditions. The active participation of native peoples whose cultural roots are linked closely with events that transpired at the site is a decided strength in the display program. Equally important is the opportunity for visitors to observe the process of archaeology and the handling of evidence to be used in determining interpretive conclusions. Sponholz provides the detail that strengthens further our appreciation of the process of balancing cultural interests.

John Foster observes a particular aspect of the historical extinction of the buffalo in Western Canada. As with many aspects of Western Canadian history, previous explanation for the extinction of the plains buffalo has been borrowed from the American experience. Foster suggests a network of causation related, but distinct from, the experience south of the forty-ninth. In the Canadian West causation focuses on native peoples and the factors that influenced their choices. Such a focus strongly suggests significant cultural change on the part of many native people in the generation preceding the demise of the buffalo. The story of the extinction begs comparison with the behaviour of Albertans and the diminution of conventional sources of crude oil, both in terms of similarities and differences. Thankfully over the past century buffalo have proved to be a renewable, if threatened, resource.

Ian MacLaren's essay places Clarence Tillenius's buffalo paintings in the context of the history of verbal and visual representations of the animal. Thoroughly if not exhaustively MacLaren traces the evolution of the images of the buffalo. The art reflects as much the coming to terms with the land and its nature as it does the improved portrayal of the buffalo in its many guises, culminating today in the work of Clarence Tillenius. MacLaren's choices of paintings and sketches provide the reader with a plethora of visual experiences. Tillenius's work deserves better than the limited format of a printed page. But MacLaren's selections and commentary attest to the richness of the experience encountered in pursuing these expressions.

Clarence Tillenius's experiences as a painter of wildlife have been many and varied. Those involving the buffalo are the subject of his essay. It is through the eye of the artist and the questions that he poses to his talent that the reader gains an appreciation both of the animal and of the artist's insight and understanding. Tillenius's adoration of the buffalo unfolds with a naturalness which is as enchanting as it is illuminating. The reader shares the events in the artist's life which furthered his appreciation and understanding of this behemoth of the midcontinent plains. Tillenius's words as well as his paintings underline the value of the artist in perceiving and comprehending aspects and essences of our world.

The buffalo in Wood Buffalo National Park and the surrounding area are a focal concern in a number of articles in this issue. Cormack

Gates, Tom Chowns and Hal Reynolds provide an historical view of
the buffalo associated with WBNP. They trace the history of the
animal from the perhaps well intentioned but now clearly ill-advised
decision to transport "plains" buffalo from the Wainwright preserve
to WBNP. It is this move which is apparently responsible in significant part for the problem of diseases in some of the northern herds.
As well it is possible that this move may be responsible for altering
the genotype of the species. On this question, however, debate continues as to whether plains and wood buffalo constitute distinct
subspecies or whether they are but regional variants of the same
population. In the account of the three authors it is apparent that the
history of the animal since the "prairie extinction" has been event-
ful. Their work sets the stage for examining various aspects of the
problem of managing the resource today and attempting to lay a policy foundation to secure its future.

Lou Carbyn identifies wolf predation as a critical factor in the life
of the buffalo in the area. Yet Carbyn cautions against too simplistic
an understanding of the apparent relationship between increased
wolf predation and the decline in buffalo numbers. He notes that the
size of the area in question holds out the possibility that natural factors could become the regulators of buffalo health and numbers
rather than outside interventions, no matter how well intentioned.

Gary Wobeser examines the history of how some diseases in domestic animals, particularly cattle, have been handled. He under-
lines the finding that anything less than the eradication of the herd
in which the diseased animal is found has proven unsatisfactory.
Less stringent measures have allowed disease to survive to strike
the animals again. Such a threat is unacceptable to the domestic
cattle industry. For those who would tolerate disease in a wild
animal population the cattle industry emphasizes the danger that
such a disease reservoir would pose to domestic animals. Wobeser's
very cogently argued work raises the question of whether those who
would choose other, more "natural" means, could be running a level
of risk that they do not fully appreciate. Can communities tolerate
such levels of health and financial risk? In terms of the buffalo itself,
is not its own survival placed in jeopardy by continuing exposure to
lethal diseases to which it has been exposed only relatively recently?

The native perspective on the issue of how to handle the problem
of diseased buffalo in the WBNP area is the subject of Theresa
Ferguson's and Clayton Burke's article. There can be no doubt as to
the danger that such animals could pose to the cattle industry and to

those people who come in contact with them. Yet Ferguson and Burke take legitimate issue with the mind set that minimizes the expertise of native people with regard to "managing" this resource. The relationship between the native people and the buffalo extends over thousands of years in the region. Have not lessons been learned that are applicable today? Or are the problems today so distinct from those of the past that the native peoples themselves stand at risk from diseased animals? The issues are such that policy makers have little room for error. As Ferguson and Burke argue it is critically necessary that the native voices be heard and appreciated.

Stacy Tessaro addresses the issue of disease in animals, including humans. Even for the uninitiated it is clear in Tessaro's discussion that humans are at risk in handling the meat of animals with diseases to which humans are susceptible. Tessaro's argument seems to add weight to Wobeser's analyses and conclusions. Domestic animals are at risk as well as humans. In view of the fact that the movement of wild animals can not be controlled as can domestic herds, is anything less than the eradication of diseased herds tenable? Yet in terms of the variation in the species's gene pool, what are the ramifications for the buffalo's long term survival, following a policy of eradicating diseased herds?

Milt Wright offers respite from current controversy by addressing one of those questions you may have wondered about but were too embarrassed to ask. Historical accounts of life on the treeless prairies attest to the use of buffalo chips as a fuel for cooking and heating. A number of questions spring to mind about the context created by the use of such fuel. Wright, thankfully, limits himself to addressing the question of the thermal properties of the fuel. One could not have envisaged the research difficulties encountered. From problems of supply to the establishing of a comparable data base, Wright recounts the challenges that his research encountered. His findings happily suggest that buffalo chips need not be viewed as a solution to our diminishing fuel reserves. But he has answered a question faced by every lecturer in presettlement western history.

A popular current view of the buffalo sees the species as an ecological success story. It has survived the trauma of the nineteenth century extinction to flourish in our northern forests. The image and reality appear as one. Yet brief inquiry demonstrates that the unity of image and reality is troubled indeed. Perhaps the survival of the animal requires image and reality to remain distinct.

J.E.F.

MICHAEL CLAYTON WILSON

Bison in Alberta

Paleontology, Evolution, and Relations with Humans

Introduction

When Napi, or Old Man, created the world, he carefully crafted the landscape, making the mountains and the prairie, and cutting places for rivers to flow. He created grass to carpet the prairie and feed the animals, which he also placed there. Among these animals was the buffalo. Out of clay, Napi crafted figures in human shape and spoke to them, saying, "You shall be people." These first people had hands like a bear and long claws. They lived on roots and berries, the inner bark of trees, and the small animals that lived in the ground.

The buffalo were black. They could kill people by hooking them with their long horns, and they would eat the people they killed. Napi looked upon this and felt badly, saying, "I have not made these people right." He changed things so that people would eat buffalo. He taught the people how to make bows and arrows and how to use buffalo jumps. He showed them how to cut meat with stone knives, and how to use fire to cook meat. From that time onward, the Siksika, Kainai, Piikani, Atsina and Tsuutina of what was to become southern Alberta were known as great buffalo hunters.

The foregoing is but a précis of the Blackfoot creation story as told to George Bird Grinnell.[1] Science has its own version of these events

1

but agrees that life had an inorganic origin, that humans have
changed in form from their ancestors, and that human hunting abili-
ties improved through time. It is also known that in the not-too-
distant past, buffalo had horns much longer than those of the modern species—horns that would have been devastating when used
upon an enemy. These buffalo, or bison, did not originate in the
New World. As with the aboriginal peoples of North and South
America, their origins are traced back to Eurasia. In North America
are plains bison (*Bison bison bison*) and wood bison (*B. bison athabascae*), although these "subspecies" are not well differentiated and
may not deserve distinct formal names. Their closest living relatives
are the European bison or wisent (*B. bonasus*) of Poland and the So-
viet Union. More distant relatives are the cattle, among them domestic cattle (*Bos taurus*), zebu (*Bos indicus*), and yak (*Bos grunniens*), as
well as wild species. The obvious differences in stance, coat, and
cranial proportions (especially horn characteristics) are to some extent illusory: bison and domestic cattle can interbreed to produce
vigorous, though often infertile, "cattalo" offspring.

Evolution and Migration

The common ancestor of *Bos* and *Bison* was probably the fossil bo-
vid, *Proleptobos*, of the early Pliocene epoch (approximately four million years ago). By the start of the ensuing Pleistocene, two million
years ago, bison were distinguishable from the *Leptobos* line, which
led toward modern *Bos*. Early bison were widespread in central and
eastern Asia, with *Bison sivalensis* and *B. paleosinensis* known from
the Indian subcontinent, China, and probably Siberia. These small,
lightly built bison resembled the modern wisent, a woodland species, more than the modern plains bison or the large extinct steppe
bison (*B. priscus*) that figured prominently in European cave art;
possibly the earliest bison were also woodland dwellers. Bison had
dispersed into Siberia and onto the steppes by the mid-Pleistocene,
so that their first spread into the New World could have occurred
a few hundred thousand years ago. By the late Pleistocene, *B. priscus* was abundant, successful, and widespread on the northern
steppes, poised to cross into Alaska whenever environmental conditions permitted.[2]

The footprints of the first bison to reach North America, like those
of the first human colonists, have been well hidden. The arrival of

the bison occurred long before the keeping of written records, and even aboriginal oral traditions do not reach back to that time. People and bison, however, apparently used the same pathway, the Bering Land Bridge, although they probably did not use it at precisely the same times. Alternative hypotheses as to the earliest human dispersal routes (for example, via trans-Pacific voyages) are, thus far, supported by little concrete evidence. What can be learned about the heritage of the bison, therefore, provides insight into human prehistory, and the reverse is equally true.

Exposure of the land bridge occurred when ice sheets built up on the northern continents, storing vast quantities of water. Sea level lowered by as much as one hundred metres at the height of glaciation, exposing the shallow Bering Platform that links Alaska to Siberia.[3] Ironically, because of airmass behavior and local rain-shadow effects associated with mountain ranges, northern Siberia, the Bering Platform, and central Alaska/Yukon remained largely ice-free even at the height of glaciation. Inasmuch as they constituted a continuous land mass at that time, the area is called *Beringia*. In Beringia, animals and people could move back and forth between the Old World and the New World, and such animals as mammoths and bison (Old World origin) as well as horses (New World origin) occupied the area in considerable numbers even when there was ice to the south. When the glaciers began to recede, a corridor opened to the south across the Canadian plains; meanwhile, rising sea levels flooded the Bering Platform and severed the tie between continents. Thus, movement of animals such as bison from Asia to the North American midcontinent was a two-stage process involving a land bridge and an ice-free corridor. In a sense, eastern Beringia was analogous to a railway station platform, where the new immigrants could wait for the first train south.

It is fascinating enough to imagine all of this having happened once, but in fact glaciers advanced and retreated several times; the land bridge appeared and disappeared repeatedly. Continental and Cordilleran glaciers last coalesced to seal off the corridor in western Canada between about 20 000 and 14 000 years ago, but similar conditions likely prevailed about 70 000 years ago and at earlier times as well. The important implication of this is that for any group such as the bison (or humans) colonization did not necessarily occur only once. Most likely, there were successive waves of migration. Complicating matters is the likelihood that, despite small-scale evolutionary change, newly incoming populations of many animal groups were able to interbreed with the descendants of earlier waves.[4] As a result, the naming and interpretation of fossil "species" is a complicated matter, oftimes extremely confusing.

Paleontological and archeological evidence suggests that bison first crossed the land bridge at an earlier time than did humans. Thus the bison were apparently free of human hunting pressures for as much as 200 000 years or even longer. However, close coordination of humans and bison, especially on the Great Plains, can be documented for at least the past 11 000 years. Some of the more recent small-scale evolutionary trends that affected *Bison bison* and its immediate precursors were likely influenced by human predatory pressures.

Some 11 500 years b.p. (before present), with ice retreat still under way, southern Alberta was a cool steppe-tundra with mammoths, horses, camels, large bighorn sheep, and large bison. By 11 200 years ago, and probably before then, their herds were attended by sophisticated human groups hunting game with spears tipped by "fluted" stone projectile points, so called because of the specialized removal of large flakes, or "flutes," from each face. Only 1000 years later, the mammoths, horses, and camels were extinct in North America for reasons that relate to climatic change or hunting stresses, or both in combination.[5]

By the mid-nineteenth century, North American scientists knew not only of the modern bison but also of some of its fossil relatives. The gigantic *Bison latifrons*, with an overall horn spread (including horn sheaths) in excess of two metres, was known from specimens found in Kentucky and Arizona. A smaller species, *B. antiquus*, was also larger than the modern form, which was soon understood to be the smallest bison to have existed in the New World. The impressive "monarch of the plains" is the smallest of its line, for reasons that are yet to be understood clearly. One must reach far back in time and well into Asia to find ancestors that are comparably small.

Studies well into the twentieth century seemed to confirm that bison evolution in North America was a story of progressive diminution, and an almost "straight-line" model emerged, with the giant *B. latifrons* earliest, and a succession through *B. alleni* and *B. antiquus* to the modern form. In the absence of direct dating techniques and with only limited stratigraphic information, this model seemed to work reasonably well.[6] However, recognition that there were multiple waves of immigration complicated the picture, and it slowly became evident that not all early bison were out-and-out giants.[7] It is possible that in the New World there have been alternating trends to larger and smaller individuals depending upon climatic conditions, as is documented in the Old World for fossil mammoths.[8] It is also possible that there were multiple evolutionary lines, allowing two or more species of bison to co-exist at one time. These alternatives seem clear enough, and the large number of bison specimens available should allow resolution; yet, the answers have not been forthcoming as rapidly as one would hope. One problem lies with the choice of characteristics for analysis. The horns provide the most obvious evidence of variation in fossil bison, the rest of the body being seemingly conservative. However, because horns, which are secondary sexual characteristics, and, thus, subject to hormonal influences, are probably the most variable characteristic within any bison population, they offer anything but the ideal basis upon which to characterize a species. Any environmental stresses that would upset the body chemistry of a buffalo during its three-year period of major growth could have affected horn size and shape.[9]

Collecting in Alberta: The Bone Pickers

Paleontologists did not collect fossil bison from Alberta in any concerted fashion until the mid-twentieth century, but the last decades of the nineteenth century saw collecting of a different kind. Commercial hunting of bison for meat and hides had rapidly expanded at a time when wild, hoofed mammals were experiencing climatic stresses, particularly in the form of severe winters, marking the culmination of a cold climatic episode. Sport hunters came in increasing numbers as the railroads expanded westward. Free-ranging bison herds stood in the way of settlement, and both the American and Canadian governments knew that Native people could remain strong only as long as their traditional food supply was secure. No-one stood in the way of the devastating, over-exploitive buffalo hunts, and the United States Army pursued a deliberate policy of encouraging the killing of bison as a strategy in the "Indian Wars." Said Colonel Richard Irving Dodge, commander at North Platte, "Kill every buffalo you can. Every buffalo dead is an Indian gone."[10] Even the Smithsonian Institution, upon learning that the buffalo were on the verge of disappearing, sent an expedition out to kill several for a stuffed and mounted exhibit.[11] Almost before detailed scientific studies could begin, the plains bison were nearly extinct. Studies of free-ranging huge herds of the sort that figured so prominently in early explorers' accounts were, therefore, never possible; now, through detailed reassembly of fragmented historical accounts that were written for other purposes, one can only try to reconstruct behavioral traits and migratory patterns.

By the late 1870s, the vast herds that had blackened the plains "as far as the eye could see" remained only as bleached white bones that littered the ground in equally prodigious quantities. A new industry of "bone picking" soon developed as entrepreneurial settlers, Indians, and unemployed Métis buffalo hunters struggled to supplement their meager earnings.[12] They shipped bones east by the boxcar load for use in sugar refining (as bone char, a filtering agent) and for bone meal fertilizer. In just one year (1890–91), the bones of some 200 000 bison were shipped from Saskatoon alone; in all, over 22 000 tons of bones were shipped from western Canada between 1884 and 1897.[13] Indians and Metis also earned money selling polished buffalo horns as souvenirs to passengers on passing trains.[14] Photographs of bison skulls stacked along the railway lines reveal greater variation in horn core characteristics than can be seen in most museum collections; regrettably, far more bison skulls were destroyed for industrial purposes than could be saved for scientific analysis. For many "bone pickers," the money received provided either a grubstake for the purchase of first seed, supplies, and equipment, or, simply, a hedge against starvation. As Leroy Barnett has eloquently stated, "with classic irony, the once great Canadian herds became, in death, the salvation for some of their own executioners."[15]

Collecting in Alberta: The Paleontologists

Aside from fossil bison skulls mentioned briefly in old annual reports of the Geological Survey of Canada and National Museum of Canada, the first detailed account of Alberta fossil bison, by W.A. Fuller and L.A. Bayrock, analyzed material collected from the Beverly gravel pits in the Edmonton area and donated to the University of Alberta and the Alberta Research Council.[16] These finds were as puzzling as they were illuminating, for they seemed to indicate, contrary to other evidence, that the giant *Bison latifrons* had existed alongside the slightly smaller *B. crassicornis* and even smaller *B. occidentalis* in early postglacial times, perhaps 8000 to 10 000 years ago. However, the date was based upon tentative correlations of river terraces. A terrace elsewhere in Edmonton had yielded radiocarbon-datable material from silts *overlying* comparable gravels, and seemed to lie at about the same level above the river as the Beverly terrace: alas, this could only be a minimum date for the gravels, even if they were the same. Fuller and Bayrock reached reasonable conclusions for their time, but more recent studies show that there are gravels of differing ages in these pits, with postglacial gravels lying atop older gravels, which were re-exposed when the valley was recut during and after the retreat of the glaciers.[17] The seeming co-occurrence of different species of bison has yet to be supported by additional finds either from Edmonton or from other localities. New discoveries from the area provide additional spice: James A. Burns, of the Provincial Museum of Alberta, is studying a sample of bison skulls that predate the last glacial advance, yet are small enough to be comparable to early postglacial bison.

The Beverly pit *B. latifrons* specimen (a single horn core) remains the only specimen of that species from Alberta, although another is known from Saskatchewan.[18] Deposits of the appropriate antiquity are scarce as a result of widespread glacial scouring, and are often masked by overlying glacial debris. Postglacial deposits, not subject to these processes, are widespread and have, by contrast, yielded many fossil bison specimens. C. Trylich and L.A. Bayrock described a partial bison skeleton collected near Taber and attributed to *B. occidentalis*.[19] The specimen, on display in the Drumheller and District Museum, was found in alluvial sands seventy-five meters above the Oldman River. Wood samples from a lower horizon were radiocarbon-dated to 11 000 and 10 500 years ago; it is not easy to judge how much younger the bones were, because the site has long since been destroyed. Trylich and Bayrock thought that no great amount of time had elapsed between the deposition of the wood and of the bison, but, as is discussed below, the size of the skull itself suggests that the bison could have been younger. Meanwhile, subsequent finds, especially in the Calgary-Cochrane area, have confirmed that bison were abundant here as early as 11 500 years ago, at a time when retreating ice still covered central Saskatchewan and northern Alberta.[20]

The Taber bison attracted attention as a possible "Early Man" site because a stone cobble interpreted by Bayrock as a chopper was found next to the broken bison skull. However, the stone has been re-examined by the present author, and it appears to him to resemble natural, glacially fractured cobbles. The skull, while broken, shows no obvious evidence of chopper impact, and the remainder of the skeleton shows no clear sign of butchering. Thus, the cultural significance of the site can be questioned. Fortunately, better sites of comparable antiquity in southern Alberta attest to the presence of humans at least 10 500 years b.p.,[21] and the distribution of fluted projectile points (of types elsewhere dated as old as 11 200 years b.p.) nicely fits the postulated 11 500 yr. b.p. Ice-free Corridor.[22] The oldest archaeological mass bison kill yet found in Alberta is the Fletcher Site, southeast of Taber, where remains of large bison have been found in association with spear points of the Scottsbluff and Alberta types.[23] This site is dated to slightly over 9000 years b.p., but older bison kill sites in Wyoming indicate that people were using sophisticated bison drive technologies more than 10 000 years ago.[24] The Lindoe Site, near Medicine Hat, exhibited a bed of bison bones that had been butchered by hunters 9900 years ago; it may not have been a kill site *per se*, but, rather, the processing site associated with one.[25]

Finds from the Cochrane-Calgary area, mentioned above, introduce an interesting wrinkle. The first material available was fragmentary; in 1968, C.S. Churcher identified it as *B. occidentalis*.[26] However, more complete skulls have since been found; they clearly differ from that species in horn core characteristics, though not in size. Thus, they are now referred by the author and by Churcher to the species *B. antiquus*.[27] The relationship between these two forms has been the subject of much debate, and resolution of the question will have far-reaching implications for the classification of fossil bison. Some authors (the "lumpers"), the present author among them, see postglacial fossil forms, including these two "species," simply as early subspecies of the modern *B. bison*.[28] Others (the "splitters") view these two forms as fully distinct and valid species, a view which suggests that the bison did not interbreed, but, rather, were isolated either physiologically or behaviorally.[29]

In 1974, the author published a paper advocating the view that there was, for all time periods, a north-south gradient in characteristics. "Northern" bison had narrow frontal bones and horn cores deflected toward the rear and upswept, while "southern" bison had broad frontals and horn cores laterally directed and downswept. In this view, *B. occidentalis* was simply the northern counterpart of *B. antiquus*, and they should be viewed only as subspecies linked by a gradient of characteristics. Some populations, such as the bison from the 10 000-year-old Casper Site, Wyoming, seemed to display intermediate characteristics.[30] There is still evidence in favor of this view; nevertheless, it is extremely interesting that the finds of *B. antiquus* from Alberta (for example, from the Bighill Creek gravels at Cochrane and Calgary) seem largely or entirely to predate 10 000 years b.p.,[31] while the finds of *B. occidentalis* (for example, at the 9600–year-old Milan Site, near Three Hills) postdate this time.[32] One way to interpret this, given that *B. antiquus* is extremely rare north of Alberta, is that the boundary between the two forms gradually shifted southward; that is, that the entire gradational series took a giant step southward. If this were the case, localities in the extreme north would show an unbroken series of *occidentalis*-like bison, while localities in the extreme south would show nothing but *antiquus*-like forms. In between, one would see *antiquus* being replaced by *occidentalis*.[33] Southward shifting of this gradient, or *cline*, could reflect climatic amelioration at the close of the last glaciation.

The alternative is equally interesting. *Bison occidentalis*, sweeping in from the north, could have replaced *B. antiquus* through genetic swamping as the two interbred on a massive scale. Perhaps the *occidentalis* morphotype conferred some advantage upon the individual or population in ways not yet understood. What makes the acceptance of either of the foregoing hypotheses difficult is that the changeover may have occurred very rapidly—possibly over a period of a few hundred years. Interestingly, it occurred, at least in Alberta, at the same time as the extinction of mammoths, horses, and camels. Thus, yet another possibility arises: that *B. antiquus* became extinct, or nearly so, at the same time as these other animals did. In this view, when *B. occidentalis* swept southward through the newly opened Ice-free Corridor, it found the Great Plains largely depopulated and ready for new colonization. If interbreeding did occur on a local scale with the few remaining *B. antiquus*, the relative population numbers were such that the *occidentalis* morphotype easily dominated.[34]

Such extinction with replacement, if it did occur, does not resolve the "species or subspecies" question. If *B. antiquus* and *B. occidentalis* were prevented by fate from interbreeding, the possibility that they *could* have done so under different circumstances cannot be ruled out. A complete extinction of *antiquus* would mean that it was the end of a lineage (however little removed biologically from other bison), and, because it was the end, it did not give rise to the modern form. Most paleontologists would probably accept this postulation as a basis for retaining a distinction between *antiquus* and *occidentalis* at the species level, although the latter's direct ancestry of, and strong similarity to, the modern bison would suggest its reduction to an early subspecies of *B. bison*, as in *B. bison occidentalis*.

All of the foregoing undoubtedly has the reader's head spinning, but serves to illustrate an important point. The classification and names that are used serve only to show "the state of the art" of our understanding of relationships. As that understanding evolves—and new finds are continually providing better information—the classification is either fine-tuned or, in some cases, abandoned entirely for a better scheme. When understandings change, often the scientific names must themselves be altered. To the public, it seems exasperating that scientists from time to time change the names of the fossils with which they deal, but the reader can now see that such changes are necessary in order to reflect current knowledge. Science does not stand still, and neither does the language that it uses.

Bison Standard Time

The complications of multiple migratory waves, interbreeding, and extinctions concluded by about 10 000 years ago—the start of the Holocene, or modern, epoch. For the past 10 000 years, North American bison have been gradually decreasing in size, particularly of horn cores.[35] Whether this alteration represents true genetic evolution or individual physiological response to environmental constraints is not clear; likely, both factors, coupled with the rising intensity of human predation, are involved. It is not clear which is more productive to ask: why Pleistocene bison were so large, or why modern bison are so small. Dale Guthrie, in tackling the former question, suggested that the large size of Pleistocene bison resulted from both high winter mortality, which kept the range understocked, and a long peak of nutrient availability during the growing season.[36] However, the first of these implies that the pressures exerted by intensive hunting would also favor large bison, but we know that bison became dramatically smaller during the period when they were intensively hunted. Guthrie believes that this trend reflects a shorter annual optimum growth period during the Holocene epoch, but the present author believes that human predation was also a direct factor; that is, the fact that the pattern of mortality (based on individual ages of animals killed) differs between the events of natural and cultural killings is probably significant. Harvesting of middle-maturity ("prime") animals by hunters, because it had the overall effect of lowering average life expectancy in a bison population, changed the selective regime. Early bison such as *B. latifrons* had such gigantic horns that they must have grown throughout the life of the animal. The horns of modern male bison, on the other hand, reach adult length in three to four years; thereafter, they increase only in robusticity, which changes their shape from relatively straight "spikes" to the familiar adult curve. The changeover from ever-growing horns to subadult horn growth could mark a change in the maturation pattern of bison. Possibly, the modern bison becomes reproductively mature at a younger age than did *B. latifrons* and other large bison; such maturation would represent a positive adaptation to the pressures of predation that shorten life expectancy.[37] Smaller size in modern bison may not, therefore, reflect a selective advantage to the size itself; rather, it may be the side effect of selection for early maturation to ensure an adequate calf crop for survival. Modern bison in managed situations live considerably longer than did plains bison that were subject to regular bison drives in late Holocene times. Unfortunately, these considerations involve factors that are difficult to discern in the fossil record; such indications are indirect and open to challenge.

Whatever the cause of the "dwarfing," the trend to smaller bison is useful in a different way, that is, in providing "index fossils." Now that the overall trend for the past 11 000 years has been documented in detail, it is possible to estimate the age of a bison skull on the basis of its size alone.[38] Of course, one does not know from the outset whether a single specimen was "average" for its population or extreme. Therefore, a date derived from bison size (it can be called "bison standard time"[39]) cannot be as precise as one determined on the basis of the radiocarbon technique; it is, however, much less expensive. Its best application would come in cases where the availability of several skulls gives a better impression of the range of variation of the sample being dated.

Development of "bison standard time" also allows critical reassessment of earlier discoveries, which, having been treated with preservative, cannot be dated directly. For example, the published tip-to-tip horn core measurement for the Taber bison, mentioned above, is smaller than the minimum documented for 10 000 or more years b.p. Even if the specimen was the smallest in its population, its comparative diminutiveness suggests that it is younger than

10 000 years old. Trylich and Bayrock used the absence of obvious unconformities in sands at the site as a basis for the opinion that not much time had elapsed between deposition of the dated wood samples and of the bison bones.[40] However, this conclusion cannot be translated easily into actual numbers of years. The published measurement of 762 millimetres suggests a maximum date of 9000 years b.p. for the bison. However, the story does not end there. In 1989, the author re-examined the specimen in the Drumheller and District Museum, discovering that some of the published measurements were taken, not from bone, but from "landmarks" in plaster where missing bone had been replaced. The left horn core, of which only the basal half was present in bone, had been restored to a length clearly shorter than the right—and the published measurement was taken using the restored tip! Taking a measurement from the good horn core tip to the midline and multiplying by two, one derives a figure closer to 780 millimeters: still not a particularly large early Holocene bison, but large enough to be as old as 9500 years b.p., and it is not unreasonable to suggest that 1000 years elapsed during deposition of the sand beds at Taber.

Samples of Holocene bison are abundant in Alberta, although many come from archaeological sites that date to within the last 5000 years, with heavily fragmented butchered bones. The best non-archeological samples are the 9600-year-old Milan Site population (twenty bison, with two incomplete male skulls and one horn core),[41] and the 3600-year-old Hitching Post Ranch sample from Bottrel, north of Cochrane in the foothills (over one hundred bison, with fourteen measurable male skulls and additional fragmentary specimens).[42] Both seem to be natural die-offs, the former in a possible quicksand trap and the latter in a bog. At Milan, a preponderance of young and old individuals with few prime adults (the identification depends upon their lower jaws and teeth) suggests attritional mortality over a period of time, while the large number of prime adults at Hitching Post, in addition to juveniles and old individuals, suggests a catastrophic die-off. In the absence of clear evidence for human predation at the latter site, one possible explanation for the bisons' demise is smoke inhalation from a major grass fire. Tooth eruption in juveniles at the site, by suggesting death in late summer to early fall, rules out the animals' foundering through thin ice. Lending credence to this hypothesis is the fact that, even today, grass fires result in significant losses of cattle through smoke inhalation; however, credence does not constitute proof.

Humans and Bison

By the time Spanish explorers first arrived within their range, the bison had increased prodigiously in numbers, and vast herds roamed the Great Plains, spilling into the patchy grasslands of the Pacific Northwest, the Great Basin, the Sonoran Desert, and the eastern deciduous forests. Observing the degree of attention accorded to the bison by aboriginal peoples, these explorers reasonably concluded that bison were the domestic cattle or oxen of the New World. While bison were never brought under the degree of control now accorded the title of "domestication," the close coordination between people and a key prey species was obvious, and verged upon pastoralism. Perhaps if Europeans had not intervened so massively in the development of New World cultures, bison would have been domesticated.

Native groups, as noted above, also came to the midcontinent via the Bering Land Bridge and the Ice-free Corridor. If bison were not able to move southward until about 10 000 years ago (in the form of *B. occidentalis*), one wonders what ramifications this constraint might have had on humans. However, it is unlikely that humans would have been as vulnerable as bison to environmental barriers: humans were more adaptable in diet and more versatile in terms of mobility. While a late incursion of bison does provide information as to the appearance of suitable habitat in the corridor, humans likely could have moved southward in advance of the bison and other relatively specialized forms. Certainly, humans on the Alberta plains have, for at least 11 000 years, depended heavily upon the bison as the basis of their economy. Ethnographic studies of historic Plains Indians show that they utilized a great range of other resources, both animal and plant; yet, their ceremonial emphasis upon the bison affirms that survival *per se* rested largely with that species. For many groups, the autumn hunt constituted the key to winter survival. Meat could be stored in dried form or as pemmican, pounded with berries, and such supplies could carry people through times of climatic severity when their mobility was minimized.[43]

Specialized communal drive strategies, utilizing natural features, such as sand dunes and gullies, were already being employed more than 10 000 years ago, although the strategies at such Alberta sites as the Fletcher Site or the Lindoe Site are not yet clear. Repetitive use of buffalo jumps was under way by 5500 years ago, as at the Head-Smashed-In Jump near Fort Macleod,[44] so for thousands of years plains bison hunters possessed the ability to kill as many as hundreds of animals in a single drive, or in repeated drives over a short time. Most drives were likely of small herds with a few tens of animals, but the potential existed for extensive impact. As suggested above, changes in the size of bisons' bodies and horns may relate, in part, to this pressure exerted by human hunters, inasmuch as, unlike wolves, they sampled the middle-age groups of the population. This practice, by upsetting the natural selection regime, likely favored rapid maturation.

Without a doubt, native people made good use of the materials obtained from the bison. Aside from food, in the form of meat, fat, bone grease, marrow, and blood, bison provided raw material for tools and weapons (bone, sinew, rawhide), shelter (hides, bone pegs), paint (fats, blood), ceremonial trappings and clothing (horn headdresses, hides, bone), dog food (bones, offal), and other uses. The near-extermination of the bison, with tacit government approval, therefore removed far more than a food source: it knocked out the underpinnings of an entire cultural pattern, from subsistence to ceremonialism. Small wonder that native groups were so vulnerable to manipulation by incoming white groups, and that their very survival in cultural terms grew so tenuous. Their prime link with the Creator disappeared, as much a memory as the unfenced open plains. The white man's simple solution to the "Indian problem," a century ago, was to kill most of the buffalo. Having done so, white law enforcement officials then complained at length to Native people about their hunting of alternative game. R. Burton Deane, Superintendent of "K" Division, North-West Mounted Police, wrote in 1890 that he

> ...was pointing out to the spokesmen of a band of Indians that they would not be allowed to molest the antelope in the breeding season, and said that if such a slaughter were permitted the antelope would soon go where the buffalo had gone. A smile, "childlike and bland," played...over the Indian's face as he replied: "Yes, but then the white men are the buffalo."[45]

Now, with the few free-roaming bison in northern Alberta's Wood Buffalo National Park already declining in numbers, a government again is being urged, by ranchers, to exterminate them—this time to protect domestic cattle herds from disease. The white man's simple solution for the "disease problem" is, again, to kill most of the buffalo.[46] This time, one hopes, the government will not acquiesce. Probably the biggest problem faced by all Albertans—and certainly by all bison—is simple solutions! Napi must surely be looking down again at the people of Alberta and the changes that have taken place. A voice in the west wind says, "I have not made these people right."

Michael Clayton Wilson is a professor of Geography at the University of Lethbridge.

Notes

1. George Bird Grinnell, *Blackfoot Lodge Tales* (1892; rep. Lincoln: University of Nebraska Press, 1962), pp. 140–44; *Blackfeet Indian Stories* (New York: Charles Scribner's Sons, 1913), pp. 150–55.
2. Jerry N. McDonald, *North American Bison: Their Classification and Evolution* (Berkeley: University of California Press, 1981), pp. 31–37; Mary Meagher, "*Bison bison*," *Mammalian Species* 266 (June 1986), pp. 1–2.
3. Richard Foster Flint, *Glacial and Quaternary Geology* (New York: John Wiley and Sons, 1971), pp. 536–38.
4. Morris F. Skinner and Ove C. Kaisen, "The Fossil *Bison* of Alaska and Preliminary Revision of the Genus," *Bulletin of the American Museum of Natural History* 89 (1947), pp. 153–57, introduced the idea of migratory waves but did not accept the idea of interbreeding. More recent perspectives are discussed in R. Dale Guthrie, "Bison evolution and zoogeography in North America during the Pleistocene," *Quarterly Review of Biology* 45 (1970), pp. 1–15; Michael C. Wilson, "The Casper Local Fauna and its Fossil Bison," in *The Casper Site: A Hell Gap Bison Kill on the High Plains*, George C. Frison, ed. (New York: Academic Press, 1974), pp. 134–42; McDonald, *North American Bison*, pp. 232–63.
5. See papers in *Pleistocene Extinctions: the Search for a Cause*, Paul S. Martin and H.E. Wright, Jr., eds. (Princeton: Princeton University Press, 1967); and in *Quaternary Extinctions: A Prehistoric Revolution*, Paul S. Martin and Richard G. Klein, eds. (Tucson: University of Arizona Press, 1984).
6. C. Bertrand Schultz and W.D. Frankforter, "The Geologic History of the Bison of the Great Plains," *Bulletin of the University of Nebraska State Museum* 3 (1946), pp. 1–9.
7. Skinner and Kaisen, "The Fossil *Bison*," p. 155.
8. Bjorn Kurtén, *Pleistocene Mammals of Europe* (Chicago: Aldine Publishing, 1968), p. 245.
9. R. Dale Guthrie, "Bison horn cores—character choice and systematics," *Journal of Paleontology* 40 (1966), pp. 738–40; Michael C. Wilson, "Problems in the Speciation of American Fossil Bison," in *Post-Pleistocene Man and his Environment on the Northern Plains*, R.G. Forbis et al., eds. (Calgary: University of Calgary Archaeological Association, 1969), pp. 180–92.
10. Qtd. in Larry Barsness, *Heads, Hides & Horns: The Compleat Buffalo Book* (Fort Worth: Texas Christian University Press, 1985), pp. 126–32.
11. William T. Hornaday, "Discovery, life history, and extermination of American bison," *Report of the United States National Museum, 1887* (Washington: Government Printing Office, 1889), pp. 493–523; Frank Gilbert Roe, *The North American Buffalo* (1951), 2nd ed. (Toronto: University of Toronto Press, 1971), pp. 447–66.

12. Leroy Barnett, "Buffalo Bone Industry in Canada, Part 2," *Alberta History* 27 (Spring, 1979), pp. 6–13.
13. Ibid., p. 12.
14. The Commissioners of the Royal North-West Mounted Police, *The New West, Being the Official Reports to Parliament of the Activities of the Royal North-West Mounted Police Force from 1888–1889* (1890; reprint, Toronto: Coles Publishing, 1973), pp. 124 (for 1888) and 119 (for 1889).
15. Barnett, "Buffalo Bone Industry in Canada, Part 2."
16. W.A. Fuller and L.A. Bayrock, "Late Pleistocene Mammals from Central Alberta, Canada," in *Vertebrate Paleontology in Alberta*, R.E. Folinsbee and D.M. Ross, eds., Bulletin 2 (Edmonton: Department of Geology, University of Alberta, 1965), pp. 1–11.
17. John A. Westgate, "The Quaternary Geology of the Edmonton Area, Alberta," in *Pedology and Quaternary Research*, S. Pawluk, ed. (Edmonton: University of Alberta, 1969), pp. 142, 146–50.
18. Ehsunallah Khan, "Biostratigraphy and Paleontology of a Sangamon Deposit at Fort Qu'Appelle, Saskatchewan," *National Museum of Canada Publications in Paleontology* 5 (Ottawa: Queen's Printer, 1970), pp. 58–63.
19. C. Trylich and L.A. Bayrock, "Bison occidentalis Lucas Found at Taber, Alberta, Canada," *Canadian Journal of Earth Sciences* 3 (1966), pp. 987–95.
20. Michael C. Wilson and C.S. Churcher, "The Late Pleistocene Bighill Creek Formation and its Equivalents in Alberta: Correlative Potential and Vertebrate Palaeofauna," in *Correlation of Quaternary Chronologies*, W.C. Mahaney, ed. (Norwich, U.K.: GeoBooks, 1984), p. 169.
21. Daryl Fedje, "Banff Archaeology, 1983–1985," in *Eastern Slopes Prehistory: Selected Papers*, Brian Ronaghan, ed., Occasional Paper No. 30 (Edmonton: Archaeological Survey of Alberta, 1986), pp. 34–36.
22. Michael C. Wilson, "Archaeological Geology in Western Canada; Techniques, Approaches, and Integrative Themes," in *Archaeological Geology of North America*, N.P. Lasca and J. Donahue, eds., Centennial Special Volume 4 (Boulder, Colorado: Geological Society of America, 1990), pp. 74–76.
23. Richard G. Forbis, "Fletcher: a Paleo-Indian Site in Alberta," *American Antiquity* 33 (1968), pp. 1–10; J. Roderick Vickers and Alwynne B. Beaudoin, "A Limiting AMS Date for the Cody Complex Occupation at the Fletcher Site, Alberta, Canada," *Plains Anthropologist* 34 (1989), pp. 261–64.
24. George C. Frison, *Prehistoric Hunters of the High Plains* (New York: Academic Press 1978), pp. 147–91.
25. Alan L. Bryan, "Preliminary Report on the Lindoe Site," *Archaeological Society of Alberta Newsletter* 10 (Fall, 1966), pp. 4–6.
26. C.S. Churcher, "Pleistocene Ungulates from the Bow River Gravels at Cochrane, Alberta," *Canadian Journal of Earth Sciences* 5 (1968), pp. 1471–72.
27. Wilson and Churcher, "The Late Pleistocene," p. 169.
28. Wilson, "The Casper Local Fauna," p. 141.
29. McDonald, *North American Bison*, p. 258–59.
30. Wilson, "The Casper Local Fauna," pp. 132–42.
31. Wilson and Churcher, "The Late Pleistocene," pp. 161–62.
32. David M. Shackleton and Leonard V. Hills, "Post-glacial Ungulates (*Cervus* and *Bison*) from Three Hills, Alberta," *Canadian Journal of Earth Sciences* 13 (1977), pp. 973–84.
33. George C. Frison, Michael C. Wilson, and Diane J. Wilson, "Fossil Bison and Artifacts from an Early Altithermal Period Arroyo Trap in Wyoming," *American Antiquity* 41 (1976), pp. 34–37.

34. McDonald, *North American Bison*, pp. 243–49.
35. Michael C. Wilson, "Holocene Fossil Bison from Wyoming and Adjacent Areas," (M.A. Thesis, University of Wyoming, 1975), pp. 229–38.
36. R. Dale Guthrie, "Alaskan megabucks, megabulls, and megarams: the issue of Pleistocene gigantism," in *Contributions in Quaternary Vertebrate Paleontology: A Volume in Memorial to John E. Guilday*, H.H. Genoways and M.R. Dawson, eds., Special Publication of the Carnegie Museum of Natural History, No. 8 (Pittsburgh: Carnegie Museum of Natural History, 1984), pp. 482–510.
37. McDonald, *North American Bison*, p. 258.
38. Michael C. Wilson, "Morphological Dating of Late Quaternary Bison on the Northern Plains," *Canadian Journal of Anthropology* 1 (1980), pp. 81–85.
39. Credit must go to Holmes A. Semken, Jr., for this entertaining name.
40. Trylich and Bayrock, "Bison occidentalis," p. 988.
41. Shackleton and Hills, "Post-glacial Ungulates," pp. 973–75.
42. Michael C. Wilson, "Canid Scavengers and Butchering Patterns: Evidence from a 3600-year-old Bison Kill Site," in *Carnivores, Human Scavengers and Predators: A Question of Bone Technology*, G.M. Lemoine and A.S. MacEachern, eds. (Calgary: University of Calgary Archaeological Association, 1983), pp. 109–17.
43. For discussion of archeological uses of bison, see papers in "Bison Procurement and Utilization: A Symposium," Leslie B. Davis and Michael C. Wilson, eds., *Plains Anthropologist* Memoir 14 (1978).
44. Brian O.K. Reeves, "Head-Smashed-In: 5500 Years of Bison Jumping in the Alberta Plains," in Ibid., pp. 151–74.
45. The Commissioners of the Royal North-West Mounted Police, *The New West*, p. 53 (for 1889).
46. Proposals (largely by ranchers) to kill a significant part of the Wood Buffalo National Park herd in order to control the spread of tuberculosis and brucellosis have been widely reported in Canadian newspapers and newsmagazines during 1990. A Federal environmental review panel recommended slaughter of the entire Wood Buffalo National Park herd, and restocking of the park with "clean" bison. Unfortunately, the "clean" population from which these animals would be drawn, having already passed through a population "bottleneck," could have limited genetic variability. One critical commentary is provided by Andrew Nikiforuk, "If Armageddon arrives, the bison are dead meat," *The Globe and Mail*, 4 October 1990.

JACK BRINK

Blackfoot and Buffalo Jumps

Native People and the Head-Smashed-In Project

Few issues in contemporary North American archaeology and museum studies are more contentious than relations between those who study and manage the information about the past, and descendants of the Native American aboriginal populations which originally produced these data. In the extreme, the scientist stresses the need to recover, curate, and analyze data pertaining to past human lifeways, and the moral requirement to store these data for future scientific study; the native community stresses the need to leave untouched ancestral objects still buried in the ground, to return to native people artifacts currently held in museums, and to bury again certain excavated materials, such as human skeletal remains.[1] So intense are the emotional issues, and so profound the legal, scientific, and cultural implications, that the leading archaeological organization in the world has recently stated that the resolution of these topics has "the clear potential to redefine the very nature of American archaeology."[2]

Few would argue that the disharmony between the archaeological community and native peoples stems from a long tradition of mutual avoidance. With very few exceptions, only in the past decade have archaeologists in North America even considered the potential concerns and interests of the native community let alone actually thought of involving members of it in their work. Previously, excavation of artifacts of native North Americans and the reconstruction of their past has proceeded in spite, rather than because, of the interests of aboriginal people. Increasingly, the message being delivered by native people of Canada and the United States is that this situation will not be allowed to continue.[3] Yet at the same time many native groups across North America have, until recent years, displayed a decided lack of interest in the workings of the archaeologists. Perhaps the latter situation was caused in part to not being kept informed or consulted by the professionals, but the net result is that native people and archaeologists seldom knew what each other was doing.

This essay provides a record of Head-Smashed-In Buffalo Jump site, a project where native and non-native individuals worked together to develop an archaeological site for public interpretation. As I believe that similar examples of close liaison between scientists and native people will be essential if we expect to continue to investigate the past, the present essay may serve to highlight some of the potential hazards, and the substantial rewards, that emerge from cooperative ventures. Thus, I will attempt to chronicle some of the more important events and issues concerning the development of Head-Smashed-In Buffalo Jump (HSI), focusing on all aspects of research and development in which members of the Blackfoot Nation played a significant role. The reason for the focus on native involvement rests with the belief that their involvement in both the developmental and operational aspects of the HSI interpretive centre distinguishes this archaeological interpretation project from similar endeavours.

I do not offer the Head-Smashed-In example as a model study. In the process of two very different cultures' attempts to deal with and to understand each other's concerns, mistakes were certainly made by all parties. Rather, I offer this chronicle as a case study from which some lessons were learned. Of necessity, the following is largely personal recollection. There exists little or nothing in published form relating to these events. My role was as both participant and observer. I was the government employee responsible for all research-related matters pertaining to the HSI project. As will be seen, the involvement with native people evolved in terms of research—both the supply of new research-related data, and the review of existing information.

Although buffalo jumps are relatively common archaeological sites on the broken country of the high plains, no site has been discovered which can match the size and archaeological richness of Head-Smashed-In Buffalo Jump, situated at the southern end of the Porcu-pine Hills in southwestern Alberta. With a time span of at least 5700 years, with cultural deposits of bison bones and stone tools extend-ing to ten metres below ground surface, with thousands of stone cairns organized into dozens of individual drive lanes serving to di-rect bison from the rich grazing area to the kill site, and with a butchering/processing area which covers more than one half of a square kilometre, Head-Smashed-In (HSI) is an incomparable site. Extrapolating from the number of bison represented in a small exca-vation in the butchering area of the site,[4] one may reasonably sug-gest that more than 100 000 bison met their death at the cliffs of HSI. To commemorate the significance of this UNESCO World Heritage Site, and to interpret the prehistory and history of HSI, the Govern-ment of Alberta constructed and operates an interpretive centre there. With its opening in July 1987 there began a period of interpre-ting the great buffalo jumps of Plains Indian culture to the general public. In the three years since that opening, over one-half million people have passed through the interpretive centre.

The Beginning

Native involvement in the HSI project can be traced to the time be-fore there officially was a "project." The *idea* to develop HSI for the public had been promoted at various levels of government since the mid-1970s by W.J. Byrne, then the Director of the Archaeological Survey of Alberta. Byrne had been a part of the archaeological team which excavated at HSI in the 1960s; as a result, he was both inti-mately familiar with the scientific importance of the site and aware of the great interpretive potential of the jump.[5] For years Byrne led the attempts, through government channels, to secure funds for a major onsite interpretive centre, but no HSI project yet existed be-cause no funding had been approved. It was Byrne who made the first overtures to the native community regarding the development of HSI.

It seemed obvious at the time that the primary group with which contacts should be established were the Peigan Indians, one of the three bands or tribes of the Blackfoot Nation. The northwest corner of the Peigan Reserve terminates only a few hundred metres south of the HSI site. Furthermore, there is little question that the Peigan were residents of the plains and foothills of southwestern Alberta at the time of initial European contact.[6] Peter Fidler wintered in the Porcupine Hills with the Peigan in 1792–93 and reported on numerous attempts by them to drive buffalo over cliffs.[7] While it seems clear that Fidler was farther north in the Porcupine Hills and probably never saw HSI, his journal nevertheless documents the fact that the Peigan were well established residents (and users of buffalo jumps) in this corner of southwestern Alberta. Given this, and the proximity of the site to the boundary of the existing Reserve, the decision to establish contacts with the Peigan Band seems reasonable. As will be discussed below, however, it was a mistake not to have established contacts as well with the Blood Band of the Blackfoot Nation during the early stages of the planning process.

In the spring of 1980, Byrne was to attend a Peigan Band Council meeting at the town of Brocket. He planned to present the *idea* of developing HSI and to express the desire to have natives participate prominently in the project. As often happens with full agenda council meetings, Byrne never succeeded in making his presentation. Instead, he was ushered into a separate meeting with Faron Strikes With A Gun, then the councilor for economic development for the Peigan Band. Initiating a concern that would often recur, Strikes With A Gun emphasized the prospect of jobs for the Peigan people. The proposed development of the jump met with polite approval, but the broader issue of native involvement was over-shadowed by the greater concern with employment.[8] A second attempt to meet with the Band Council was made in the fall of the same year. Again, Byrne, who by now had become the Assistant Deputy Minister for the Historical Resources Division, was unable to make an appearance before the council. This time he was redirected to the office of the Peigan Cultural Centre where he met with Reg Crow Shoe, who expressed considerable interest in the entire concept of public development of the buffalo jump, seeing the proposal as one which could benefit the Peigan in a number of ways, including employment.[9] These early attempts at contact with the Peigan Band represented a serious effort to initiate native involvement in the HSI project prior to any formal approvals for it. There was still no funding for development of the jump, nor was there any compelling reason to believe that funding was imminent. It is fair to say that serious contacts with, and involvement of, native people in the HSI project did not develop as an after-thought once the project was under way.

The points at which it can be said that the concept to develop HSI became a reality were two events which occurred in the years 1981 and 1982. First, in late 1981, an application compiled by the Historical Resources Division of Alberta Culture and submitted by Parks Canada to the UNESCO World Heritage Committee was approved. With this success, HSI joined an elite list of natural and cultural sites, such as the pyramids and Stonehenge, which are regarded as having universal historical significance. Such a designation carries a great deal of weight when applications for major funding are brought forward to government finance committees. The successful UNESCO application was therefore instrumental in hastening the second critical event—the approval of funding, which occurred in 1982 when the Alberta government allocated some ten million dollars for the development of an onsite interpretive centre at HSI. Prior to the UNESCO designation, repeated submission of the same funding request had met with no success. Now, HSI was a project.

Beginning Again

Subsequent to Byrne's initial attempts to contact the Peigan Band, I assumed responsibility for the anthropological and archaeological research requirements associated with the HSI project. I functioned as part of a government planning team which included planners and designers.

Efforts to involve native people in the HSI project next moved to a meeting held in Lethbridge in 1981. This meeting, billed as a "Think Tank," brought together people recognized as authorities in several related fields, such as archaeology, anthropology, display, interpretive design and project management. An invitation also was extended to the Band Council of the Peigan Indians. Two representatives of the band were sent to attend: William Big Bull and Nelbert Little Moustache. Over the course of two days, the discussion centred around this fundamental question: given the opportunity to interpret a large and complex prehistoric site, what should be the themes and storyline of the interpretive programme? More generally, the planning team was seeking advice on the whole structure of the presentation of the thematic statements. At the time of this meeting there were few firm ideas as to the intended nature of the interpretive programme for HSI.

Of relevance to this paper was a lengthy presentation made on the second day of the Think Tank by William Big Bull. This presentation portrayed traditional Peigan native culture as a series of seasonal decisions and events. Big Bull discussed the important happenings of each season, linking events with characteristic environmental and ecological conditions. This presentation had a strong impact on the members of the planning team who realized that in the search for a central structure for the displays, an alternate reality—that of the native people—could (and more importantly, perhaps should) form a part of the story of HSI. This reality was distinct from the one gleaned from the archaeological and anthropological textbooks, and excavated from the earth below the jump; rather, it existed in parallel to the more scientific sources of information, and it had remained largely untapped by the individuals in government who had controlled the development and interpretation of other historic sites.

The direction obtained from the Think Tank was one of structure for the interpretive programme, and not content or specific storyline. Government personnel left Lethbridge knowing that in some yet undefined way the HSI Interpretive Centre would present more than just a textbook view of Plains Indians culture and the story of the buffalo jump. Furthermore, it seemed clear that there was a critical need to explore the range of knowledge of living Blackfoot people; what was still remembered about the glorious days of the great buffalo hunts?

Obviously, the interpretation of a prehistoric archaeological site would be essentially a story about native people. For this, standard information sources were already available. These included the archaeological literature pertaining to HSI and to buffalo jumps generally, the historical records of early western Canadian explorers, fur traders, and missionaries, the anthropological literature about the Plains Indians, and so forth. Consultation and integration of these data into a display format could be achieved without any more involvement of the local native groups than as an advisory body, providing approvals during the various stages of the development project. But would such an approach make native people feel like essential contributors to the development of this interpretive centre? Without necessarily questioning the accuracy of data contained in traditional anthropological sources, native people the fact remains often view these data as "white man's knowledge," collected and presented through the filter of the white man's culture. As a project of the Alberta Government, and its non-native staff, HSI could never entirely circumvent this filter, but it was also clear that a greater legitimacy, in the eyes of native people, could be obtained if the contemporary members of the Blackfoot Nation could make direct and meaningful contributions to the information to be contained in the centre. With this in mind, and with the additional goal of seeking any new or alternate information to that already available in the standard reference works, we decided to initiate a series of interviews with elders of the various Blackfoot reserves.

To gain the necessary approval for conducting interviews with Blackfoot elders, I attended a meeting in 1982 with the Peigan Band Council, presenting to it and the Chief the nature of the HSI development project, an indication of some of the anticipated native participation, and a request that interviews with elders be initiated to collect information on all aspects of the buffalo jump. Although not the first attempt to meet with the Band Council, this was the first successful effort to present officially to the Peigan governing body the project's aims. Development of the jump was presented as a project which, by preserving and interpreting native past, would be of benefit to contemporary natives and non-natives alike. Reaction to the proposal was generally favourable, although the plan to develop the site met with scepticism. In light of the number of times that native people have discovered the fallacy of government agents' promises, the sceptical reception was understandable.

Questions at this meeting focused on what kind and number of jobs for native people would result from the eventual development. Moreover, would people be paid for the interviews? If so, how much, and would any native people be hired to actually work on the interview project? The Band Council recommended that the proposal be approved on the following conditions: that one part-time person be employed as an assistant to the anthropologist; that the salary for this person be $500.00 per month; that the Band Council select this person (Joe Crow Shoe Sr. was chosen at the meeting) and that the Peigan Cultural Centre be identified as the coordinating agency for the project. Subsequent contact with the Cultural Centre touched off a series of problems and debates highlighting some of the frustrations encountered and lessons learned during the early stages of gaining native support and cooperation.

Late in 1982 I contracted the services of a cultural anthropologist, Dr. Roger McDonnell, who, with Joe Crow Shoe Sr. as his assistant, conducted interviews with Blackfoot elders. In the first meeting with the staff of the Cultural Centre, however, a major obstacle arose when McDonnell offered to pay all informants at a rate of $10.00 per hour, compared to the Centre's demand of $75.00. Such a wide discrepancy could not be bridged with the financial resources available to McDonnell. Permission to conduct interviews with the Peigan elders was therefore denied. There are historical reasons why this impasse was reached, which are particular to the people under study.

Beginning about fifteen years ago, a non-native individual began publishing popular books about the Blackfoot people. Whether it is true or not, the *perception* among many of the Blackfoot is that this person made a considerable fortune by writing about their cultural ways. Some native people view this practice as a "rip off" of a resource which is precious and should be owned by the natives. They think, not so much that this information can not or should not be communicated to the outside world, but rather, that the native people should benefit from the publications. A member of the Band Council provided a comparison: if a consulting geologist, who is an expert on a particular topic, is paid for what he knows, a Blackfoot elder should be paid for what he knows. Unsurprisingly, as a result of this historical precedent, suspicion arose that the HSI project aimed at personal gain for non-native people. At more than one meeting, in reference to the popular writer, a native person announced that, "we don't want another one of these guys." Frequently, it was asked if there would be any books published as a result of the interviews, or if profits would be made in any other way from this project. (I was even asked if this material would be used in the production of my own graduate thesis, as this too was seen as a form of personal, albeit not monetary, gain.) Furthermore, this situation explains the insistence on the high rate of pay demanded by the Cultural Centre for interviews with the elders. Despite assurances that any information collected would be used solely for the betterment of the story to be told at the HSI interpretive centre, the sour taste of the previous experience resulted in a refusal to relax the identified rate of pay. Clearly, assurances were not enough to remove the deeply ingrained belief that personal benefit would accrue to the non-native people involved in this project. What happened next is an interesting lesson in the independent operation of individuals within the loose structure of Reserve government.

Still in 1982, in a stroke of good fortune, the Band Council directed me to see Joe Crow Shoe Sr., whom noted plains historian and native researcher Hugh Dempsey advised me to secure for the project if I could. Crow Shoe was then and continues to be one of the most respected spiritual leaders among all the Blackfoot, and indeed among all Northern Plains Indians. By the time the Band Council had rejected the proposed interview programme, anthropologist McDonnell and I had already met with and informed Crow Shoe about the nature and purpose of the project. As a result, he became a strong supporter of the need for this work, pointing out that young Blackfoot people no longer possess information about the past and that the elders are dying off rapidly.[10] Convinced, as well, the project was a legitimate one from which no one would personally benefit, Crow Shoe agreed to work with McDonnell. Early in 1983, Crow Shoe, McDonnell, and two other respected Peigan elders met privately to work out new terms of reference. Informants would be paid at a rate of \$18.75 per hour (exactly one quarter the rate identified by the Cultural Centre), McDonnell would urge me not to publish the report which resulted from these interviews (as this might bring in revenue which would be contrary to the spirit of the endeavour), and finally McDonnell was to write a second report which was to be owned solely by those who assisted him with the project. Although the revised terms were agreed upon by Crow Shoe and the other two elders, McDonnell, and myself, the Peigan Cultural Centre never approved them. It was clear that interviews would have to be conducted on the other Blackfoot reserves.

Ironically, the one Blackfoot group that Alberta Culture staff had chosen to work with was now the one that had to be avoided. As a rule, McDonnell and Crow Shoe were warmly received on the reserves of the Blood, Blackfoot, and the South Peigan in Montana— groups which had never been formally approached about the project. The key was Crow Shoe, a respected elder and spiritual leader, rather than a white government employee, who approached the authorities and informed them of the nature of the mission. It would have been a great act of disrespect to him not to grant permission to conduct the interviews. Had Crow Shoe made the initial presentation about this project to the Peigan Cultural Centre, approval likely would have been received.

The net result of this research was a final report,[11] which, as requested, was never published, and a large collection of tape recordings with partial transcripts. In truth, little of the collected data had a direct effect on the HSI project, and little was ever used in the subsequent displays. Much more significant were the project's demonstration that there still existed a considerable body of knowledge about the ancient buffalo jumps, and, by its informing many of the elders throughout the Blackfoot Nation of the intentions to develop the HSI site, the winning of their support. The influence this support would have in smoothing the process of seeking additional co-operation and contributions from native people proved critical to native involvement with HSI.

Interpretation

Research and Development
Preliminary contacts were necessary with the Peigan and, eventually, others of the Blackfoot Nation, through the discussions of the Think Tank, the meetings with the Band Council and the Cultural Centre, and the subsequent informant interviews. The interviews accomplished much in the way of disseminating knowledge of the project and good public relations, but they lacked a focus for application to an actual thematic structure for the interpretive centre. The integration of contemporary native information and standard reference data into an interpretive framework was precisely the next step in the evolution of the HSI project. This led full circle, back to the Peigan Band Council, the Cultural Centre, and to more informant interviews.

In 1985, after a hiatus of about a year, we again made contact with the Peigan Band Chief and Council. We explained that our office now wished to establish a formal means of having the Peigan participate in the HSI project, as an advisory body to review proposals for displays, artifacts, text, and so forth, and as a source of information, to provide data on themes and storyline for the interpretive centre. The Band Council recognized that the advice needed was better offered by the elders than by a political body. Accordingly, we were referred, through the Peigan Cultural Centre, to a weekly meeting of elders at the town of Brocket. (Interestingly, the previous, unofficial, interviews conducted by McDonnell and Crow Shoe at the other Blackfoot reserves were never mentioned despite the fact that the "small town" communication system of Reserve life precludes anyone's not having learned of them.) Joanne Yellow Horn, the Centre's director, arranged for me to attend an initial meeting and present to the elders the nature of the HSI project, and to discuss the various functions which native people might play in this process. Because of a lack of funding, neither I nor the team of McDonnell and Crow Shoe had ever met with the Peigan elders at the Cultural Centre. And since the initial project was forced to avoid working on the Peigan

Reserve, these elders, while aware that the interviews had taken place, remained largely unaware of the details of the HSI project.

The Peigan elders greeted the initial presentation positively yet cautiously. All who spoke to the issue (typically a small number of those present, and limited to the most respected males) applauded the concept of interpreting the buffalo jump as a way of preserving aspects of native heritage which were quickly being lost. Interestingly, they often noted that the proposed facility would serve as a means to educate *native* children about their heritage; the benefits of educating the non-native populace were seldom mentioned. Yet, at the same time, the native reaction to the proposal seemed rather abstract and distant because of their longstanding suspicion of overtures from non-natives.

At the same meeting, we told elders of the intention to involve the native community with aspects of the site development, and we outlined some of the steps involved in this process. Discussion included the conduct of further research among Blackfoot elders, the involvement of the elders in the review of information to be presented in the interpretive centre, including text, display concepts, and artifact content, and the role of native people in actually presenting the interpretive programme at HSI. It was at this meeting that the statement—"as long as it is done right"—was made. It set the tone for much of the native participation on the project. Nearly all the elders could recount numerous examples, drawn from major museums across the country and even abroad, where native heritage was displayed incorrectly. These errors ranged from the inappropriate juxtaposition of artifacts that did not belong together, to incorrect placement of artifacts in a display or diorama (such as a tipi door facing in the wrong direction), to the playing of the wrong native music with a particular artifact display. These errors have created a serious credibility gap between native people and the museum community. The elders made clear that their meaningful involvement with HSI required the assurance that this time "things would be done right."

Early relations with the Peigan were certainly hindered by the fact that the opening and operation of the interpretive centre was so distant that economic benefits for the native community amounted to mere promises of some unspecified horn of plenty. With no intent to avoid the issue, we nevertheless had no answers to these questions. With the exception of a likely opening date (which proved to be inaccurate by a margin of several years), there was no information available on when and how many natives might be hired. But the commitment was clearly presented at the initial meeting with the elders; employment would exist, would be substantial in number and, most important, would be meaningful both to the operation of the site and to the historical traditions of Blackfoot culture. Still, this amounted to no more than another white man's promise. The elders' abiding apprehension was understandable.

The initial meeting had established the Peigan Cultural Centre as the meeting place for a series of interviews, and the elders who assembled there as both a review body and a source of information about the site itself and native culture in general. This time the research would be conducted with a preconceived plan for incorporation of information into a display format. All Peigan who met the band definition of an "elder" were invited to attend periodic meetings late in 1985. Sam Good Rider and Reg Crowshoe acted as interpreters and translators of tape recordings, for although command of English ranged from excellent to very limited, most elders were more comfortable speaking in Blackfoot. Moreover, it became clear that discussion of certain topics—the traditional history of their people, ceremonial life, and story telling about "the old days"—was deemed more appropriate in Blackfoot. Thus, interviews were taped during afternoon sessions, and Good Rider and Reg Crow Shoe translated them in the evenings. As the conversations tended to stray over a wide range of topics, many of which were of limited interest to our purposes, translations were provided only for relevant stories.

When money again arose as an issue, all concerned reached a new compromise whereby $75.00 would be paid to each person for each session regardless of its duration. Typically, interview sessions lasted from 10:00 AM to 2 or 3:00 PM. At the outset, money was a minor concern, since an average meeting involved about a dozen people. As word of the sessions spread, however, the numbers grew until, at one point, nearly forty people attended a single meeting. Many of those in attendance at sessions did not contribute to the discussions about traditional aspects of Blackfoot culture. It is tempting to suggest that increased attendance was a response to the spread of the word across the Reserve that money was available for simply being at the meetings. No doubt, this was partially true; with high unemployment on the Peigan Reserve, especially among the elders, the funds involved were significant. This, however, is only part of the story.

That many in attendance said little or nothing, indicates a continuation of certain Blackfoot social rules and values. First, gender played a part: with a few exceptions, women often said little and clearly were expected to remain silent on most topics. For the most part, the questions I posed involved traditional forms of buffalo hunting—essentially a male activity, requiring answers from men. But, moreover, because so much of Blackfoot culture was male dominated, even a question regarding a specific female activity might be answered by either a male or a female; the same taboo about not speaking of matters pertinent to the other sex did not seem to apply equally to the males. Second, age played a part. The younger members of the elders deferred to the senior members, either by hesitating to speak or by awaiting and then supporting the seniors' statements. Third, only a few elders were clearly recognized as the real sources of traditional knowledge. Because the words of these individuals carried more weight than anyone else's, it was deemed inappropriate for other, less knowledgeable, individuals to speak in the presence of these senior elders. When pressed to speak (during a protracted silence on a particular issue, Good Rider or Reg Crow Shoe would go around the room urging people to talk), many of the elders declined, saying that they did not possess the requisite knowledge. Frequently, they added that they were in the presence of the really knowledgeable elders, and that the latter should do the talking since they would "tell it the right way." One's inclusion in this select group of elders appeared to depend heavily on the conditions under which the individual was raised. Having been raised by grandparents (who, it could be established, did in fact participate directly in the last of the great buffalo kills) instead of by parents, and not having been forced to attend residential school (where great efforts were made to eliminate all vestiges of traditional native culture) were two important attributes of the most respected elders, Billy Strikes With a Gun and Nick Smith. Often, a topic would produce a general round table discussion for a considerable time until a number of the elders agreed that Billy or Nick should tell the story. While egalitarian, this procedure was very time consuming and costly. After several months of meeting every week or two, it was decided to hold a few final meetings with only the more senior elders.

Integration: The Napi Stories

Informant interviews, combined with archaeological and historical research, provided much material for development of the interpretive thematic structure and storyline. Much of the material to be presented in the centre would be straightforward information concerning the plains environment, Plains Indian culture, the operation of the buffalo jump, and so forth. The earlier decision to augment this material with contemporary information acquired directly from the Blackfoot raised the issue of how to present this new material to the general public. Should Blackfoot oral history be presented in like manner and alongside anthropological and other scientific text material? If indeed some of the newly generated information represents a different, but equally valid, order of reality when compared to the traditional scientific and historical literature, then perhaps the presentation of displays should reflect this separate reality.

As was noted above, the second series of interviews with the elders was conducted with a preconceived plan for incorporating new information with actual text and displays. This plan involved the use of "Napi Stories." Napi is the creator of the Blackfoot people. Somewhat like a god, but with a human element of prankster thrown in, Napi created the earth, the animals, men and women, and so on. Napi also interacts with the things around him, makes mistakes, and loses as often as he wins. For the purposes of the interpretive centre, Napi stories provide an element of interpretation based on nonwestern thought. (As an aside, part of Blackfoot oral tradition has it that Napi stories were always told at night, not during the day. Thus, during the recording sessions at the Cultural Centre, the curtains were carefully closed when a Napi story was about to be told.)

Two important questions arose: how to present the Napi stories within the display area of the interpretive centre, and which version of a particular Napi story to use. Regarding the former, the fact that many if not all of the guide staff would be native people allowed for the possibility of the preferred delivery system—first-hand telling by Blackfoot people. It could not be assumed, however, that staff would always be available in various galleries in the building to present these stories. An automatic delivery system was needed. It seemed inappropriate to put Napi stories, part of oral history, onto display panels alongside text based upon anthropological and archaeological information.

Two nonwritten delivery systems were employed. First, using native speakers, tape recordings were made of several Napi stories. Today these are presented in the centre in both Blackfoot and English. Second, slide projectors mounted on the ceiling project short versions of Napi stories onto sandstone boulders at a number of locations on the first three levels of the building. These levels, because they deal with the environmental and cultural conditions prior to contact with Europeans, offer the most appropriate settings for the traditional Napi stories. Never written down in the past, the Napi stories presented in the Interpretive Centre continue to be passed on as a form of story telling, not as written history.

The second issue concerned which version of Napi stories to use in the displays. During the past century, Napi stories have appeared in the anthropological literature.[12] It would have been a simple task to extract, from the published anthropological sources, the relevant Napi stories for use in the displays. In many cases, the Napi stories told by the elders were astonishingly similar to those recorded nearly a hundred years ago. In some cases, however, there were important differences in the old and modern versions of the same story. These variations often reflect European influence in native religion. For example, one story tells how Napi created the land. In the older versions, Napi floats on the water, encouraging various animals to bring up mud from the bottom of the water. In one contemporary version told during an interview, Napi was floating on a cloud. The influence of the Christian concept of God in the latter version seems clear. The contemporary version of the Napi stories, it was argued, would be more relevant, if potentially less "traditional," to the Blackfoot people themselves.

Undoubtedly, all oral history has been subject to a certain amount of change through time, even when there has been an expressed attempt to recount stories exactly as they were learned. All too often, traditional (precontact) native culture is seen as a static entity which persisted unaltered for thousands of years. As Trigger has noted, the culture of the North American Indians has been, and continues to be, seen as a part more of the natural environment than of the cultural achievements of ancient people in other parts of the world.[13] Using the contemporary, rather than the "traditional" Napi stories, was an intentional recognition of the dynamic nature of culture and of the fact that no particular period in the history of a cultural group is more valid or authentic than any other.

The Interpretive Centre's displays of the Napi stories present an alternate, and sometimes conflicting, interpretation of information when compared with western knowledge systems. For example, on the first level of the building a display panel presents a brief interpretation of the glacial erratics which line the prairie immediately east of the jump. A display panel bearing the standard geological explanation indicates that the erratics were deposited by glacial ice. Immediately adjacent to this panel is a sandstone boulder, onto which is projected the Napi story of the origin of the erratics. In this version, Napi leaves his buffalo robe with a large rock which was feeling cold. Later, Napi himself grows cold and wants his robe back. The rock becomes angry and starts chasing Napi across the landscape. Pieces of the rock are broken and thrown at Napi during the chase, leaving the glacial erratics that can be seen today. The two explanations employ very different concepts of reality, so vastly different in foundation that visitors to HSI seem clearly to grasp the fact that the issue is not which explanation is correct, but, rather, that two cultures have devised their own means of understanding the matters of the universe.

This, then, is how the project evolved. Meetings were held, questions asked, wide ranging discussion ensued, Napi stories were told, recordings were translated and selected parts were taken and fitted into the overall themes of the Interpretive Centre. By prior arrangement with the Cultural Centre, all original tape recordings of meetings with the elders were retained by the centre, while HSI kept the English translations. This arrangement reflected, and was sensitive to, the continuing fear that some misuse—especially profit—might result from the release of original material.

Other than the problem of payments for increasingly high attendance at the meetings, the first function of the Peigan elders committee, that of suggesting and supplying information for displays (in the form of oral history) succeeded, in the eyes of all parties. After an initial nervous hesitation by both the researchers and the elders, the meetings became a source of great pleasure and were eagerly anticipated. Although the Peigan Reserve has witnessed its share of the usual individual anthropological studies over the past century, with researchers disappearing, neither them nor their work to be heard from again, nothing similar to this project had been tried before. This time, there was an end product which had tangible meaning for those involved: some of their own words and ideas would soon make their way into a building located just a few kilometres from their homes, to be read by thousands of visitors. By late 1985 this fact was dramatically underscored, as heavy machinery rumbled across the prairie and huge cranes towered over the cliffs where bison had once plunged to their death. The promises were visibly coming true; there truly would be a a place to commemorate and celebrate the proudest moments—the great buffalo hunts—of Plains Indian culture.

As the reality of the HSI interpretive project became accepted, so did a deep sense of responsibility. The elders knew that their words would stand for, and would be seen by, a much larger group of people than their own, native people in particular. This prospect reinforced the elders' conviction that HSI "had to be done right." Moreover, it would present a tangible testimony to the value that other members of society place on their deep knowledge. Meanwhile, the work of the second dimension of the elders committee, that of reviewing material prepared by government staff, continued through the latter part of 1985 and all of 1986. A few interesting debates occurred; they are discussed in the following section. In reviewing and commenting on concepts for displays, all text material, and all proposed artifacts to be used throughout the building, the elders recommended few changes. Since the HSI building is truly an interpretive centre, lacking the extensive curatorial requirements of a museum, there is very little use made of original artifacts, so replicas had to be made for the displays. The great majority of these were prepared by skilled Blackfoot people, whom the elders recommended. In the case of some replicas native involvement was mandatory; for example, a decorated ceremonial buffalo skull could be made only by an individual of high spiritual status.

Debates and Controversies

It would be misleading to imply that all flowed smoothly. One of the most contentious issues in the design of displays was native religion and ceremony. There were essentially two sides to this discussion. Many aspects of Plains Indian culture are steeped in religion and ceremony;[14] was this fact to be discussed and portrayed, or ignored? Omission of it would deny visitors the knowledge that religion permeated most aspects of daily life, and would imply that Plains Indian culture was devoid of religious beliefs and customs. The counter argument, however, was that public presentation of this topic trespassed on areas of culture which modern native people deem highly sensitive and private. In fact, the evolution of the concept for the displays led to the proposal of several ideas specifically concerned with religious themes. For example, in the gallery where the operation of the jump is explained, the "Iniskim" ceremony is presented. Iniskim is the Blackfoot word for the buffalo stones—

fragments of ammonite fossils which occasionally take the shape of various animals—used in ceremonies designed to lure the bison to the trap. Sacred paraphernalia associated with the Iniskim ceremony include the buffalo stone itself, a medicine pipe, sweetgrass or needles of sweet pine, sometimes a rattle, buffalo fur, red ochre, and so on. A second display of an even more sensitive nature concerned the sacred medicine bundles of the Plains Indians. Medicine pipe bundles are today considered the most sacred artifact among the Blackfoot[15] and have probably been regarded as such for quite some time.[16] In the early planning of displays for the interpretive centre, the discussion of the role and importance of the medicine bundles, as well as the exhibition of some form of a bundle, were proposed.

As was standard procedure for all displays, Peigan elders reviewed and commented on the text and a list of the artifacts required for the bundle display. All displays involving a religious theme yielded much discussion, but none more so than the bundle. Whereas the inaccuracies in the design and display of less important ceremonies at other museums could, the elders thought, have been averted by greater involvement in the work by natives, the issue of the bundles was much more complicated. Indeed, the issue of the display and interpretation of a medicine bundle drew more attention than all other displays combined. On the one hand, there were those who felt that it was inappropriate to display a medicine bundle and to discuss its role in native culture, for to do so would be to treat a sacred matter in a profane way. Others felt that not to discuss the significance of the bundles was to ignore the most important part of native religious life, and, consequently, to distort the presentation of this part of their culture. All elders agreed only that a *real* medicine bundle should not be displayed within the interpretive centre; and all would have firmly opposed the idea had it been proposed.

After much debate, a compromise emerged: the display and interpretation of a *replica* of a medicine pipe bundle. While most elders agreed that this would not compromise the sanctity of the artifact and its function, they still attached many prerequisites to this solution. First, it was essential that the replica bundle be made by a qualified elder; that is, the owner of a real bundle had to construct the replica. This apparent solution generated further debate. Did not a replica made by a legitimate bundle owner become essentially a real bundle? Did not such a "legitimate replica" then require the care and attention given a real bundle, such as the annual renewal of tobacco and blessing at a sun dance?

These concerns led to the second prerequisite: the replica would be made to look like a real bundle from the outside, but the inside would be empty except for the pipe stems, which, in order for the bundle to look authentic, would have to protrude out of the hide shell. An empty bundle should not require the same renewal and care as a real bundle. Third, only a person with the requisite spiritual qualifications could install the bundle properly in the display, and any subsequent attention to the bundle (such as its removal for occasional cleaning, photography, and so on) must also be performed by a qualified person. Fourth, it was imperative that the text for this display make particular note of the fact that the artifact on display was in fact a replica, not a real bundle, and that it had been made by a person of high spiritual standing: the elders did not wish other native people visiting the interpretive centre to think that a real bundle was on display, for such an inference would reflect badly on their guidance of the interpretive programming. Thus, the text for the medicine bundle display, as for no other display in the interpretive centre, explicitly states that this item is a replica and that it was made by a spiritual elder. To this day, however, the display remains controversial in that some native guide staff disagree with its inclusion in the displays, and do not interpret it to the visiting public.

Not all elders will necessarily agree on issues of great importance. The point was made above that the Blood Band was not consulted early in the history of the research and development of HSI. Further evidence that this was an error arose in 1986, when, after the Peigan elders had agreed to the display of a replica bundle, I met with two influential members of the Blood Band, the respected spiritual leader, Dan Weasel Moccasin, and Wilton Good Striker, then leader of the Horn Society. At this meeting, these Blood Band members strongly disagreed with the presentation of the replica bundle, all prerequisites notwithstanding. Had the non-native members of the HSI planning team proposed its display, the Bloods would have intervened to oppose it, but since the idea had been endorsed specifically by the Peigan elders, the Blood Band members limited their disagreement to a refusal to involve themselves with the display in any way. Aside from learning not to expect consensus among elders even of closely related native bands, several other important lessons offer themselves. Perhaps most important is the power of a native elders committee. This meeting with the Blood showed how vitally important approval from the Peigan elders was for the bundle display. Without their consent and strict supervision of it, a serious difference of opinion between HSI and the Blood Band would have emerged. No amount of persuasion and rationalization by non-natives as to the potential need or value of such a display would have impressed the Blood elders. The Blood tolerated this situation with benign indifference only because the idea had the backing of individuals who possessed status equal to their own. Another lesson is the need, from the outset, to form a committee comprising elders from any reserve that a project will affect.

Ongoing Native Involvement

This paper primarily concerns native participation in the events and processes which led to the research and development of the HSI Interpretive Centre. Elsewhere in this issue, the role of native people in the operation of the building is discussed in detail by Ed Sponholz. One aspect of the continuing operation of the site remains relevant to this paper, however. The role of native people in the ongoing archaeological research at HSI also offers lessons about the role of native people in discovering their own past. Since the opening of the site in 1987, a summer program of archaeological field research has been presented in a setting accessible to the visiting public. Including the pre-opening field work, eight seasons of archaeological excavation have now been completed; all have included native people as members of the project. Aside from providing meaningful employment in the exploration of native heritage, this involvement has yielded several important observations.

First, as more native staff are brought through the archaeological program, spending weeks digging and listening to the site interpretation provided by the archaeologists, they become trained in interpretation as well. Clearly, the general public (composed largely of non-natives) finds it preferable to receive information on the site from a native person. It is widely accepted in archaeology that the past is less a discovery than a creation. As Potter and Leone have noted, "There is little knowledge of the past that is not filtered or shaped by the present, and none that is unquestionably true or value-free. This does not mean that the past did not exist, but that whenever it is reached for, the reaching shapes."[17] Furthermore, the presentation of the past to the public is itself an act of creation: "... the entire presentation, not just the facts about the past, or excavation, or analytical techniques, becomes an entirely new artifact, a piece of modern material culture, one to be analyzed for what it tells about the culture creating it, not about the past *per se*."[18] If indeed the presentation of the past is shaped, to some extent, by the cultural background of the interpreter, then it is fair to say that native interpretation will differ in some unique way from the story of the past told by non-natives. Experience suggests that a typical visitor to HSI will be more interested in the unfamiliar and seemingly exotic story, as shaped through the cultural filters of native people, than in the already familiar cultural sieves of his or her own background. Thus, even though the native staff deliver much the same factual information as do the archaeologists who train them, the *interpretation* by a native person creates a past which the public seems especially interested in learning. As an example, natives interpreting the archaeological project often relate statements about what their parents or grandparents have told them; thereby, they bring to their interpretation a human dimension that non-natives seldom present in such an intimate way.

A second observation is that native staff find interpretation more interesting and rewarding than excavation. To recount for the visitors the truly astonishing story of cunning, sophistication, and knowledge that went into the operation of a prehistoric buffalo jump is clearly a source of pride to the native interpreter, a sentiment difficult to glean from the excavation of fragmented individual artifacts. Furthermore, it is clear that the telling of this remarkable story, as a form of oral history, is both a subject and an activity which lies much closer to the familiar cultural background of the Plains Indians than does the essentially foreign activity of field archaeology. Certainly not applicable to all archaeological situations or to all cultural groups, the experience from Head-Smashed-In suggests that to dig is to have a hot, dirty job that yields a pay cheque; to interpret the dramatic saga of the buffalo jump is to be an Indian (see Figs. 1 and 2).

Finally, it should be noted that the continued involvement of native people on the HSI archaeological project has largely eliminated the issue of artifact ownership and repatriation. During the past eight seasons, native people have consistently made up a significant portion of the staff. Furthermore, in recent years the excavations have commenced and concluded with a ceremony in which a Blackfoot elder administers a blessing to the crew, the artifacts, and the work done by the archaeologists. For my part, I stress to the spiritual leaders both that the excavations done by our crew aim to under-

Fig. 1. Peigan Indian John Holloway excavating at Head-Smashed-In Buffalo Jump. (Archaeological Survey of Alberta)

Fig. 2. Peigan Elder, Joe Crow Shoe Sr., blesses a kill site dig, 1989. (Archaeological Survey of Alberta)

stand better the ways of their ancestors, and that the artifacts removed from the earth will never be owned by anyone personally, will never be traded, sold, or used for any purpose other than to help interpret the past. Perhaps this context helps explain how the issue of repatriation diminishes in importance. Quite simply, when native people play an integral role in the discovery of their own past, they do not feel that something either has been taken away or, therefore, needs to be repatriated. Yet, the situation remains far from ideal: employing native people as crew members and interpreters is an important start but their movement into the more substantive roles of the professional archaeologist must ensue.

Concluding Remarks

North American archaeology finds itself needing to decide how to make the study of the past relevant to those whom the discipline serves, without further exacerbating a growing sense of discontent, especially among native people who continue to watch the past uncovered in spite, rather than because, of them. Furthermore, academics, as well as museum and government scientists realize in increasing numbers that innovative attempts to interpret the past to the general public will likely meet with resounding success. The one-half million visitors to HSI in the past three years demonstrates such success. That related attempts at bringing the past to the public with the help of native people are now progressing in Canada, is indeed encouraging.[19]

The HSI project marks an attempt, admittedly flawed at times, to integrate the knowledge, beliefs, values, and life experiences of native and non-native people for the common purpose of telling a story about the past. Critical now is the opportunity for additional attempts.

Acknowledgements

Support for the work reported in this paper has come from both the Archaeological Survey of Alberta and the Historic Sites Service. My thanks go to present and former staff of the Historical Resources Division of Alberta Culture, especially to Drs. W.J. Byrne, P. Donahue, J. Ives, D. Burley, F. Pannekoek, T. Nicks, and M. Magne, for long years of assistance. Ms. Liz Connell, formerly of the Historic Sites Service, was instrumental in organizing, assisting with (and paying for) the interviews with the Peigan elders at the Brocket Reserve. Comments on an early draft of this paper were supplied by W.J. Byrne, J. Ives, M. Magne, M. Nagy, and two anonymous reviewers. While I have taken to heart many of their suggestions, the opinions expressed remain my own. I extend my thanks to the editors of *Alberta: Studies in the Arts and Sciences* for their interest, patience, and assistance.

I wish to acknowledge the assistance and advice that I have received from many members of the Blood and Peigan bands. Interviews and review sessions at the Peigan Cultural Centre were facilitated by Joanne Yellow Horn and Bryan Yellow Horn. These two individuals also coordinated all meetings with the elders during the many discussions of the requirements for displays and artifacts at HSI. Assistance with interviews and translations of tape recordings was provided by Reg Crow Shoe and Sam Good Rider. Although many participated in the interviews, the important contributions of Billy Strikes With a Gun and Nick Smith require special acknowledgement. My thanks go as well to the Peigan Band Chief and Council for permission to conduct interviews with elders and for assistance in establishing the Peigan elders as an advisory body.

My sincere thanks to Louisa Crow Shoe, Leo Pard, Kenneth Eagle Speaker, Linda Eagle Speaker, Lorraine Good Striker, Murray Small Legs, Walter Crow Shoe, Eldon Yellow Horn, Willy Big Bull, Sandra Aberdeen, Reg Crow Shoe, Sam Good Rider, Wilfred Yellow Wings, Lorraine Jackson, John Holloway, Rita Morning Bull, Ester Tail Feathers, Dan Weasel Moccasin, Wilton Good Striker, and Josephine Crow Shoe. Finally, my thanks to Joe Crow Shoe Sr., who shared the most.

Jack Brink is an Archaeologist with the Archaeological Survey, Provincial Museum of Alberta.

Notes

1. See articles in *Who Owns the Past?*, Isabel McBryde, ed. (Melbourne: Oxford University Press, 1985); and articles by Bruce Trigger, Julia Harrison, Richard Hill and Michael Ames in *Muse* 6, no. 3 (1988). For a thorough listing of related publications, see "American Indian Sacred Objects, Skeletal Remains, Repatriation and Reburial: A Resource Guide," Rayna Green and Nancy Marie Mitchell, ed. and comp. (Washington: The American Indian Program, National Museum of American History, Smithsonian Institution, 1990).

2. Anon., "Redefining the Nature of American Archaeology" Society for American Archaeology *Bulletin* 8, no. 2 (April 1990), p. 1.

3. See Robert McGhee, "Who Owns Prehistory? The Bering Land Bridge Dilemma," *Canadian Journal of Archaeology* 13 (1989), pp. 13–20; and Jack Brink, "Site Significance: Preservation, Zen and Indians," paper presented to the Association of Heritage Consultants, Toronto, 1989.

4. Jack Brink and Bob Dawe, *Final Report of the 1985 and 1986 Field Seasons at Head-Smashed-In Buffalo Jump, Alberta,* Archaeological Survey of Alberta Manuscript Series No. 16. (Edmonton: Alberta Culture and Multiculturalism, 1989).

5. See Jack Brink, *Dog Days in Southern Alberta.* Archaeological Survey of Alberta Occasional Paper No. 28 (Edmonton: Alberta Culture and Multiculturalism, 1986), Hugh A. Dempsey, *Indian Tribes of Alberta* (Calgary: Glenbow Museum, 1986), John C. Ewers, *The Blackfeet: Raiders of the Northwestern Plains* (Norman: University of Oklahoma Press, 1958), and Clark Wissler, "Material Culture of the Blackfoot Indians," *Anthropological Papers of the American Museum of Natural History* 5, pt. 1 (1910).

6. Peter Fidler, "Journal of a journey overland from Buckingham House to the Rocky Mountains in 1792 and 1793," unpub. ms. on file, Provincial Archives of Alberta, Edmonton.

7. W.J. Byrne, personal communication, 1990.

8. Ibid.

9. R.F. McDonnell, "PIS'KUN: Some Ethnohistorical Considerations of the Blackfoot Communal Buffalo Hunt," unpub. report on file, Archaeological Survey of Alberta, Edmonton (1984), p. 9.

10. Ibid., p. 10.

11. Ibid.

12. See C.C. Uhlenbeck, *Original Blackfoot Texts from the Southern Peigan Blackfoot Reservation, Teton Country, Montana* (Amsterdam: J. Muller, 1911), and George Bird Grinnell, *Blackfoot Lodge Tales* (Lincoln: University of Nebraska Press, 1962).

13. Bruce Trigger, "The Past as Power," in *Who Owns the Past?* p. 21.

14. See Clark Wissler, "Social Organization and Ritualistic Ceremonies of the Blackfoot Indians," *Anthropological Papers of the American Museum of Natural History* 7 (1911), pp. 3–64, Clark Wissler, "Ceremonial Bundles of the Blackfoot Indians," *Anthropological Papers of the American Museum of Natural History* 7, pt. 2 (1911), pp. 65–289, and Ewers, *The Blackfeet.*

15. J. Crowshoe, personal communication, 1987.

16. Wissler, "Ceremonial Bundles."

17. Parker B. Potter, Jr. and Mark P. Leone, "Archaeology in Public in Anapolis: Four Seasons, Six Sites, Seven Tours, and 32,000 Visitors," *American Archaeology* 6 (1987), p. 52.

18. Mark P. Leone, "Archaeology's Relationship to the Present and the Past," in *Modern Material Culture, The Archaeology of Us,* Richard A. Gould and Michael B. Schiffer, eds. (New York: Academic Press, 1981), p. 5.

19. See Gerald T. Conaty, "Canada's First Nations and Museums, A Saskatchewan Experience," *The International Journal of Museum Management and Curatorship* 8 (1989), pp. 407–413, and William A. Fox, "Native Archaeology in Ontario: A Status Report," *Arch Notes* 89.6 (Nov./Dec. 1989), pp. 30–31.

ED SPONHOLZ

Head-Smashed-In Buffalo Jump

A Centre for Cultural Preservation and Understanding

At a remote location in southwestern Alberta, several millenia before European settlement began in western Canada, a ten-metre high and three hundred-metre long sandstone cliff became a meeting place for prehistoric hunters. Archaeological research over the past fifty years has revealed that Plains Indians employed this precipice, now named "Head-Smashed-In Buffalo Jump," to stampede herds of buffalo to their death. There the Peigan (Blackfoot) Indians of historical times and their predecessors hunted buffalo for at least 5600 years and possibly as many as 9000.[1] Today, Head-Smashed-In (HSI) is the site of a major interpretive effort to chronicle and preserve the saga of this ancient cultural landmark, which continues its role as a meeting place, but now serves, as well, as a locale for a variety of scientific and multicultural activities. A visitor's centre acts as the interpretive centre's focal point. Managed by the Alberta Government, Department of Culture and Multiculturalism, this centre provides many services: exhibits and displays with replicas of artifacts, on-site archaeological research during the summer, Blackfoot-speaking interpretive guides, cross-cultural employment, special events promoting the preservation of Plains Indian heritage, a "Friends Society" for encouraging community involvement, and facilities for other types of gatherings. In order to focus on the life of HSI since the official opening of its interpretive centre in July 1987, one

Fig. 1. Head-Smashed-In Interpretive Centre.

must begin with a brief look at the past role of Head-Smashed-In Buffalo Jump.

According to Peigan Indian legend, the Head-Smashed-In Buffalo Jump owes its name to a young Indian who fell victim to his own curiosity. The boy, too young to participate in the hunt, decided to conceal himself beneath the cliff and watch the bison plummet to their deaths in front of him. Unfortunately for him, the hunt was very good that day. As the bodies piled up in front of him, he was trapped against the cliff and crushed by the tremendous weight of the beasts. Later, when the buffalo carcasses were pulled away, the boy was found with his skull crushed. In his memory, the jump was named "Itsipa̱'ksikihkinihkootsiiyapo'pi'" (where-he-got-his-head-smashed-in).

The Plains Indians depended on the bison for all the essentials of life: food, clothing, shelter, fuel, and tools. But this relationship between humans and the buffalo went beyond the natural world. As a symbol of spiritual worship the

> buffalo stood very high among the animals revered, . . . and was *Nayote* (of the sun), i.e. sacred. . . . The importance of the buffalo to the survival of the Plains Indians consequently gave the buffalo

a prominent role in the religious life of the Plains tribes. This role was very evident in the mythology and ceremonies of the Plains tribes.[2]

Over several millenia, hunters developed truly sophisticated methods for luring the buffalo into drive lanes and stampeding them to their deaths. In addition,

> their hunting methods required more sophisticated social mechanisms than many scholars have been prepared to credit [them with].... For all their deceptively simple material culture, these earliest plainsmen were at the same time excellent organizers and daring coordinators when many of the white man's ancestors were still simple hunters and gatherers in the chill forests of Mesolithic Europe.[3]

Executing these hunts would have required extensive knowledge of the natural landscape, the climate, and the behaviour of bison. Before the construction of Stonehenge or the pyramids of Egypt, Plains Indians were employing sophisticated techniques in their communal buffalo hunts.

Head-Smashed-In Buffalo Jump today remains an important landmark in our understanding of the ancient lifestyles of the Plains Indians. Unique in its size, age, and complexity, it was only one among the scores of such sites on the North American Plains.[4] The last recorded use of Head-Smashed-In as a buffalo jump is the middle of the nineteenth century. The arrival on the Northern Plains of the horse, followed much later by European settlement, brought the need for buffalo jumps to an end. The cliff site and area surrounding Head-Smashed-In remained virtually abandoned until 1938, when the first professional archaeological study of it was made by Junius B. Bird, of the American Museum of Natural History.[5] Later studies, in the 1940s, 1950s, and 1960s, have unearthed historical treasures that Head-Smashed-In has held for thousands of years.

In 1981, Head-Smashed-In Buffalo Jump was declared an UNESCO Cultural World Heritage Site because of its important example of cultural and in-situ preservation. It is one of four cultural World Heritage Sites in Canada, and 240 world-wide, forming the apex of perceived value in global history.[6] A plaque erected at the entrance to the present interpretive centre records that, "Head-Smashed-In Buffalo Jump was placed on the World Heritage list at the 1981 meeting of the UNESCO World Heritage Committee as a site of outstanding universal value forming part of the cultural heritage of mankind." That designation helped Head-Smashed-In Buffalo Jump to endure as a symbol of the technological and social development of a rich prehistoric culture; although Canada declared it a National Historic Site in 1968, and Alberta a Provincial Historic Site in 1979, the UN-ESCO designation prompted Alberta Culture, also in 1981, to commit itself to the interpretive development of Head-Smashed-In both for the benefit of the public and for the protection of the site itself. Construction began in 1985, and the interpretive centre was officially opened on 23 July 1987 by the Duke and Duchess of York. The ten-million-dollar facility houses five levels of exhibits and displays, over two kilometres of outdoor interpretive trails, an eighty-seat theatre with film presentations, interactive computer displays, other audio visual presentations, a sixty-seat cafeteria, and a gift shop featuring native arts and crafts.

The centre functions chiefly to introduce visitors to the site safely and comfortably. Built into the hillside in order to blend with its natural surroundings and reflect Alberta Culture's commitment to in-situ preservation, the centre initiates the visitor's tour into two worlds of knowledge: the oral traditions, religion, and mythology of the Blackfoot; and archaeological as well as other empirical evidence of how the great communal hunts developed over several millenia. Visitors enter at the base of the building (Exhibit Level 5) and are encouraged to begin their tour by ascending to the uppermost level. Closely tied to the information presented is the centre's educational and interpretive mandate: to chronicle the buffalo hunting culture of the Plains Indians from prehistoric times to the arrival of the first Europeans. The story line for each of the five exhibit levels corresponds with the five major themes of this mandate.

Level One, entitled *Napi's World*, encompasses the theme of "The Ecology of the Northwestern Plains." Display panels present scientific data on the social behaviour of the buffalo, as well as the geography and climate of the Northern Plains. These are combined with the traditional Blackfoot explanations, or "Napi legends," for these natural phenomena. A central character in Blackfoot legends, Napi was "put here on Mother Earth by Creator Sun, an exact image of himself.... Creator Sun was always worrying about the life of his chil-

Fig. 2. The Interpretive Centre houses five levels of
exhibits and displays. (Archaeological Survey of
Alberta)

dren, a good life he wanted them to lead. Creator Sun sent a disciple
[Napi] to lead them into a better way of living. . . ."[7] Because Blackfoot legends are oral, these stories of Napi are projected by lights
onto large sandstone rocks, which are located throughout the three
upper levels of the building.

Level Two, *Napi's People*, complements the theme of "Head-
Smashed-In Buffalo Jump: A 6000 Year Record of Cultural Development and Adaptation in the Northwestern Plains." Display panels
reveal the natural world as paramount in the Plains Indians' world
view. Each season of the year signifies a different social, cultural,
and ceremonial importance. Rock projections of Napi stories com-
bine with the scientific messages presented. Visitors can also exam-
ine what life was like during the Dog Days, before the (relatively
recent) arrival of the horse, when hide tipis provided shelter and
dogs served as the beasts of burden for these nomadic tribes.

Level Three, *The Buffalo Hunt*, examines the processes involved in
"The Dynamics of Buffalo Jumping at Head-Smashed-In." Visitors
learn how clans gathered for the hunt, how the camp was organized
before the hunt, and how buffalo were hunted and then processed,

Fig. 3. Level Three: The Buffalo Hunt (Archaeological Survey of Alberta)

Fig. 4. Visitors view the exhibits from one level to another. (Archaeological Survey of Alberta)

part by part, into the essentials of life. Also featured is a ten-minute film, which imaginatively recreates a prehistoric hunt from the points of view of a holy woman who leads the hunt, and of a young buffalo runner who lures the animals to their deaths.

Level Four, entitled *Cultures in Contact*, documents the drastic changes that occurred when European settlement began in the nineteenth century. "The Buffalo Jump in Historical Perspective" tells how a way of life that had existed for thousands of years vanished in a few short decades with the arrival of the horse, the gun, and the white people. The Plains Indian became a rootless soul, his traditional way of living forever changed. In the twentieth century, most buffalo jumps on the Plains were severely damaged or destroyed, their bones literally mined from the earth for use in the manufacture of fertilizer and munitions. A short video documents the near extinction and recovery of the buffalo in recent times.

Level Five, *Uncovering the Past*, returns the visitor to the present day. The exhibits in "Uncovering the Past: the Sciences" relate how the science of anthropology and the related fields of archaeology, ethnology, and ethnography are unravelling the mysteries of the past, providing enlightenment for present and future generations. A multiprojector audio-visual presentation takes the viewer into the history of HSI through contemporary archaeological study. The presentation leads to the conclusion that we are all players in the course of human history. Level Five also houses the research laboratory for the archaeology crew during their summer operation. Visitors are invited to observe and ask questions of the staff here and at the outdoor excavation area. Both locations provide excellent opportunities for visitors to experience, firsthand, interpretation of the ongoing archaeological research at HSI.

The centre's interpretive style possesses sufficient flexibility to permit the delivery of information at a range of detail and intensity: thereby, it respects visitors' different levels of education, interest, and time. The average group or self-guided tour takes about two hours. The media presentations and trail walks provide a more challenging experience for those visitors who desire them. But beyond all the display text, fine visuals, and flashing lights, stand the centre's greatest asset—its interpretive guides—who are recruited from the nearby Peigan and Blood Indian Reserves. Their ages vary from eighteen to sixty-five. Criteria for the selection of staff include a strong background in the Blackfoot language and traditions. Those

Fig. 5. A training session for Native interpreters.

Fig. 6. A trail from the Centre's entrance level leads to a spectacular view from the bottom of the Head-Smashed-In Jump. (Archaeological Survey of Alberta)

selected undergo an intensive two-week training seminar, which includes sessions in oral traditions, archaeology, story telling techniques, hands-on demonstrations, visitor relations, offsite presentations, and use of audio-visual equipment.

Elders from both reserves play an important role in this seminar. In providing spiritual and moral guidance, they shape the new guides' understanding of the two worlds of knowledge that exist inside the centre. At the end of the seminar, they conduct a pipe-smoking and face-painting ceremony in which the new guides are given spiritual purification and blessing, and are reminded of the importance of educating non-native visitors about the history of the Blackfoot and their predecessors. All native and non-native staff at the centre are encouraged to attend these ceremonies.

Guides conduct scheduled tours at the interpretive centre, and answer individuals' concerns in the building and on the outdoor trails around the site. Guided or unguided interpretive walks include the Cliff Top Trail, which leads from the top of the centre approximately 180 metres to the edge of the cliff. Visitors can enjoy a dramatic view of the prairies to the east and the Rocky Mountains to the south. Another trail, a one-kilometre loop, accessible much of the year, departs from the centre's entrance level. It includes a spectacular view from the bottom of the HSI cliff and a walk through the campsite area where, during the summer months, the archaeological dig takes place. Along with interpretive panels, both these walks take the visitor into the prairie and its flora and fauna. Tours to more sensitive areas beyond the trail system may be arranged. Guides are also qualified to deliver interpretive programmes for adults, seniors, or special-needs groups, and educational programmes ranging from the preschool to the university level. The presentation of factual information is liberally combined with opportunities for participants to handle replicas of artifacts or even to create their own. For example, in "History Underground," the Grades seven to nine programme, students can learn firsthand the processes involved in an archaeological dig. Educational programmes are designed to meet the curriculum requirements of the Alberta Department of Education.

The interpretive guide's role is to give life both to the artifacts and displays in the centre and to the natural surroundings of the buffalo jump. While living in the modern world of science and technology, these guides are still linked through tradition to their ancestors who

Fig. 7. "Naming Ceremony" at the annual Pow Wow and Tipi Village in July. (Archaeological Survey of Alberta)

Fig. 8. Joe Crow Shoe Sr., Peigan Elder and Ceremonialist at Head-Smashed-In. (Archaeological Survey of Alberta)

hunted buffalo on the plains. Thus, they blend two bodies of knowledge to break through the ignorance and stereotyping of the past and educate visitors, both native and non-native, about the wealth of human history around them.

While virtually all interpretive staff employed at Head-Smashed-In are native, the proportion of native and non-native employees is about even among the staff employed in management and administration, scientific research, public works, the cafeteria and gift shop (both privately operated), and the Friends Society. Such a native/non-native mixture creates a unique employment opportunity. For many of the staff, both native and non-native, the centre's working environment offers the first close contact they have had with each other in a work situation. This cooperative effort abets the promotion by HSI of multicultural understanding.

Special events held year-round not only support the centre's educational and interpretive mandate, but also act to promote cultural preservation on the part of the Blackfoot people. Equally important is that these gatherings provide a festive meeting point for natives and non-natives. Summer begins with the "Dog Days Presentation Series." Each Saturday in July and August features weekly speakers on a wide variety of topics relating to HSI and Plains Indian history. Blackfoot elders, native artists, university professors, archaeologists, and museum professionals have been some of the featured speakers. July also features HSI's premier event: the annual "Pow Wow and Tipi Village." This three-day event includes a traditional Blackfoot encampment, dance competitions, special ceremonies, and numerous other activities. The Pow Wow plays a dual role as both a traditional gathering and celebration for native peoples, and an event to promote cultural tourism. Native and non-native visitors can freely mix and participate in special "honour dances" held throughout the event. The Pow Wow is almost unique in Canada, being one of the few traditional gatherings of its kind held off an Indian reserve. The 1990 Pow Wow provided particular interest. It included a Mongolian Yurt Exchange Ceremony, which symbolically linked indigenous peoples of Asia and North America.

Late summer features "Stones and Bones." This weekend event in early September promotes archaeological awareness generally, as well as specifically at this site. Young and old alike are encouraged to bring their treasured artifacts for identification by site archaeologists. Related displays and demonstrations are included to enhance the visitor's educational experience. Fall includes a youth art competition. Local schools are encouraged to enter students' art work that pertains to a selected theme relating either to Head-Smashed-In or to Blackfoot culture. The many entries received are judged by a panel of three and the winners' art works are displayed in the centre for the following year. Winners are invited to attend a ceremony to honour their accomplishment.

A "Mini Events Series," held on Sundays from December through March, features a different monthly event. Along with artifact displays, craft demonstrations, games, and film presentations, this series includes two other important annual events. One is "Heritage Through My Hands," a pre-Christmas showcase and sale of traditional arts and crafts. The public is invited to view works and demonstrations by well known Blackfoot artists and craftspeople. The other, the "Miss Buffalo Jump Princess Pageant," is held in late March. A young Blackfoot woman is selected to represent HSI on the Pow Wow Trail and other cultural events during the coming year. The contestants for Miss Buffalo Jump are judged on their knowledge, appreciation, and practice of their heritage.

Elders' gatherings and luncheons are held regularly for business or for purely social reasons. In these activities, Mr. Joe Crow Shoe Sr., a Peigan elder and ceremonialist, plays an important role for the centre by offering blessing and purification for many of the centre's ceremonies and special events. The sudden and unrelated deaths, due to heart attacks, of two visitors in the spring of 1989 prompted the closure of the interpretive centre for a day in order for Mr. Crow Shoe and other elders to perform a purification ceremony. On a lighter note, the elders are regular guests of the centre for special events and luncheons. All staff are invited to eat and socialize with these respected members of the native community. The role of elders and ceremonialists has been, and continues to be, paramount in nearly every facet of the development of HSI. (The article by Jack Brink in this volume provides greater focus on their involvement since the 1970s.)

A nonprofit agency, the Friends of Head-Smashed-In Buffalo Jump Society was formed in 1987. Governed by a volunteer board of directors, the Society provides a liaison between the Alberta Government and the communities surrounding HSI. The Society's primary responsibility is to administer income collected from visitors' admission fees, memberships, and rent from the gift shop and cafeteria (both privately run). These monies are channelled back into activities at HSI in order to provide such services as an onsite shuttle

Fig. 9. Visitors observe an archaeological dig during the
summer months. (Archaeological Survey of Alberta)

bus, marketing and promotional ventures, a university scholarship,
and financing for special events.

The HSI interpretive centre thus serves four important functions.
The first is its role in the lives of the Blackfoot people: it serves as a
meeting place for young and old to promote preservation of their
heritage at and beyond this site. The second is its ongoing project of
in-situ preservation, as demanded for an UNESCO World Heritage
Site, and the third, closely linked, is the scientific research conducted by archaeologists. The fourth is the role of this site as an
important centre for public education. The immediate and ever
evolving challenge for the interpretive centre's management comes
in trying to satisfy all these functions. While its roles as a World
Heritage Site and archaeological research facility can find common
ground with conserving Blackfoot heritage, these three stand in potential conflict with the centre's role as a high-profile tourist facility.
Meanwhile, the educational and interpretive mandate for the centre
is considered by some to be too rigid for creating new development
opportunities; maintaining it, however, is crucial for preserving the
integrity of the Head-Smashed-In site, as called for by the UNESCO
World Heritage Site designation. Moreover, it has been argued, another primary aim is being realized: "With the prime mandate of the

interpretive centre being [public] education, tourists [and indeed everyone involved] are beginning to understand their role in preservation."[8]

Maintaining an equilibrium, one that satisfies the aspirations and goals of all parties concerned, can occur only through negotiation and compromise on all sides. When one considers some of the players involved—natives (primarily Peigan and Blood tribes), nonnatives, scientists, visitors from and representatives of the private sectors, non-profit groups and the general public—the inevitability of conflicting political agendas and challenges to HSI's mandate are evident. So far, the interpretive centre's management has met these challenges with success. It may be that "Head-Smashed-In is fortunate since its theme of Native Indian culture is presented not as entertainment but as instruction."[9] The interpretive programmes themselves act as vehicles for preservation, providing a necessary human dimension for the historical drama that occurred here. The interpretive guide serves as the backbone of this endeavour, providing guidance and understanding not only about what happened here over the millenia, but also about how closely this history relates to the present and the future; thereby, tensions created through stereotyping and cultural generalizations, occurring in both native and non-native groups, can be eased.

Over a half million people have visited Head-Smashed-In Buffalo Jump since the interpretive centre opened in 1987. Its potential for multicultural education is enormous. Particularly interesting is the remark often heard from visitors that the Head-Smashed-In development is a fine example of "government money well spent."

The buffalo hunters of the northern Plains may have long since vanished, but HSI continues to live a dynamic life. While one wonders if the challenges faced today would seem trivial in comparison to those faced by prehistoric hunters fighting for their survival on this windswept prairie, it appears that this lonely sandstone cliff in southern Alberta will remain a meeting place for cultural activities, a significant landmark in the course of human history.

Ed Sponholz has served as Education and Special Events officer for Head-Smashed-In Buffalo Jump, Fort Macleod, Alberta.

Notes
1. B.O.K. Reeves, "Six Milleniums of Buffalo Kills," *Scientific American* 249 (Oct. 1983), p. 2.

2. Eleanor Verbicky-Todd, *Communal Buffalo Hunting Among the Plains Indians*, Occasional Paper no. 24 (Edmonton: Alberta Culture, Historical Resources Div., 1984), p. 197.

3. Reeves, "Six Milleniums," p. 11.

4. The works by Reeves and Verbicky-Todd may be consulted by those readers wishing a more detailed account of the site's prehistory and history.

5. Reeves, "Six Milleniums," p. 2.

6. Alberta Culture, *Head-Smashed-In Buffalo Jump: World Heritage Site Annual Report* (Edmonton: Alberta Culture, 1984), p. 1.

7. Percy Bullchild, *The Sun Came Down: the History of the World as my Blackfeet Elders Told It* (New York: Harper and Row, 1985), p. 86.

8. Debbi Cannon, "Head-Smashed-In Buffalo Jump: A Case Study in Developing Cultural Tourism in the Context of Cultural Conservation," paper presented at the "Geography of Tourism" seminar, University of Toronto (1990), p. 18.

9. Myra Shackley, "World Heritage Site Designation and its Meaning for Tourism: A Canadian Case Study," unpub. paper prepared for UNESCO (1990), p. 8.

J.E. FOSTER

The Metis and the End of the Plains Buffalo in Alberta

A frequently encountered and enduring historical truism, addressing an aspect of the Western Canadian experience, is the statement that the "whiteman" was responsible for the destruction of the buffalo on the Canadian prairies. Like most historical truisms this one needs clarification. If by "whiteman" the truism identifies the commercial system rooted in the industrial cities of eastern North America, which for a time seemed to offer an insatiable market for buffalo robes and a cornucopia of material goods in return, the statement has much validity. If on the other hand it purports to identify the "trigger-men" in the hunting of the buffalo in the Canadian West it is wrong. The overwhelming proportion of buffalo hunters in the decade before extinction, the 1870s, were native peoples. Even among the traders who encouraged hunting activity, in the wintering villages, native peoples were a majority. The willingness, even enthusiasm, with which native hunters pursued the buffalo to the point where this critically important resource became extinct raises questions about the context in which they acted and how they assessed their interests in relation to the buffalo as a community resource.

In his recent book Paul Thistle suggests "cultural continuity" rather than "cultural change" marked the behaviour of many Indian bands in the fur trade.[1] Prior to the 1840s Thistle argues, cultural change was minimal with altered behaviour merely reflecting the expression of traditional attitudes and values in a fur trade context. For Thistle this cultural continuity on the part of a number of Indian bands was a function of choice derived from two underlying fundamental principles. The first principle, as old and as widespread as the human species itself, was "the principle of least effort" expended in the harvesting and distribution of resources essential to life. Tools and procedures responsive to this interest could be adopted with alacrity with apparently little impact on attitudes and values. The second principle, the "Zen road to affluence," was a philosophy frequently encountered among mobile hunting bands, which minimized, beyond the necessities of life, the acquisition and consumption of material goods in living the "good life." In Thistle's analysis these two principles alone are sufficient to understand the "cultural continuity" of Indian behaviour in a fur trade context before the 1840s.

It is in the subsequent generation that native behaviour, in what would become Western Canada, appears to challenge the cultural continuity explanation. Various native peoples responded to the burgeoning opportunities in the buffalo robe trade when the geographical isolation of the Hudson's Bay Company's territories crumbled in the 1840s. It was to the cities of eastern North America, not the cities of Great Britain and Western Europe, that the Euro-Canadian and Native Traders would look to market their product. In return an exponentially expanding array and number of goods were manifest in the lives of Native peoples. By the 1870s behaviour would suggest that, rather than the "Zen road to affluence," material goods were of much importance in the lives of native peoples. Old and new products were consumed in increasing amounts. Significant risk was undertaken to sustain the flow of goods. Behaviour in many areas no longer reflected cultural continuity; rather, it manifested cultural change.

Four "tribal" groupings; the Blackfoot Confederacy, the Sarcee, the Cree and the Metis, hunted the buffalo on a frequent and regular basis on the prairie and in the bordering parkland in what is today Alberta. In the south between the Red Deer, a principal branch of the South Saskatchewan River, and the Missouri River were the members of the Blackfoot Confederacy; that is, the Blackfoot, the Blood, and the Peigan, and their ally, the Sarcee. In the central region were the Plains Cree and Metis. In time and with increasing frequency a fifth group, the Stoneys, from the foothills region appeared. These were the peoples whose ways of life and circumstances attracted them to the buffalo robe trade. As bed covers and sleigh throws, and occasionally as material for winter coats and boots, buffalo robes enjoyed a market in the eastern cities that expanded from a few hundred robes annually in the 1820s to more than a 100 000 robes annually in the 1860s. As yet it is not clear whether the upsurge in the market in the rapidly growing cities of eastern North America represented increasing product familiarity or increasing purchasing power, or both, on the part of the emerging middle classes. An expanding transportation network, linking frontier and eastern markets, also played a role. Of the four tribal groupings responding to the opportunities in the buffalo robe trade, the Plains Metis of the Upper Saskatchewan country are of particular interest.[2]

It is only recently that historians have come to appreciate the importance of the Metis experience in the buffalo robe trade in laying the foundation for later events and developments in Western history. Previously historians of the later settler society emphasized the "progressive" nature of agriculture as opposed to the "primitive" nature of the hunt. Thus the subsistence peasant farmers in the Red River Settlement in the nineteenth century became the heroic pioneer forerunners of the modern Canadian West while the entrepreneurial native hunters and traders of the same region and era, who had responded quickly and effectively to a market opportunity, were portrayed as historically inconsequential, an antiquarian curiosity of no current relevance.[3] This historical assessment is in the process of being revised.

The Metis of the Upper Saskatchewan country owe their existence to the buffalo. As a people they originated from the servants of the fur companies, Canadien, British (mostly Orkneymen), and "Eastern Indians" (Iroquois and Ojibwa), who contracted as hunters, trappers and canoeists and their "country wives" (mostly Cree). A very few of these men, when they ended their obligation to the companies as *engagés* or contracted servants, decided not to return to Britain or Lower Canada. They chose to become "free men" and remain in the West. With their country wives and children they became *les gens libres* who hunted and trapped on their own account and marketed their production through the trading post. For those freemen in the valley of the North Saskatchewan River, the buffalo quickly became their raison d'être.[4]

While always interested in trading furs the posts along the North Saskatchewan River had the cardinal function of obtaining provisions in surplus amounts to fuel the crews of the york boat brigades and to supplement the diet of fish at northern posts. The major source of provisions was buffalo meat, fresh in winter and rendered as dried meat, fat, and pemmican in summer. In the early years of the nineteenth century the Plains Indians had minimal need for, and interest in, manufactured goods. In contrast to the "Bush" Indians to the north and east, guns on the prairie were a weapon of war and not a hunting tool: thus the Plains Indians' need for shot and powder was much less than the "Bush" people. Visits of the Plains Indians to the trading posts were at their own discretion, not at the dictates of the fur trade companies.[5] In such circumstances the "Bourgeois" of the fur forts looked to more regular suppliers of essential provisions. The free men and their families, les gens libres, were such suppliers. By the second quarter of the nineteenth century the generational succession of these people created the Plains Metis.[6]

The buffalo robe trade in the Hudson's Bay Company's territories arose in the 1820s out of the Company's attempt to tie the Blackfoot commercially and politically to their forts on the North Saskatchewan River rather than allow the Blackfoot to seek such ties at much better prices with American traders on the Missouri River.[7] The Missouri River traders, with their water and railroad network to eastern markets, enjoyed much competitive advantage over the Hudson's Bay Company.[8] From before the 1820s American traders had been accepting buffalo robes as an auxiliary product in their fur trade. During the 1820s and early 1830s the Blackfoot and American Mountain Men (trappers) had clashed over the beaver resources in the Rocky Mountains to the south of the Hudson's Bay Company's territories. In this commercial war significant amounts of beaver moved through the Blackfoot to the Hudson's Bay Company's posts on the North Saskatchewan where they were exchanged for goods including guns and ammunition. In attempting to pacify the Blackfoot the Missouri River traders offered generous terms for beaver as well as less valuable furs such as buffalo robes, a by-product of Blackfoot hunting in winter. Even after the Rocky Mountain beaver hunt dried-up in the 1830s Missouri River traders continued to encourage the Blackfoot. The Hudson's Bay Company viewed with alarm the defection of the Blackfoot to the Missouri River traders.[9] While the Blackfoot were not as regular as the Metis as visitors to the Company's forts their numbers made them important suppliers of provisions. In order to maintain at least a partial commercial loyalty on the part of the Blackfoot, the Company had to be prepared to accept the by-products of provision hunting, hides and robes.

There was a limited market for buffalo hides within the Company's service as tenting material and as packaging for fur bales. Robes were another matter. Despite a major effort the Company did not succeed in developing a market in Britain or Western Europe. Robes had to be transhipped to North American cities. At a later date the Company would avail itself of American railroads in marketing its robes. Prior to the late 1860s the Company's robe trade was only minimally profitable at best.[10] As a result it attempted unsuccessfully to limit its purchases of robes to the Blackfoot and then only as a sideline to a principal trade in provisions and furs.

From the time competition between the fur trade giants, the North West Company and the Hudson's Bay Company, ended in 1820 there had been tension between the newly revitalized Hudson's Bay Company and the freemen. In a major effort to cut ruinous costs and return profitability to the trade, the Company over the decade of the 1820s had cut its labour force by two-thirds. At the same time it had eliminated the premiums it had traditionally extended to freemen but not to Indians. In the face of what they viewed as the "tyranny" of these agents of the British metropolis, hundreds of former servants and their families, as freemen, directed their course during the 1830s towards the Red River Settlement. Seeing themselves as unfairly treated hinterland residents they pursued the possibility that farming and the presence of missionaries would offer a degree of independence from the Company's dictates.[11] Those freemen and their families who remained in the interior shared their compatriots' view. Both in their own way were aware that the new and "modern" Hudson's Bay Company looked to the efficiency of its commercial process and not, as previously, the socioeconomic interests of the participants as its focal criterion in determining commercial success.[12]

The Metis encountered a formidable antagonist in the service of the Hudson's Bay Company. On the Saskatchewan Chief Factor John Rowand, known to his men as "One-Pound-One" (from the sound of his lame walk on the wooden walkways of the Fort) and to the Blackfoot as "Iron Shirt," directed the Company's interests. Seen physically to be as thick as he was tall Rowand was a formidable defender on what he defined broadly as the Company's interests. Should he feel the situation called for it he would not hesitate to use his fists. He was feared by all and respected by some. Only a very few regarded him with affection. The freemen and their families were not in this number. With rigour and at times ruthlessness

Rowand significantly slimmed the Company's largesse on the Saskatchewan—but not with the Blackfoot.[13]

Although himself a Roman Catholic, Chief Factor John Rowand did not welcome their missionary presence in the freeman settlement at *Lac Ste-Anne*, a day's journey to the west of Fort Edmonton. His defensive alertness to what might transpire there suggests that he foresaw missionaries stabilizing social relations and thus laying the foundation for an expanded settlement. As well the missionaries would "legitimize" the community and the actions of individuals who could be seen as acting in the community's interest.[14] And one community interest was a "return" to the more rewarding days of the trading competition before 1820. This goal, though, necessitated commercial ties outside the Company's control with private traders in Red River who had commercial relations with industrial markets.

The "Sayer Trial" in the Red River Settlement in 1849 had dramatized the breakdown of the Company's splendid geographical isolation. It had been this isolation which had given substance to the monopoly provisions in the Company's royal charter, granted in 1670. Access in and out of the Company's territories, a large part of northwestern British North America, had depended upon the Company's good will and services. The advance of the American frontier, still distant by the 1840s but within communication and transportation contact, offered hinterland residents alternatives to the Company's ways and means in establishing relations with outside markets.[15] And the Metis with their technological skills and their entrepreneurial ethos had the cultural capacity to respond quickly and effectively to the new-found opportunity.

The tripmen of the Saskatchewan york boat brigade had carried word of the changes in the Red River Settlement, symbolized in the events of the Sayer Trial, to the peoples of the Upper Saskatchewan country. As House Indians these men, known as *"Blaireau"* (Badgers), did not take a primary interest in the buffalo hunt. But they did have kinsmen among les gen libres, now the Metis, who would respond. Among them was Isidore Dumont, alias *Eccapo*, the younger brother of Gabriel Dumont the elder (or "Alberta"). Isidore took his wife, Louise, the former country-wife of a fur trade officer, and children to Red River and joined the buffalo hunts out of that Settlement for a period of years. His son Gabriel the younger (or "Saskatchewan") would learn the ways that would make him a paramount *Chef Métis* and take him to the battlefield at Batoche in 1885. Early in the 1850s Metis entrepreneurs on the Saskatchewan initiated trading adventures to Red River, attempting to "fine-tune" already existing skills and relationships to take advantage of the commercial opportunities there and south to St. Paul in Minnesota Territory. As the decade advanced the market for buffalo robes, harvested between mid-November and mid-March, became more apparent. With this market came the Metis who specialized in harvesting them, "*les hivernants*" (the winterers).[16] The summer provision hunt, supplying the Company's fur brigades and northern posts, would remain. But now *les villages hivernements* (wintering villages) would appear at wooded oases on the prairie. In the West the last great fur extravaganza was building momentum. The buffalo robe was emerging in the product position previously held by coat beaver.

The founding of the Roman Catholic mission at *St-Albert* (Big Lake) in 1861 marked a significant development in the experience of the buffalo-hunting Metis in the Upper Saskatchewan country, particularly those who tended to focus their commercial interests on Fort Edmonton (known to the Metis at this time as *Fort des Prairies*). Located where early frosts were less likely than at *Lac Ste-Anne* to frustrate attempts to grow grain to supplement the fisheries and the buffalo hunt, the St. Albert Mission continued the role that the Roman Catholic missionaries began two decades earlier. In so doing it became the base for the largest number of buffalo hunters in the region.[17]

The presence of the Roman Catholic Missionaries strengthened social stability in a community dependent upon the expectations associated with kinship and friendship to direct social intercourse.[18] Even with recognized elders mediating disputes and established traditions guiding social interchange, incidents exacerbating social relations could occur. It was difficult to hold large groups together for any length of time. Incidents giving rise to social tension encouraged families in conflict to distance themselves one from the other. Yet in the buffalo country south of the North Saskatchewan River small family groups were vulnerable to attack by the Blackfoot or Sarcee. And beyond the Battle River, a day's ride farther south, the danger increased appreciably. Thus small family bands were unable to avail themselves of the opportunities open to larger groups who could hunt buffalo on the prairie with much less fear of attack. Even large hunting parties, however, profited from the presence of a priest whose religious office gave him significant social authority. He could use his social prestige to mediate conflicts. The need for families to distance themselves from each other was reduced. With his presence, larger more stable hunting parties were possible. And the attractions of the larger hunt were obvious to the participants. With it came the opportunity to capitalize on the material and other rewards that access to outside markets promised.

While the 1860s marked the road to Confederation in three of Britain's self-governing colonies in eastern British North America, it marked the first appearance of itinerant pedlars from Fort Benton on the Missouri River in the neighbourhood of Fort des Prairies.[19] In part they dealt in whisky. But they dealt in other products as well— attractive products—in greater number and variety than those available on the Company's tariff. This expanding cornucopia of material goods suggested a hopeful future. In contrast other events and developments heralded a future of much darker consequences.

The decade preceding the extinction of the buffalo in the Canadian West began with "The Transfer," the joining of the Hudson's Bay Company's territories to the Canadian Confederation. The events of the Transfer in the Red River Settlement ushered in a decade of uncertainty for the people of the North West, particularly the Metis.[20] Uncertainty lay in the juxtaposition of the opportunity for material well-being which in turn suggested sociopolitical consequence for themselves with the threat that the coming of the Canadian settlers and their institutional ways would deny these opportunities to the Metis. Not a few Metis had opposed Louis Riel's stand during The Transfer in Red River. They had welcomed the approach of the Canadians and what they believed were the opportunities to establish more direct commercial contact with Canadian markets. The Metis merchants heading extended family-networks of hunters had the technological and entrepreneurial skills necessary to direct the harvesting and marketing of buffalo robes and thus profit handsomely from enhanced contact with Canadian markets.[21] But after the Transfer violent incidents involving the Metis and the Canadian military in Red River did not bode well for the future; neither did the appearance that summer of *la picotte* (small pox) in the Saskatchewan Country.

Picture if you will at the end of July 1870 the St. Albert summer provisioning hunt returning to Fort des Prairies, bringing reports of la picotte far out on the prairie.[22] Their stay would only be a matter of weeks as they traded summer provisions and outfitted themselves for the autumn hunt. Many families would remain out on the prairie in *islets de bois* (wooded oases) during winter in order to harvest buffalo robes. More rumours cast a pall over *la caravane* (the hunt) as it

Fig. 1. Buffalo butchering diorama at the visitor
reception centre, Batoche National Historic Site,
Saskatchewan. (Photo courtesy I.S. MacLaren)

passed by the Fort to cross the North Saskatchewan River. Already
access to the Fort was restricted and several servants and officers
were sending their families away in the hope they would escape the
onslaught of the epidemic. A day's journey south of the River, at
Jolie Butte, la picotte surfaced in the hunters' camp.

Three encampments farther south and already reeling in the face of
the small pox epidemic, la caravane was threatened by an onrushing
prairie fire. Some took to a nearby slough; others, no doubt responding to their leaders' directions, piled baggage, probably wetted from
the nearby slough, in the face of the approaching flames. Joining
their missionary, Fr. Vital Fourmond, in prayer, they watched the
fire meet the barricade and then part around the camp, causing neither injury nor loss of life and only minor property damage. The momentary sense of deliverance gave way to the realization that la
picotte remained. And their quarry would now prove even more elusive than previously as the burnt prairie would drive the buffalo to
more distant hunting grounds.

The toll from la picotte would be heavy throughout the West. Unlike the epidemic of 1836–37 during which mixed ancestry seemed
to offer a fair chance of surviving the disease, la picotte of 1870 was
deadly, taking a toll of Euro-Canadians as well as Metis and Indian

peoples.[23] Over the course of the St. Albert fall hunt of 1870 three different cemeteries were established to receive more than 120 dead. Le Chef de la caravane, Louison Montagnais, lost four children and later that winter his young wife Angele Dumont. Others had similar experiences. Two-thirds of the Metis would become ill; half of these would die. The demographic and emotional legacy of la picotte 1870 would be extensive and enduring.

Success did not greet the continuing efforts of the St. Albert hunt as September gave way to October. Word of their plight reached Chief Factor William Christie at Fort des Prairies. He dispatched a relief party with necessities, enabling the hunt to remain out on the prairie. But the herds continued to remain elusive.

At the end of October le Chef called a council to determine the hunt's course of action. A minority informed the hunt that they would break off to winter with relatives at the St. Albert Mission. No doubt they reasoned that la picotte preoccupied the Blackfoot as much as themselves; thus, there would be little likelihood of encountering a larger hostile party on their journey. The majority, in view of the poor returns from the fall hunt, opted to winter in the valley of the Battle River where they would be much closer to the herds, the source of provisions and robes. With the onset of winter la picotte slowly abated and the herds seemed to return. The traders who appeared among them with their wares offered a distraction from the memory of fire and epidemic. Even the Canadians, and the threat that their institutions and ways suggested, would hold little interest for the Metis of the Upper Saskatchewan Country that winter.

It was two years later when the fall hunt of the St. Albert Metis, now led by le Chef Abraham Salois, again experienced severe hardship.[24] In this instance, however, the near disaster may well have been the experience that laid the foundation for the meteroric rise of one of the most noteworthy of the robe hunt wintering villages, *Lac du boeuf*. Buffalo Lake drained southward through Tail Creek into the Red Deer River at its grand bend southward. Buffalo Lake had long been noted as a favourite buffalo hunting ground by the Blackfoot, Sarcee, and the Cree as well as the Metis. In the autumn of 1872 the missionary accompanying the hunt on *une mission ambulante* was Fr. Joseph Dupin.[25] It is his account of the 1872 autumn hunt which recalls memories of the disastrous hunt two years earlier.

At the end of September, several days travel to the southeast of Fort des Prairie, a small herd offered momentary respite to the otherwise unsuccessful St. Albert hunters. Following a successful run on the herd dissension emerged with a small group breaking away to winter at St. Albert. The majority chose to stay out on the prairie, seeking to fill their scant larders before the onset of winter. On 26 October a blizzard of several days duration caught the hunt far out on the prairie. When the winds abated after several days snowfall, intense cold threatened life itself. In desperation the hunt began the grim trek to the shelter of the trees in the parkland. The journey took a heavy toll in equipment and animals. No doubt the hunt fragmented into extended families as it trekked. In such circumstances it was obvious they would not have to fear an encounter with the Blackfoot. After some fifteen days the largest group stumbled into the shelter of the trees and hills on the northeast shore of Buffalo Lake. Taking what steps they could they threw up log shelters. The cold continued until the end of February, cutting an increasing swath through the hunters' livestock. In such circumstances the hunt furnished only sufficient returns to ensure survival. When warmer days and new shoots of grass assured sustenance for the few surviving horses the winter village at Buffalo Lake dissolved in a surge of hunters and their families moving southeastward toward the prairie and the herds. In subsequent years they would remember their winter haven.

Over the next two winters *Lac du boeuf* grew to over eighty cabins with more cabins close at hand in the valley of the Red Deer River.[26] At Buffalo lake Louison Montagnais emerged as le Chef and apparently as a principal trader. Remarried to the widow Marguerite Allary his cabin would have functioned both as residence and trade store. Together with the cabin of the priest, "*l'église*," it would have centred a cluster of cabins of various kinsmen including some of his former wife. No doubt it was this Dumont connection that facilitated the movement of Dumont kinsmen from the South Saskatchewan river parish of *St-Laurent*, later to include the village of Batoche, to Buffalo Lake for the winter robe hunt.[27] Other traders would attract their clusters of cabins while acknowledging the primacy of Louison Montagnais as Le Chef. Cuthbert McGillis, originally of Red River, had traded extensively north of Fort Pitt toward Lac la Biche during the 1860s. Now he and his extended family looked to robes rather than furs to make their fortune. Other traders included Addison MacPherson and Charlie Smith whose commercial base was Fort Benton and Louis Marion and John Kerr, *Le Petit Canada*, whose ties were to Red River. A few itinerant pedlars such as James Gibbons and Joseph Lamoureaux were occupied in different activities near Fort des Prairies during the summer but in the winter they journeyed from encampment to encampment peddling their wares.[28]

As the decade advanced the wares of the traders became more numerous and more varied. The Indian tariff of the Hudson's Bay Company with its limited numbers and choices was becoming an increasingly distant memory. Farther south in the valley of the Bow River where Fort Benton based traders were more frequently encountered, the Blackfoot were doing the unheard of; they were trading for luxury foodstuffs, particularly high quality flour and molasses.[29] Both the traders and the hunters seemed to be testing the capacity of nomadic peoples to consume the vast array of trade goods, including whisky, at their disposal. There appeared to be no end in sight to the increasing bonanza of wealth.

In the wintering villages traditional practises lent stability to the good times that abounded. The memory of disease, prairie fire, and blizzard could not dampen the enthusiasm for the hunt. Neither could incidents such as sudden violent death, some criminal and some accidental, raise questions as to the long term benefits of the course they pursued. While the Canadians remained a concern to the residents of the wintering villages they were not a preoccupation. At Buffalo Lake John Kerr, le Petit Canada, behaved as a trader and as a guest while enjoying the protection of the Dumonts from St-Laurent.[30] After 1874 the Mounted Police were an occasional presence. Even the annoyance of their searches for whisky could be enjoyed when a clever stratagem hid a keg from their poking and peering.[31] Only momentarily did events suggest a pause in the pursuit of robes.

When the hunters gathered about their traders' stores conversation quickly turned to the usual topics, horses and the prices of robes.[32] Only occasionally did the talk include the observation that the buffalo were fewer in number. Perhaps this was the factor that explained the increased frequency of incidents of confrontation among various groups.[33] Similarly reports of the absence of calves with some herds suggested that hunting pressure was beyond the capacity of the resource to endure.[34] As well talk of disease among domestic animals and the possibility of its spread to the herds attracted attention only momentarily.[35] The bonanza had become a fantasy that seemed to be without end.

But it did end! The Hudson's Bay Company's robe sale in Montreal in November, 1875 signaled problems in the robe trade.[36] Supply had caught demand and passed it. The sale was unsuccessful as large numbers remained in the hands of the Company and the wholesalers whom they supplied. The same experience was apparent in American markets. While the Company tried to support prices by stopping the flow of robes from its warehouses the inevitable price decline began. It would take several months for word to reach the traders who had already paid premium prices during the winter of 1875–76. For many bankruptcy would result.

The casual observer might have predicted a decline in robe production with the fall in prices. In this view native hunters, Indian and Metis, would simply cease to hunt to produce robes in surplus amounts and return to a strategy of an earlier generation of hunting for subsistence. Such was not the case. The Metis particularly had never been subsistence producers. Rather than diminishing the production of robes the fall in prices increased production. More robes were necessary to attempt to sustain the flow of material goods from the east.[37] But with the increase in robe production prices tumbled further.

It was apparent that in the minds of a large number of native hunters and their families the material goods acquired in the robe trade were no longer luxuries but necessities. The nomadic native hunters of the northwestern plains had joined their middle-class coresidents in eastern North America as consumers. Consumerism had become institutionalized in their cultures. It had become inextricably linked with cultural ways which identified individuals and families of social and political consequence.

The catastrophic fall in prices was cut short by the extinction of the resource itself.[38] With the end of the 1875–76 winter hunt the focus of activity shifted to the valley of the Bow River and southward to the Cypress Hills. Over the next three years wintering villages appeared intermixed with the camps of the Indian peoples. The dramatic events of the treaty signing in 1876 and 1877 seemed to promise "famine relief" in the critical days ahead. All the participants had thought in terms of a decade before the crisis in provisions would be upon them. They had no such wait. It was the early spring of 1879 when the crisis would be at hand.

Near the end of March native hunters broke their various winter camps and set out southeastward along the Bow River valley in pursuit of the dwindling herds.[39] Several runs by different hunts encountered fewer and fewer buffalo. By the end of April there were none. The enormity of the disaster was probably not immediately

apparent. Only when word returned that there were no buffalo anywhere including the Cypress Hills would the sense of disaster become manifest. Many Indians and Metis would surge southward in
pursuit of the dwindling herds in Montana Territory. The respite
would be only of two years duration before the Canadian experience
was repeated.

Some Metis would turn to other traditional activities, particularly
freighting, in an attempt to provide the means of a livelihood. Others would try cowboying on the ranches now appearing where the
buffalo had roamed. Most would turn northwestward, pursuing for
the moment the woodland hunt. In time they would join the surge in
commercial activity associated with the major upswing in the fancy
fur trade in the Athabaska and Peace River countries in the last quarter of the nineteenth century. Most Metis in the succeeding generation would not be able to recreate the golden years of fur trade
consumerism that had marked their community life during the last
decade before the extinction of the buffalo.

Recent writing in fur trade studies has argued that prior to the
1840s there had been little change in the "cultural core" of the native
peoples of Western Canada as a result of their participation in the fur
trade.[40] But after that date, if the Metis of the Upper Saskatchewan
country are an indication, there was profound and significant
change. The area and direction of that change was in the increasing
amount and variety of goods consumed. As well, native peoples
demonstrated a willingness to alter their behaviour to generate an
increasing number of buffalo robes. Such an alteration in behaviour
suggests the consumption of the industrial world's material goods
had become inextricably linked with "understandings" of the "good
life." The importance of these understandings was such that the fall
in robe prices, rather than lessening the production of robes, height-
ened the hunting pressure on the buffalo resource to the point of extinction. In their behaviour the Metis heralded the future settler
society not the past. The Metis of the 1870s in Alberta were the precursors of the consumerist, single-commodity, boom and bust economy of the twentieth century West, especially in Alberta.

John E. Foster is a professor of History at the University of Alberta. As Professor Foster is a co-editor of this Journal an independent specialist in this field was engaged to
conduct the usual process of editorial assessment and independent evaluation of this
article.

Notes

1. Paul C. Thistle, *Indian-European Trade Relations in the Lower Saskatchewan River Region to 1840* (Winnipeg: University of Manitoba Press, 1986).
2. An adequate scholarly history of the buffalo robe trade remains to be done. In the Canadian context popular histories have focussed on the whisky trade in which the emphasis has been on criminality rather than commerce. No doubt this orientation has shaped the perspective of more scholarly works, explaining in part the inadequate treatment of the subject there. In recent years the robe trade has taken on greater significance. Note particularly Bob Beal, "The Buffalo Robe Trade," appendix B in R.F. Beal, J.E. Foster, and Louise Zuk, "The Metis Hivernement Settlement at Buffalo Lake, 1872–1877" (Edmonton: Historical Report prepared for Alberta Government, Department of Culture, Historic Sites and Provincial Museums Division, 1987), pp. 80–107.
3. See particularly Gerhard Ens, "Dispossession or Adaptation? Migration and Persistence of the Red River Metis, 1835–1890," *Historical Papers 1988* (Ottawa: Canadian Historical Association, 1988), p. 120–144.
4. For a discussion of the origins of the Plains Metis see J.E. Foster, "The Plains Metis" in R. Bruce Morrison and C. Rod Wilson eds., *Native Peoples: The Canadian Experience* (Toronto: McClelland and Stewart, 1986), pp. 375–403.
5. The standard work for the Indian experience in the pre-settlement fur trade in what is today Western Canada remains A.J. Ray, *Indians in the Fur Trade: The Role as Trappers, Hunters and Middlemen in the Lands Southwest of Hudson Bay, 1660–1870* (Toronto: University of Toronto Press, 1974). Of particular interest to this paper is A.J. Ray, "Indians as Consumers in the Eighteenth Century" in Carol Judd and A.J. Ray, eds., *Old Trails and New Directions: Papers of the Third North American Fur Trade Conference* (Toronto: University of Toronto Press, 1980), pp. 255–71.
6. Foster, "The Plains Metis," pp. 382–83.
7. The history of this particular aspect of the fur trade seems to have fallen victim to national historical blinkers. Canadian fur trade historians have kept well north of the forty-ninth parallel of latitude while American fur trade historians have remained firmly rooted to the south. As a result cross-border traffic not subject to diplomatic comment has remained little more than a scholarly curiosity. Source materials for such a study are known.
8. David J. Wishart, *The Fur Trade of the American West, 1807–1840* (Lincoln: University of Nebraska Press, 1979), pp. 83–87, p. 108.
9. Hudson's Bay Company Archives (hereafter HBCA), A.12/1,Gov. Geo. Simpson to Chief Factor John Rowand, 18 December 1830.
10. Beal, "The Buffalo Robe Trade," p. 85.
11. This relatively extensive migration during the 1830s from various posts to the Red River Settlement remains to be studied. An earlier examination of "Hudson Bay English" in this time period appears in J.E. Foster, "The Country-born of the Red River Settlement, 1820–1850," Ph.D. dissertation, University of Alberta, 1973, pp. 119–26.
12. E.E. Rich, *The History of the Hudson's Bay Company, 1670–1870*, II (London: The Hudson's Bay Record Society, 1958), pp. 290–94 remains the best study of the Company in this period. Yet it can be argued that Rich fails to appreciate fully the significance of Lord Selkirk's "takeover" of the Company and the installation of "modern" business managers in key positions.
13. HBCA, A12/2, Simpson to the Governor and Committee, 6 June 1845.
14. Ibid., D.5/12, Rowand to the Governor [Simpson], Chief Factors and Chief Trad-

ers Northern Dept. 4 December 1844. When Rowand threatened a freeman for trading illicitly he replied, "Take me prisoner. This is my country. I shall have justice." Also see ibid., D.5/22, Rowand to Simpson, 21 July 1848.

15. The most useful account of the "Sayer Trail" and its consequences can be found in W.L. Morton, ed., *London Correspondence Inward from Eden Colvile 1849–1852* (London: The Hudson's Bay Record Society, 1956).

16. See Beal, Foster, Zuk, "The Métis Hivernement..." Also see Stuart Baldwin, "Wintering Villages of the Metis Hivernants: Documentary and Archeological Evidence, in Metis Association of Alberta, The Métis and the Land in Alberta Land Claims Research Project, 1979–80 (Edmonton: Metis Association of Alberta, 1980). Also see M.F.V. Doll, R.S. Kidd and J.P. Day, *The Buffalo Lake Metis Site: A Late Nineteenth Century Settlement in the Parkland of Central Alberta* (Edmonton: Alberta Culture and Multiculturalism, Historical Resources Division, 1988).

17. A documentary source on this subject, equal in importance to those in HBCA, are those in Provincial Archives of Alberta (hereafter PAA), *Congrégations des oblats de Marie Immaculée* (hereafter OMI). Note particularly the "Papiers Personnels" of individual missionaries.

18. The argument in this paragraph is developed more fully in J.E. Foster, *"Le Missionnaire and Le Chef Métis,"* Etudes oblates de l'Quest/Western Oblate Studies 1 (1990) pp. 117–27.

19. These free traders were introduced to the area through the miners who flocked to the region in this period. See J.G. MacGregor, *Edmonton: A History* (Edmonton: Hurtig Publishers, 1975), p. 66.

20. PAA, OMI, Papiers Mgr. Vital Grandin, Divers, boîte 1, Cahiers, Copies de Lettres, 1874–77, Grandin au Ministre de l'Intérieur á Ottawa, St-Albert, 5 avril 1875, fo. 19.

21. Gerhard J. Ens, "Kinship, Ethnicity, Class and the Red River Metis: The Parishes of St. Francois Xavier and St. Andrew's" (Edmonton: Ph.D Thesis, University of Alberta, 1989), pp. 105–7.

22. The source for this account is R.P. Vital Fourmond á T-R.P. Superieur Général 26 décembre 1870, as "Mission du lac Sainte-Anne," in *Missions de la Congregations des Oblate de Marie Immaculée* X, 39 et 40, sept. et déc. 1872, pp. 473–506.

23. There is general agreement on the death toll in the small pox epidemic of 1870. For the Metis at St. Albert see P.E. Breton, *Vital Grandin: la merveilleuse aventure de l'Eveque des Prairies et du Grant Nord* (Montreal: Librairie Artheme Fanard, 1960), p. 236. Also see PAA, OMI, Papiers R.P. Léon Doucet, Journals 1868–1890, boîte 15, item 5, fo. 11.

24. Abraham Salois was a noted "plains trader" usually under contract to the Hudson's Bay Company. He was a kinsman of the High Eagles, a prominent family among the Blackfoot. Two of his sons were married to daughters of prominent Metis traders, the McGillises and the Brélands.

25. See F.C. Jamieson, "The Edmonton Hunt," *Alberta Historical Review* I, no. 1, April 1953 and *Missions . . .* XII, 1874, p. 505.

26. Beal, Foster, Zuk, *The Hivernements . . .*, pp. 18, 22, 35.

27. Compare entries in St. Albert Roman Catholic Parish Offices, *Registre St-Albert, Actes de Baptemes, Mariages, Sepultures, 1872–78,* for Buffalo Lake and environs with PAA, OMI, *Paroisse Duck Lake, Liber Animarum des Indiens et des Metis de Duck Lake Jusqu'a 1940 1,* item 1, fo. 727.

28. Beal, Foster, Zuk, *Les Hivernements . . .*, pp. 20, 48.

29. Glenbow-Alberta Institute Archives (hereafter GAA), Richard Hardisty Papers, M477, item 595, Leslie Wood to Richard Hardisty, 12 Sept. 1875, item 604, John Bunn to Hardisty, 14 Dec. 1875, item 605, Wood to Hardisty, 15 Dec. 1875 and item 611, Francis Whitford to Hardisty, 29 Oct. 1875.

30. Beal, Foster, Zuk, *Les Hivernements* . . . , p. 39.
31. Jock Carpenter, *Fifty Dollar Bride: Marie Rose Smith* (Sidney, B.C.: Gray's, 1977,) p. 112.
32. GAA, M477, item 773, John Sinclair to Hardisty, 22 January 1876.
33. For the most notable event in these years see George F.G. Stanley, "The Half-Breed 'Rising' of 1875," *Canadian Historical Review* XVII, no. 4, December 1936, pp. 399–412.
34. See Gilbert Roe, *The North American Buffalo: A Critical Study of the Species in its Wild State* (Toronto: University of Toronto Press, 1951), Chapter XVII, "The Numbers of the Buffalo, the Final Extermination in Western Canada." Roe did not use Hudson's Bay Company documents nor the "Richard Hardisty Papers" in the Glenbow-Alberta Archives. His questioning of "last buffalo" reports is excellent.
35. R.P. Lestanc au R.P. Aubert, Assistant Général, 30 juillet 1879, in *Missions de la Congregation* . . . XVIII, 1879, p. 171.
36. GAA, M477, item 665, Extract of a Letter from James Bissett to J.A. Grahame, 22 November 1875. Also see Ens, "Kinship, ..." pp. 273–76.
37. Beal, "The Buffalo Robe Trade," pp. 98–100.
38. Ibid., pp. 102–3.
39. R.P. Lestanc au R.P. Aubert, Assistant Général, 30 juillet 1879 in *Missions de la Congregation* . . . , XVIII, 1879, p. 183, p. 188.
40. See particularly Thistle, *Indian-European Trade* . . . .

I.S. MacLAREN

Buffalo in Word and Image

From European Origins to the
Art of Clarence Tillenius

The buffaloes are gone.
And those who saw the buffaloes are gone.
Those who saw the buffaloes by thousands and how
    they pawed the prairie sod into dust with their
    hoofs, their great heads down pawing
    on in a great pageant of dusk,
Those who saw the buffaloes are gone.
And the buffaloes are gone.[1]

When Carl Sandburg wrote "Buffalo Dusk" in 1920, no buffalo were roaming free; they were gone from their largest natural habitat, and no peoples were still living chiefly by hunting them. They were not, however, gone for ever. Between 1907 and 1912, Michel Pablo of Ravalli, Montana, and Charles Konrad of Kalispell, Montana shipped 716 buffalo by rail to parks at Banff, Elk Island, and Wainwright. By the time Sandburg published his poem, this number had grown, mainly at Wainwright, to several thousands. Then, between 1925 and 1928, 6673 buffalo of that Wainwright herd were transferred, under the direction and supervision of Col. J.K. ("Peace River Jim") Cornwall, to the newly created Wood Buffalo National Park.[2] Although not the short grassland prairie of the plains buffalo habitat, Wood Buffalo National Park, nearly the size of Nova Scotia, continues today to provide a prodigious range for the great symbol of the wilderness West. There, as well as at Elk Island National Park east of Edmonton, and the Waterhen Wood Bison Ranch in Manitoba, Clarence Tillenius captures their pageants of pawing, stampeding, wallowing, roaming, and vitally being buffalo naturally. Perhaps the most devoted and gifted of all who have painted the beast, Tillenius knows them today with an intimacy that Carl Sandburg and many others who built them into a symbol of doom would have thought impossible. But to understand Tillenius's achievement, one needs a context: the preceding four-and-one-half centuries' attempts to image the animal visually and verbally in the traditions of Western Civilizations.

I

Like trees, to which they were compared in one of the first accounts of them by a European, buffalo have fallen in massive numbers, numbers which nineteenth-century travellers had imagined to be infinite. Sixteenth-century writers found them and their habitat incredible. The second Spanish expedition to reach the prairie in what is today the United States was Francisco Coronado's (the first was Alvar Nuñez Cabeza de Vaca's, in 1534). Travelling as far north as Kansas in search of gold in 1540–42, Coronado was accompanied by Pedro de Castaneda, of Najera, the translation of whose account reads in part as follows:

> The country they [cibola: buffalo] travelled over was so level and smooth that if one looked at them the sky could be seen between their legs, so that if some of them were at a distance, they looked like smooth-trunked pines whose tops joined, and if there was only one bull it looked as if there were four pines. When one was near them, it was impossible to see the ground on the other side of them.[3]

The image is a bemusing one, partly because it requires the reader to imagine trees, however figuratively, on the treeless prairie of the American southwest. In our more recent habit, derived from the nineteenth century, of visualizing buffalo "realistically," the first European picture of the bison (probably Bison bison bison, the southern Plains buffalo[4]) demands considerable imaginative accommodation. Driving past Elk Island National Park on the Yellowhead High-

Fig. 1. First known illustration by a European of a
Buffalo. 1552-53. Woodcut engr. In Francisco López de
Gómara, *La Historia general delas Indias*.

way, for example, one would be surprised indeed to encounter
anything resembling the specimen in Figure 1 along the park fence,
either alone or (the earth shakes at the thought) in a herd. As if with
Castaneda's description in mind, the unknown engraver of this picture, which appeared with another in Francisco López de Gómara's
Historia delas Indias in 1552–53,[5] has endowed the beast with disproportionately huge hooves (the base of pine trees?) and an under-
belly that appears to have suffered the purges of a modern-day
weight-loss clinic (the better to disclose the prairie beyond?).[6] Meanwhile, the rest of the animal looks to have endured the attentions of a
hairdresser's wizardry, so uniformly, decorously, even regally are
its locks arrayed. The eyes seem human, the tail borrowed from a
horse and long enough to trip over. And yet, the boss (or hump) and
horns render it a buffalo as much as, say, a lion, a gryphon, or any
other creation of the Renaissance European imagination. Indeed,
rather than representing an animal, the illustration seems more
concerned with symbolizing the exotic in terms that are at once
recognizable and recognizably foreign. (Amerindians, of course,
would undergo a similar pattern of representation over the next four
centuries.[7])

López de Gómara's woodcut profits by comparison, for its image
more nearly approximates to what we think of as buffalolike today

82   I.S. MacLaren

Fig. 2. Possibly the first illustration by a European of a
Buffalo in Canada. 1575. Woodcut engr. In André
Thevet, *La Cosmographie Universelle*. (Courtesy National
Archives of Canada C-99345)

than does another (Fig. 2), published two decades later in André
Thevet's *La Cosmographie Universelle* (1575).[8] In the French rendition,
two beasts appear to be placed on the lawnlike grounds of a chateau,
which is meant to represent the France of the New World, perhaps
Quebec,[9] but likely owes its inspiration to the Mannerist elegance of
the first Fontainebleau School. In the figure of the chateau itself there
lies an allusion perhaps to the Royal Palace of Fontainebleau, which
was decorated during the reign of Francois I (1515–47), just before
Thevet's alleged travels to the New World.

If only by chance, this marginally more recent specimen has somewhat more realistic, unkempt hair, although its appearance cannot
overcome the stately, nearly statuesque effect of the animals. Certainly, the buffalo in the foreground is huge compared to the scale on
which its attacker is drawn—this tendency will endure in depictions
right through the nineteenth century—but its bulging eyes (even

more pronounced than usual) diminish the terror we feel for the pyr-rhic hunter by suggesting the bull's imminent collapse. Meanwhile, the boss has receded so far from the head as to lend the animal a dromedarian air, or worse: visually, the representation is to a buf-falo what, to the modern eye, a stretch limousine is to an automo-bile. More notable is the exception that this early picture constitutes. Invariably, buffalo are pictured on open prairie of the short grass-lands. Only in the twentieth century, with painters like Tillenius, has the forested portion of the species' habitat provided the land-scape scenery in painting. In terms of the visual stereotype, buffalo and trees have appeared together no more frequently than has re-search on the eastern extension into the deciduous woodlands of the buffalo's habitat.

Equally uncertain remains the derivation of the name *buffalo*. The popular practice, including the naming of Wood Buffalo National Park by an Order in Council of the federal government in December 1922, has ever been at odds with the animal's scientific classifica-tion. David Dary explains how the popular name came into being:

> To the Spanish explorers the animal was frequently called *cibola*. Some Spanish writers spoke of it as *bisonte*. Others called it *armenta*. Early French colonists usually called buffalo *Bison d'Amérique*. Canadian voyageurs used the term *boeuf* —"ox" or "bullock." Later French explorers called the animal the *bufflo* and later *buffelo*. It may have been from these terms, adopted by the English colonists, that the word *buffalo* originated. Although the word was used by the colonists beginning around 1710, it first ap-peared in print in 1754 in Mark Catesby's *A Natural History of Carolina*.[10]

It would be many years before the term approved by science—bison—was insisted upon; of course, it has never supplanted buf-falo in popular usage.

The same year that it was appearing first in print down in the United States, Anthony Henday, the first white man to travel in the lands now known as Alberta, was using it in his field notes. On 15 September 1754, while travelling with his guide, Attickasish, and other Plains Cree through east-central Alberta, Henday went "a Buf-falo hunting, all armed with Bows & Arrows: killed seven, fine sport. We beat them about, lodging twenty arrows in one beast. So expert are the Natives, that they will take the arrows out of them when they are foaming and raging with pain, & tearing the ground up with their feet & horns until they fall down."

The next day, on the way west, "the Buffalo [were] so numerous [that the riders were] obliged to make them sheer out of our way."[11] But Henday was not the first to write the name. If by no others, he was preceded by Henry Kelsey, the Hudson's Bay Company trader and first white man to see the northern prairie. Uses of it in both his famous verse journal of 1691 and his prose journal of 1692 are the first recorded appearances in the English language.[12] Recently described as a "humble Argonaut" by D.M.R. Bentley, who sees his chief function as that of a "namer and a marker,"[13] Kelsey will be remembered chiefly for having been the first to attempt in English a poetic description of a portion of what today is Canada. The same may be said for his attempt to describe buffalo in the northern prairies, where

> . . . you leave the woods behind
> And then you have beast of severall kind
> The one is a black a Buffillo great
> Another is an outgrown Bear which is good meat . . .
> This plain affords nothing but Beast and grass
> And over it in three days time we past.[14]

In both Kelsey and Henday's accounts, one remarks how the buffalo acts synecdochically: the buffalo *is* the prairie; there is nothing but beast and grass through which one must pry, sheering them out of the way. The definition of geography in terms of an animal thus represents one strain in the early verbal accounts that explains why the buffalo came to assume such symbolic significance in the cultures of both Native and European Americans. Clearly, one cannot overlook their crucial importance as a source of sustenance for Indian and (especially in the form of pemmican) fur trader alike, but the symbolic prominence is there as well.

In 1795, more than one hundred years after Kelsey's report, trader John McDonnell spent a day on the Qu'Appelle River of southern Saskatchewan counting carcasses of drowned buffalo: by nightfall, 7360—more than were shipped from Wainwright to Wood Bison park in this century—had passed him.[15] Eleven years later, on the upper Red River in what is now North Dakota, Alexander Henry the Younger observed from a perch in an oak tree outside his post a landscape "covered at every point of the compass, as far as the eye could reach, and every animal was in motion."[16] In such numbers, how could they have been effectively hunted on the "barren ground" of the short grassland prairies? Buffalo jumps, where the geography permitted, provided one answer. Where it did not, the stratagem was likely the one described by Kelsey in his prose journal: "they surround them with men[,] which done they gather themselves into a small Compass Keeping the Beast still in the middle & so shooting them till they break out at some place or other & so gett away."[17] This form of hunting provided a massive provender, which, by means of turning the panic-stricken buffalo against one another, could be realized without rifles.

Tribes and others with horses could make the most "sport," as Henday first calls it, of the hunt. They lived, according to fur trader Daniel Harmon, nearly a paradisiacal existence. Camped with Crees and Assiniboine on a hill in the prairie between the upper Assiniboine River and Last Mountain Lake (in modern east-central Saskatchewan) in February 1804, Harmon wrote of the prospect and of the lives of his hosts:

> ... thousands of buffaloes were to be seen grazing, in different parts of the plain. In order to kill them, the Natives in large bands, mount their horses, run them down and shoot, with their bows and arrows, what number they please, or drive them into parks [i.e. pounds] and kill them at their leisure. In fact, those Indians, who reside in the large plains or prairies, are the most independent, and appear to be the most contented and happy people upon the face of the earth. They subsist upon the flesh of the buffalo, and of the skins of that animal they make the greatest part of their clothing, which is both warm and convenient. Their tents and beds are also made of the skins of the same animal.
>
> The Crees and Assiniboins procure their livelihood with so much ease, that they have but little to confine them at home.[18]

No doubt, the Eurocentric cast of Harmon's perspective, or, at least, that of his book's narrative (it was rendered more "literary" by an editor), describes the native way of life as carefree because the buffalo seems both to furnish the life normally thought of as commensurate with a gentleman's—replete with leisure and sport—and to satisfy, Eden-like, *all* the needs of those who subsist on it. Only by reading any one of these narratives in its entirety does one come to an understanding of the hardship, the penury suffered by those whose reliance was so exclusive, when the buffalo did not come.

Despite the sublime prospect of a panorama consummately animated by a single species, few of the early visual depictions attempted what the verbal ones had.[19] None attempted to rival in paint what Henry Brackenridge had provided in prose: a scene of multitudes of buffalo bulls in combat over cows. Boating up the upper Missouri River in 1811, he and his party suddenly found their ears

> assailed by a murmuring noise. As we drew near it grew to a tremendous roaring, such as to deafen us. On landing we discovered the grove crowded with buffaloe, the greater part engaged in furious combat—the air filled with their dreadful bellowing. A more frightful sight cannot easily be imagined. Conceive several thousand of these furious animals, roaring and rushing upon each other, producing a scene of horror, confusion, and fierceness, like the fight of armies: the earth trembled beneath their feet, the air was deafened, and the grove was shaken with the shock of their tremendous battle.[20]

Such an account is not without its sublime effect, especially in view of Brackenridge's decision not to stay on the river but to go ashore and, thereby, increase the risk of being overwhelmed by the fracas. But there is abundant, stylized control in the description, as well. This effect derives from the personification of the animals through the analogy that Brackenridge strikes between combative bulls and armies; as well, it arises from the use of the word "grove" to designate the brush, since the word carries connotations of gardens (because it refers especially to trees cleared of their underbrush[21]), civilization, stately terrain. Moreover, the double use of the rhetorical device of tricolon—first, with nouns: "horror, confusion, and fierceness"; then, with independent clauses: "the earth trembled beneath their feet, the air was deafened, and the grove was shaken"—exerts a narrative poise over the allegedly "wild" scene, effectively marshalling its sublimity into a simultaneously enthralling but nearly decorous image of the exotic.

The earliest picture of a buffalo by a European emigrant to the northern prairies is Peter Rindisbacher's *Buffalo* (Fig. 3).[22] Like most of Rindisbacher's work owned by the Manitoba Museum of Man and Nature, this watercolour dates from the 1820s. Rindisbacher was one

Fig. 3. First illustration of a Buffalo by an artist resident in Western Canada. Peter Rindisbacher, *Buffalo*. 1820s. Watercolour. (Courtesy Provincial Archives of Manitoba, Winnipeg N3755)

of the contingent of Swiss emigrants lured to Red River by purple promises of arable land in the land of plenty. Arriving in the fall of 1821 by way of Hudson Bay, Rindisbacher, who had already shown promise as an artist in his boyhood, grew so discouraged by his five years of starvation, his crops ruined from the Red River's regular flooding, especially in 1826, that he left for Gratiot's Grove, and later, St. Louis in 1826. Five years' residence, however, yielded the first accomplished pictorial record of what would become the Canadian West.[23] His buffalo picture possesses understandings of mass and proportion (especially of the head to the torso) that strike the late twentieth-century eye as true; indeed, his training as a miniaturist stood him in good stead for such a specimenlike rendition, with the animal virtually unrelated to the background. The animal's musculature in the fore legs is well represented, aided, no doubt, by the low point of view, which permits the viewer to address the enormity of the animal's girth, rather than to either minimize or exaggerate it. A sufficiently good artist of animals and Indians to have his work lithographed and published in London,[24] albeit without credit, and in *The American Turf Register and Sporting Magazine*,[25] Rindisbacher here eliminates the problem that would most often beset painters of the animal: its appearance when in motion, either singly or in groups.

Fig. 4. Peter Rindisbacher, *Blackfeet Hunting on Snowshoes*. 1833. Watercolour. (Courtesy Amon Carter Museum, Fort Worth, Texas 1966.51)

However, such a study came early in Rindisbacher's life in the New World. He would go on to paint hunting scenes, haltingly at first, as in *Indian Hunter Killing a Bison* (1823), where the buffalo retains the appearance of being frozen in motion, and then more confidently, as in two watercolours from 1833, *Blackfeet Hunting on Snowshoes* (Fig. 4) and *Blackfeet Hunting on Horseback*.[26] His maturation as a painter involved retaining his idea for detail and the development of it for anatomy. Such maturation yielded three-dimensional buffalo, which, if they are somewhat stylized, certainly advance a strong sense of realistic, violent action, such as buffalo running necessarily involved. That all of the foreground buffalo, dogs, and cumbersomely-shoed hunter strain their muscles while in full run, attests to Rindisbacher's growing confidence in expressing action. As a critic of his day wrote, "His bison or so called buffalo hunts instruct us in the very temper of that animal. . . . tracked and pursued by hunters, they flee with powerful leaps through the high grass of the prairies and bushes or through deep snow."[27] Certainly, some of the drama captured by Brackenridge's prose account is caught by Rindisbacher, if in another context and on the scale of only one buffalo. It is worth noting, as well, that the variation that he brings to his representation of the animal's body marks a further source of his art's expressiveness. Unlike the entire hirsuteness of the early Spanish and French illustrations (perhaps exacerbated by the demands exerted

Fig. 5. Edward Finden, after George Back, *A Buffalo Pound. Feb. 8, 1820*. 1823. Lithograph. In Capt. John Franklin, *Narrative of a Journey to the Shores of the Polar Sea...*, opp. p. 113.

by the technique of woodcut), Rindisbacher's early and, to a greater extent, later watercolours cut the lower body's hair sufficiently short to permit the muscles to exhibit themselves. On a cold prairie night, though, would one benefit from the comfort that a robe from the back of a Rindisbacher buffalo could provide?

Whereas Rindisbacher's art evolved beyond problems with depicting buffalo in motion, the art of George Back, a visitor only and not a resident, did not. Neither Back, one of the midshipman-artists assigned to John Franklin's first overland expedition to the Arctic Ocean,[28] nor Edward Finden, Back's engraver, solved it in *A Buffalo Pound: Feb. 8, 1820* (Fig. 5).[29] Although Back's original pencil and watercolour study (private collection) shows him able visually to capture a buffalo in motion, in this scene he and his engraver encounter difficulty generating any convincing proportions. Two-dimensional bodies stuck on four sticks do not come up to the standard set by the landscape surrounding them. Still, interest is generated by the centre figure on three legs, the body of which is the least exaggeratedly elongated of the six. Its apparent sighting of the man up the tree in the pound also lends the picture a dramatic dimension, as do the shadows cast on the snow. The partially clothed Plains Cree in the foreground strike a bizarre, if accurate, note in a winter scene, and the very regular structure of the fence conforms rather to an English than to an Indian idea of fencing.[30] Still, for an explorer who was an artist only secondarily, working in a subject matter yet new to the European eye,[31] the creation is a credible one. It is not, however, a representation, since Back saw neither buffalo in the pound nor a man in the tree, singing prayers to the presiding spirits, when he and Franklin made their visit.

To a considerable degree, the mere naming of the animal and, by analogy, the simple outline of it pictorially still sufficed. Rindisbacher's work marks the early exception, Back's the rule. Complementary to Back's depiction is the appearance of buffalo in a list of North American species that occurs amid the wooden menagerie of couplets in Thomas Cary's *Abram's Plains* (1789), at a point where the rich resources of the St. Lawrence River watershed are being enumerated in descending order of commercial worth:

> What tho' no mines their gold pour through thy stream,
> Nor shining silver from thy waters gleam;
> Equal to these, the forests yield their spoils,
> And richly pay the skilful hunter's toils.
> The beaver's silken fur to grace the head,
> And, on the soldier's front assurance spread;
> The martin's sables to adorn the fair,
> And aid the silk-worm to set off her air.
> Gems of *Golconda* or *Potosi*'s mines,
> Than these not more assist her eyes' designs.
> The jetty fox to majesty adds grace,
> And of grave justice dignifies the place;
> The bulky buffalo, tall elk, the shaggy bear,
> Huge cariboo, fleet moose, the swift-foot deer,
> Gaunt wolf, amphibious otter, have their use,
> And to thy worth, O first of floods! conduce.[32]

The point perhaps to be emphasized here, however, is that the European traditions did not equip these painters or writers with precedents. Horses and, less so, dogs in motion are also notoriously difficult to paint well, but at least with them, the nineteenth-century painter had a long tradition to which to turn for ideas and precedents, including the famous works of the Englishman George

Stubbs, whose career began in anatomy studies.[33] Even so, because the painted record from Europe inclined far more often to stationary representations, the artistic attempts at matching the better travel writers' accounts in their descriptions of a whole landscape in motion demanded not just superior skill, but a direction in painting that, if it was not entirely new, was not yet practised to a point or with a frequency that made it widely known.

II

In taking the imaging of the buffalo beyond the cataloguing stage, Rindisbacher's paintings heralded a new phase, one which would reach its apotheosis in the works of the American George Catlin, and, in the wake of their success, those of Paul Kane. Catlin made buffalo an artistic subject, if not always an object for close study. In 1844, to compress his six hundred-odd paintings made from his travels in the American mid-West during the previous decade, he chose to represent buffalo in over half of the twenty-five plates selected for lithographed-and-hand-coloured publication in *Catlin's North American Indian Portfolio*. He hoped that this work, which he had published in London, by its emphasis on *Hunting Scenes and Amusements*, as his subtitle puts it, would be widely acquired by the British audience at whom it was directed. On the one hand, Catlin had trained himself as an artist along the guidelines of the tradition of the artist-naturalist, a tradition that reached its apogee among the scientists of Philadelphia in the years when he worked there. On the other hand, when it came to selling his works abroad—they formed the basis of his sole source of income—he had to take into account the tastes of "European audiences, whose distance from American shores," remarks William H. Truettner, "made them both more objective and more extravagant in their notions of savage life."[34]

For the most part, Catlin's consideration of European taste exerted a greater effect on the representations of his Indians than on those of his buffalo, for the former had to be made both more noble and more savage than his own experience had shown them to be. But, in choosing to emphasize hunting scenes in his chief publishing scheme—intended to reach a wide audience so as to clear his substantial debts—Catlin necessarily drew the buffalo into the reworking's aesthetics. The upshot, unsurprisingly, is a series of pictures depicting gigantic bulls (much more often than cows or calves); bulls represented for their dramatic spectacle, at the point of death, or, if

Fig. 6. McGahey, after George Catlin, *The Buffalo Hunt*
"Chase." 1844. Hand-coloured lithograph, printed as
Plate 5 in *Catlin's North American Indian Portfolio*.
(Courtesy Bruce Peel Special Collections Library, Javitch
Collection, University of Alberta)

not death quite yet, then pretty certain doom. Catlin did not choose
to use his tableaux to chronicle life beyond civilization; instead, he
exaggerated the life of the wilderness, both in subject and style.

Figure 6 shows *The Buffalo Hunt "Chase,"* the fifth plate in the *Indian Portfolio*. It is typical for its sensational drama, deriving not only
from the action depicted—both horse and bull are fully airborne, all
hooves ungrounded[35]—but also from the opposition of the dark beast
on the right half of the picture with the light-coloured Indian and
horse on the left.[36] What is not exaggerated, Catlin claims in the an-
nexed note, are the buffalo's wide-open eyes (he says nothing about
the Indian's or the horse's):

One of the most remarkable peculiarities of the Buffalo is the formation and expression of the eye, the ball of which is very large
and white, and the iris jet black. The lids of the eye seem always
to be strained quite open, and the ball rolling forward and down,
so that a considerable part of the iris is hidden behind the lower

lid; while the pure white of the eyeball glares out over it in an arch, in the shape of a moon at the end of its first quarter.[37]

Perhaps the influence of the popular humanized animal faces of Edwin Landseer's contemporary wildlife and sportsman's paintings can be traced to this depiction and testimony, but Catlin's observation rings true in this instance, despite the inclination of his prose to wander into romantic bombast. A further suggestion of close attention to detail, Catlin's notorious reputation for quick work notwithstanding, comes in another note, where his reader is counselled on taxonomical discrimination: "the American Buffalo is a very different variety of the Ox species from the buffalo of the Eastern continent, and probably closely allied to, if not exactly the same as, the European Bison."[38] Such statements make one pause before dismissing the apparently exaggerated scale of the bull in Figure 6. Indeed, aware that the scale might strike even the avid British sportsman as far-fetched, Catlin buttresses his depiction verbally:

> The very great disparity in size between the horse and the buffalo, in this instance [i.e. Fig. 6], which is much more than is usual, nevertheless correctly illustrates the actual difference that often occurs between an Indian poney of thirteen or fourteen hands, and a huge bull, as is here represented, weighing, as they sometimes do, 1800 or 2000 pounds.[39]

The point is that the sensational, the *unusual*, is Catlin's aim here. To the extent that it is, his yielding to European taste for the gigantic in the wilderness, however much his buffalo paintings seem realistic, aligns his works with those of the engravers preparing woodcuts in the sixteenth-century editions. If, moreover, his publishing scheme did not net him a profit, it did help to sponsor what Truettner calls "the invasion of the Great Plains [as well as the Prairies] by English sportsmen in the second half of the nineteenth century."[40]

Catlin embraced the idea of further embellishments, including scenes of a winter buffalo hunt which he never witnessed, never having spent a winter on the prairie. It may further be said that, by representing the single buffalo so often as a huge bull, he fit the beast into his unvarying theme of the nobility of life in the "'Far West'." The buffalo thus takes its place alongside the "noble and dignified-looking Indians," who, he tells his reader, gave his life a

Fig. 7. McGahey, after George Catlin, *Buffalo Hunt, Surround*. 1844. Hand-coloured lithograph, printed as Plate 9 in *Catlin's North American Indian Portfolio*. (Courtesy Bruce Peel Special Collections Library, Javitch Collection, University of Alberta)

purpose when, after he had taken up painting in Philadelphia, they "suddenly arrived in the city, arrayed and equipped in all their classic beauty; with 'shield and helmet,' with 'tunic and manteau,' tinted and tasselled off exactly for the painter's palette." Not only did the buffalo take up this station, it occasionally seems almost to have taken the place of the Indian. The following remark gives the impression of nothing so much as of the blending (confusion?) by Catlin of the two:

> From the noble bearing and fine proportions of this animal, one instantly admits his gigantic strength, and estimates his splendid utility to man, provided he could be made to bear the yoke. Almost endless efforts have been made by eager and avaricious man to enslave this noble Animal, and humble him to the drudgery of the plough; but with the like result as with the noble Men of the same free country, (almost the only living exceptions;) [sic] who, if they lack the merit of meekness and docility, have had and maintained the virtue of courage to contend for their lives with civilized man, and the sternness to resist his slavery.[41]

Contending for their lives with civilized man was not, however, the theme of Catlin's paintings. Indeed, in *Buffalo Hunt, Surround* (Fig. 7) one of the best from the *Indian Portfolio*, the contention lies between nearly five dozen Hidatsa and three times as many buffalo. It provides the scene's fine drama, affording the first illustration of Kelsey's prose description of the surround technique.[42] By pitting nobility against nobility, then, he uses the hunting scenes to enhance his dominant, romantic representation of "the vast and pathless wilds which are familiarly denominated 'The Great Far West' of the American continent."[43]

While the work of Karl L. Bodmer, Alfred Jacob Miller, and John Mix Stanley—other nineteenth-century painters of buffalo on the American plains—might also be considered in this study,[44] more central still to its purposes is the work of another Catlin-inspired artist, Paul Kane, whose travels across the British North American West and Oregon Territory in the years 1846–48 resulted, in part, from his viewing Catlin's Indian Gallery in London in 1842. Kane's travels furnished the first paintings (apart from a couple of Back's) of what is now Alberta. In his oil painting, *Assiniboine Hunting Buffalo* (Fig. 8), for example, the influence of Catlin's *Buffalo Hunt "Chase"* (Fig. 6), which appeared in the *Indian Portfolio* even before Kane headed west in 1846, and which, therefore, could well have taught him how to see and paint the animal, is readily apparent. It may be argued, moreover, that Kane's studio painting is even more romantically transfigured than Catlin's lithograph, insofar as the colour values are subdued and harmonious (almost, contradictory to all the action, in harmonious repose); the clouds ease past in Constable-like succession, and the horses, groomed and ready for their equestrian dressage, prance like European steeds, not prairie ponies.[45] Perhaps, it may be argued, in this painting and in *Buffalo at Sunset* (Fig. 9), Kane had particularly in mind the Edenic image of the West that accompanied the spirit of expansionism pervading Canada West (soon to be Ontario) in the 1850s, when, in that decade, he made his first studio paintings of his travels and sold them to the Parliament of Canada, the prominent voice of that expansionism.[46] On the other hand, all the romanticism notwithstanding, the buffalo itself receives less exaggerated treatment by Kane than by Catlin; the Canadian's bull is neither in full flight nor disproportionately gigantic.

The same cannot be said, however, of a companion painting, *Buffalo at Sunset*. On a point in the North Saskatchewan River valley—or is it the Loire or the Thames?—at the close of day, the "cattle" take

Fig. 8. Paul Kane, *Assiniboine Hunting Buffalo*. c. 1851-56. Oil on canvas. (Courtesy National Gallery of Canada, Ottawa 6920)

Fig. 9. Paul Kane, *Buffalo at Sunset*. c. 1851-56. Oil on canvas. (Courtesy National Gallery of Canada, Ottawa 6919)

Fig. 10. Paul Kane, *A Buffalo Pound*. c. 1850. Oil on canvas. (Courtesy Royal Ontario Museum, Toronto 912.1.33)

their ease. The oval structure frames and pronounces the courtly tone of the work: no wildness, indeed, no wilderness here. The cows are pretty well appropriated into a domesticated scene, as if trained to take up their assigned positions in, not a vast, open prairie, but the picturesque, moderately-scaled confines of a river bend. The nostalgia cast by the time of day achieves "Keeping" by lending a further sensation of tranquility to the representation, which, it must be said, comes as a relief after so many depictions of the buffalo simply being hunted down.

For the most part, Kane had his troubles with scenes of action. As can be seen from his rendition of a buffalo pound (Fig. 10), which he visited at its location south of Fort Carlton in 1846 (perhaps the same one that Franklin and Back had seen in the same vicinity twenty-six years earlier), the animals receive unrealistically uniform presentation, all in the same gait. J. Russell Harper may exaggerate when he nominates Kane "the outstanding painter of the vast buffalo herds on the Canadian prairie during their last phase."[47] Not only did he never paint herds of any number (a point noted by Robert Thacker[48]), but, like Back, he probably did not witness the scene here depicted. Kane's famous book, *Wanderings of an Artist Among the Indians of North America* (1859), certainly boasts that he did—"Whilst the buf-

Fig. 11. Paul Kane, *Wounded Buffalo Bull*. 1846.
Watercolour on paper. (Courtesy Stark Museum of Art,
Orange, Texas 31.78/119, PWC 8)

faloes were being driven in, the scene was certainly exciting and picturesque; but the slaughter in the enclosure was more painful than
pleasing"[49]—but it is highly unlikely that Kane authored that or any
other claim in his book.[50] More dependable for what Kane himself
saw, is the entry in his field notes' uniquely written account, which
gives no indication of any action occurring during his visit:

> 12 of September I viseted a Buffalo pound the manner of cilling
> they Buffalo in a pound is as follows one man gous out in till he
> seese a a [sic] Band of Buffalos he starts a hed of them in the derec-
> tion of the pound they Buffalo trys to cross a hed of him whitch is
> all ways the case with them now the pound is made like a try
> angle with one side opene bilt witch logs and brush wood it has a
> gate or dore whitch is shut when they get in on eatch side of the
> opening to the pound is sticks put up whitch is called ded men
> the branch of fur about 4th of a mile thare is men behind these frs
> to friten them with skings and haullowing and when they get in
> the Straat thakn with arrows . . . .[51]

Two *real* occurrences supplied Kane with sketches which provided models for many of the buffalo paintings he would do once he returned to Toronto in October 1848. In each case, the buffalo in question remained stationary (or almost), thereby getting Kane round what Harper and others judge to be his "constant trouble in sketching moving objects."[52] The first came during his famous participation in a Metis spring buffalo hunt to the southwest of the settlement at Red River. *Wounded Buffalo Bull* (Fig. 11) is Kane's watercolour sketch of the second bull he ever shot for himself—shot, but did not kill straightaway, since his shot found the bull's stomach. As the following passage from his field notes attests, the frontier painter's avocation could prove a tricky business at times:

> Mounted agane and started in pursute came up with a Bull and shot him started in pursute of another fired and wounded him he stoped and turned round cocking his tale I thought this a good time to take cetch so laid my gun down on the pummal of the Saddle. tuck out my cetch Book and just as I was commenceing the Bull made a furious charge on me I let go gun cetch book and all I returnad, fired and wounded him in the side whitch stoped him he stud long anph for me to take a cetch and fele.[53]

Were it not for the truth rung by this tale, one might suppose Kane's sketch to have been modelled on one of Catlin's: Plate 16 in *Catlin's North American Indian Portfolio*, and reproduced often by Catlin. But, in fact, this occasion gave Kane—latterly, at least—the sort of opportunity for draftsmanship that his artistic education lacked. Having made his living for a time by painting portraits, and studious of portraiture when in Italy, he profited from this chance to sketch the proportions of a plains buffalo bull as it presented itself for such portraiture. It is as fine a rendition as Rindisbacher's early effort (Fig. 3), from a quarter century before, and likewise profits from not having to correspond in scale to a landscape background.

Kane came by his other opportunity to sketch a stationary bull less precariously. On his return from the Pacific Ocean in 1847, he spent the winter on the prairies, making a variety of trips out from Fort Edmonton, where he also enjoyed the Christmas dinner of which a Victorian ghost writer made a sumptuous—and now famous—verbal feast.[54] During the first of these forays, along the North Saskatchewan River valley (up- or downstream of the fort is unknown), he shot a gigantic bull and had its head brought back to the fort, where

Fig. 12. Paul Kane's
Buffalo Head.
Photograph. 1990.
(Courtesy Manitoba
Museum of Man and
Nature, Winnipeg)

Fig. 13. Paul Kane, *Two
Buffalo Heads* (detail). c.
1848. Watercolour on
paper. (Courtesy Stark
Museum of Art, Orange,
Texas 31.78/121, PWC 10)

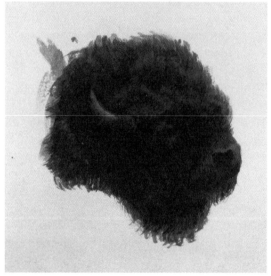

he put it on the scales and found it to weigh 202 pounds, or so his
book tells us.[55] The head survives; a photograph of it (Fig. 12) helps
to show how realistically Kane endeavoured in watercolour (Fig. 13)
to paint it. Its chin hair has disappeared under the taxidermist's art,
but, otherwise, it appears pretty well as Kane drew it in his field
sketches, and survives as a splendid specimen for study of the species.

Despite Kane's varied styles over the entire corpus of his works, the representation of buffalo in his large, romantic oil paintings would remain regarded as his contribution to the history of the animal's image. In his wake in Canada would come Frederick Arthur Verner, English-trained, who sought a realistic rendering of buffalo and achieved it, from time to time, as in his watercolour, *Buffalo Grazing* (1889), despite his foreign training.[56] Even more than Kane, he chose to de-emphasize the buffalo as victim, so that, in his best known work on the subject, *The Last of the Herd* (which owes at least a titular debt to Albert Bierstadt), the buffalo remains the occupant of an Edenic landscape rather than the game of sportsmen or the sustenance of Indians. But the buffalo herds, because they were dying out in the 1870s, when Verner came west, necessarily take on a nostalgic cast, one that British audiences, in particular, remarked and approved. By the last decade of the century, with Riel defeated and hanged, central Canada was viewing the West in terms of railways and settlers, and did not find the tone of regret commensurate with their taste and expectations for the hinterland. Put another way, Ontario was beginning to look at the West practically; romantic art, which, by definition, the Victorians saw as ennobling for the human spirit, began to look impractical, untrue.

Ushering in a more realistic rendering of the buffalo were some retrospective prose accounts, not issued until the twentieth century, recalling the famous semi-annual Metis buffalo hunts. Unlike Kane's book, though not his field notes, the descriptions given by John George "Kootenai" Brown of the last hunts, in the mid-1870s, do not glorify the event in the manner of some exotic riding-to-hounds spectacle. Instead, it is seen both dramatically *and* practically, in the context of the needs of Metis life, with which Brown had come into contact by marriage in 1869. The adventure of running buffalo consisted less in sport than in risk and hard work:

> It was some experience for a new hunter—dust flying, horns clashing, buffalo bellowing, men yelling, and all going at top speed. The buffalo dare not stop as the rest of the herd would trample over them. There was hardly ever a drive in which someone was not hurt. It rarely ever happened that a hunter was shot but sometimes he would be knocked off his horse and another rider would run over him. We had to be very careful and at the same time we had only a few minutes to do our execution . . . .

In running buffalo a hunter with a good horse would kill only prime animals. No calves or yearlings were ever killed—nothing but full growns, three, four, five, and six years old. Buffalo live, barring accidents, to about the same age as domestic cattle. We always preferred front quarters of a buffalo because they were fatter and as we boiled our meat in summer front quarters made the best food. Of course, it was a rule in all half-breed hunting camps that every part of every animal must be used unless it was diseased. Mange was the principal disease, but we frequently found buffalo with lump jaw and occasionally with wounds inflicted in drives or by the arrows of roaming bands of Indians. These diseased or maimed animals were only killed by accident.

The run of the herd would average about one mile. Some of the slow or long-winded horses might run a couple of miles but most of the killing was done in five hundred yards. It was just a miniature battle but the killed were always of the fleeing army of buffalo. A hunter would occasionally be hurt....Each hunter must look after the animals he has killed and his woman is on hand to haul it away with a cart. The drive begins as early as possible in the morning. This gives plenty of time to dress the killing and get it to camp before dark at night. A cow and a half was considered a good load for a cart, which of course, was hauled by only one horse. It was the hardest kind of work skinning and cutting up buffalo in the boiling sun of a midsummer day and we were always glad when the carts came back for another load as our women always brought a keg of water. We were always very thirsty.[57]

There is no vision of heroic men of the frontier in Brown's account; indeed, he all but forgets to mention the skill required of the hunter, so many other factors seeming to be equally important, including the regimen of the hunt.

In a different practical respect, Charles Mair, poet, Orangeman/ Imperialist, and civil servant, offered what may well be the first Canadian taxonomical descriptions of "The American Bison" to a meeting of the Royal Society of Canada, held in May 1890. Wisely basing his remarks on the verbal reports of Indian hunters, which he had collected himself or had had passed along to him, Mair included a delineation of three types of plains buffalo—the southern or "Missouri" cattle, the northern or "Prairie beast," and the diminutive

"Beaver River" buffalo—and one type of wood buffalo—the "thickwood buffalo."[58]

Mair's paper occasions the entry of the buffalo into Canadian academic discourse as the bison. This discourse continues to the present day, of course, fascinating scientists because its sufficiently adaptable character apparently rendered it capable of living anywhere in North America where space permitted; it simply altered its physical appearance to take local factors into account. Indeed, perhaps it is the right animal to be the one known by the "wrong" name—buffalo—so adaptable has it proved in most other respects.

William Rowan, a professor at the University of Alberta, took the prudent measure in September 1925 of travelling to the unscientifically-named Wood Buffalo National Park in order to study the wood buffalo before the shipments there of the plains buffalo from Wainwright had had the opportunity to introduce themselves to the indigenous animals to any intimate extent. One of Rowan's guides, Susie Marie, who had guided Ernest Thompson Seton in 1907, took the party to Salt River by horse and democrat from Fort Smith. The men followed many buffalo trails over a ten-day period in September, using the ranger's buildings at Pine Lake and the Mission as a base camp. However, few animals were actually seen. Rowan's party killed two old bulls for specimens, but, as stipulated in the agreement by which he had gained his permits, Rowan did not shoot the young bull that he saw up close.[59] The graphite sketches that Rowan made, based on these specimens and related photographs—one of the drawings appeared in print four years later[60]—attest to his skill as a draftsman, but one cannot straightforwardly compare his depictions to the paintings by Rindisbacher, Catlin, or Kane, let alone those of the Europeans: simply, the animal is manifestly distinct in outward appearance. Only the common name of *buffalo* occasions their being brought together for comparison.

Figure 14 presents a wood buffalo with a remarkable head, almost barbered with quite blunt features, and positions the animal imposingly at the edge of a bluff overlooking a train of ten other buffalo in the river valley below. Figure 15 appears to have used other models altogether, for there is a faintly dromedarian protuberance of the skulls. Perhaps the domestic arrangement of the two animals makes for a more imaginative than realistic and draftsmanlike presentation; certainly the mountainous background intimates as much, the romantic effects of landscape, as with Kane's *Buffalo at Sunset* (Fig. 9),

Fig. 14. W. Rowan, untitled. [Buffalo on river valley bluff] 1925? Graphite on paper. (Courtesy University of Alberta Archives, 69-16. Reproduced by permission of the Archivist.)

Fig. 15. W. Rowan, untitled. [Buffalo in mountain landscape] 1925? Graphite on paper. (Courtesy University of Alberta Archives, 69-16. Reproduced by permission of the Archivist.)

Fig. 16. C.W. Jefferys, *A Typical Buffalo Bull*. 1924.
Coloured pencil on card. (Courtesy Robert Stacey,
Toronto)

seeping back, even into the drawings of a scientist. At least one may
infer that the bluff, river bank, and mountains of the three landscapes demonstrate how dramatically Rowan regarded the animal.
Alternatively, he may intentionally have been hypothesizing that, at
one time or another, the buffalo occupied all the habitats of western
North America, and that to stereotype the buffalo as a beast of the
short grassland prairies only, is misleading.

C.W. Jefferys, best known as the first Canadian painter systemati-
cally to go beyond the conventions of the picturesque in prairie landscape painting, was studying the buffalo at Wainwright the summer
before they began to be shipped north to Wood Buffalo. In his excellent introduction to and study of Jefferys' prairie art, Robert Stacey
quotes two letters by the painter, written during his stay at Wainwright during the last week of July. In one, he marvels at the animals, "remarking that he had had 'no idea their lines were so fine'."
In another, he tells Lorne Pierce, of Ryerson Press in Toronto, that,
"'If you've never visited Wainwright Buffalo Park, you've never

seen a buffalo. . . . And if you think the buffalo is a sluggish creature, just try to sketch one; I chase them with a Ford and they can show speed'."[61]

In the context of other buffalo paintings, what strikes one about Jefferys' *A Typical Buffalo Bull* (Fig. 16) are the signatures of all his western work—the "sun-saturated" quality of his vision, and the ample range of colour and hue. In his typical bull, the shape is familiar, as, of course, is the open eye, but the prairie light accentuates four different colours of the pelage. Jeffreys thereby brings out, not its uniform bulkiness, as a Catlin or Kane would have done, or as Kelsey's verse—"The one is a black a Buffilo great"—puts it, nor some sombre, subdued demeanor (as if the species were, in and of itself, surly and skulking), but a livelier beast than had hitherto been depicted. In addition, taking his cue from the Impressionist school's fascination with shadow even while he adjusts their rules for composition,[62] he integrates his typical bull into the terrain with a shadow, which, though shadows accompany most of the earlier pictures of buffalo discussed above, stands out here both for the contrast it makes to the colour of the ground, and for the sense it somehow gives of having been as carefully studied and represented in tone and shape as the buffalo itself. Realistic in a new way, a way still influenced by European style, however, Jefferys' effort marks a noteworthy achievement when one considers it as the product of only one week's work, and without, probably, his ever having seen a buffalo before.

III

By no means has this provision of a context attempted to place on view all the attempts at recording the buffalo in word and image up to the time of its near extinction and necessary placement in captivity. But it is hoped that it will have prepared a sufficient ground for a discussion of the works of the most important painter of the animal, Clarence Tillenius. Unlike all others discussed to this point, Clarence Tillenius is a naturalist, a student of wildlife. Not only is it his avocation, it is his vocation, and it is his genius. Moreover, the West is not for Clarence Tillenius the destination in a summer's or several months' travels, after which he retreats, Kane- or Catlin-like, eastward in order to make over his impressions in the images dictated by non-Westerners. This is not to say that he has not studied widely the styles and techniques of others, but they do not condition and control his art; an intimate connection with nature does. His Winnipeg studio, Trails of the Interlake, is as far as he "retreats" from the wilderness West and North, which lure him in every month of every year, a "hidden... world coexistent with ours, one that we may never completely understand, but that lives out an existence fully as rich and significant as our own."[63]

Born on a homestead near Sandridge, in the Manitoba Interlake, in 1913, Tillenius grew up with an intimate awareness of animals, powerfully reinforced by an early introduction to the works of Ernest Thompson Seton, including *Pictures of Wild Animals* (1901) and *Rolf in the Woods* (1911). Although he had already sold his first magazine cover in 1934, when an industrial accident cost him his painting (right) arm in 1936, he found himself with more time and an unrelinquished passion to paint wildlife. After an approach to Lionel Lemoine Fitzgerald, a native-born Manitoba artist of European descent and then Principal of the Winnipeg School of Art, to paint wildlife did not work out, Tillenius arranged to meet and study with Alexander J. Musgrove. Musgrove had come from Scotland in 1913 to serve as the first Principal of the Winnipeg School of Art.[64] His own training had occurred under Maurice Greiffenhagen at the Glasgow School of Art after the heyday there of the painters known as the Glasgow Boys.[65] Musgrove's own early art does not, however, evince that famous group's interest in rustic naturalism, and the contemporary trends of the Hague School and French Impressionism; while his early work most nearly resembles the landscapes of James Paterson, it remained, Nancy Dillow states, "relatively conservative, reflecting the romantic traditions of Scottish painting," with restrained use of colour and subdued light. On the other hand, his Canadian paintings, which he had more time to create after stepping down from the principalship in 1921 and beginning his own Western Art Academy, reflect an adaptation to the light and high colour of the West without ever breaking from the conservative temperament.

What Musgrove offered Tillenius as his tutor over a three-and-one-half-year period (1936–40) was a quick, fluid technique, which sought to capture moods rather than define characters fully. Never overworking sketches, watercolours, or oil paintings, Musgrove used line to develop a scene's pattern and design. Seldom dwelling on social scenes, he concentrated on landscapes, but in them he "rejected the rough, primeval elements of the Pre-Cambrian Shield" because, in his search to express the harmony he wished to find between man and nature, the shield country proved jarringly inap-

propriate. Instead, he emphasized the intensity of light in his landscapes, must have approved of the work of C.W. Jefferys, and certainly looked with a jaundiced eye on the Scandinavia-derived styles
and subject matter of the Group of Seven.[66]

Of course, not all this attitude was appropriate to the direction
that Tillenius's art would take, but Musgrove succeeded in bringing
to Tillenius's attention not only ways of painting landscape, but also
the consummate draftsmanship of two portrait painters, the Wel-
shman Augustus Edwin John, and the expatriate American John
Singer Sargent. At about the same time, Tillenius writes, he made
the "electrifying discovery of the paintings of that superlative
painter of the wilds, Sweden's incomparable Bruno Liljefors [and
those of] Harald Wiberg, Sweden's other great animal draughts-
man."[67] Each of these influences on Tillenius's training confirmed
one thing: the importance of draftsmanship in wildlife studies.
Meanwhile, as his own remarks repeatedly suggest, Tillenius was
fully convinced that only careful and prolonged study of animals in
their habitats, *in-situ*, as it were, with the painter patiently awaiting
their unprovoked appearance and movements, would permit him to
realize the realistic representations of the "truth" of the animals he
sought out. Thus, to learn that he spent over five years studying buffalo and, then, preparing and completing the *Red River Buffalo Hunt*
diorama in time for the opening of the Manitoba Museum of Man
and Nature in July 1970, is not so surprising.

The Manitoba Museum diorama was not Tillenius's first. That had
come a decade earlier, when he prepared the *Fundy Bay Moose* diorama for the National Museum in Ottawa. Not very far along in his
painting career, he had taken a great interest in the work of the diorama artists—particularly at the American Museum of Natural
History—including that of Carl Rungius, the German-American
and, from 1921 to 1958, summertime Albertan,[68] the influence of
whose style may be detected in Tillenius's work.[69] Further trips to
museums were made. In 1962, for example, Tillenius studied Sargent's paintings in London; in 1966, he studied Charlie Russell and
Frederic Remington's work in Phoenix (on the same trip, he visited
Ernest Thompson Seton's widow in Santa Fe). But the trips for artistic study were always outnumbered by the wilderness sojourns that
Tillenius undertook in the 1950s, 60s, and 70s to the Rocky Mountains, the Yukon, and the near and far North. These, together with
his art, won him election to the Explorers Club of New York in 1967.

Only lately have his travels assumed a less hectic pace, but by no means have they halted: for Tillenius, to paint is to travel.

Clarence Tillenius's interest in (indeed, fascination with) buffalo has figured in his art throughout his career, but more prominently at particular points, including the present.[70] After intermittent studies of them over a number of years in his native province's Riding Mountain National Park, and an intensive session there in July 1966, he spent June and August 1967 at both Elk Island and Wood Buffalo parks, and made further trips in 1968. All these pertained, if not strictly, to the *Red River Buffalo Hunt* diorama. What material and knowledge he could not use for that plains buffalo setting was added to his studies in 1971 for his diorama, *Wood Bison, N.W.T.*, at the National Museum. As much as, or perhaps more than, paintings, dioramas accentuate motion and mobility, animals interacting with landscape. Tillenius's rules for representing action are, therefore, important and instructive:

> never try to study or draw details such as fur texture, feather patterns or horseshoe nails on anything in motion. If it is motion you are after, look *only* for the things that express that motion—big sweeping curves, short, choppy movements, blurring of arms, legs or wings, dust stirred up behind, mane, hair or tail flying in the breeze. All of these things belong to motion—get them down in the fewest possible lines.[71]

These are his words of advice to neophytes, of course, but they also indicate his own practice. He does not, like Kane and others, wait for the buffalo to stand still; on the contrary. (See his own description, elsewhere in this issue, of his practice.) Capturing essence with careful draftsmanship is his forte. In an analogous way, to "get them down in the fewest possible lines" is the strength of Sandburg's nostalgic poem: "Their great heads down pawing / on in a great pageant of dusk." Out of such restraint, by concentrating on essence, issues eloquence of line in image or verse.

Sketches from Life 1 (Fig. 17), a page from Tillenius's February and March 1990 sketchbook, demonstrates the consummate practice of his preaching. The line dominates but nothing is overdone. The taut hind legs of the bull in the lower right are captured by the straight line of the inside right and outside left legs. Then, the outstretched tail, emblematic of an alerted and enlivened state, seems to act as a

Fig. 17. Clarence Tillenius, *Sketches from Life 1*. 3 March 1990. Charcoal on paper. (Courtesy the artist)

Fig. 18. Clarence Tillenius, *Sketches from Life 2*. 3 March 1990. Charcoal on paper. (Courtesy the artist)

Fig. 19. Clarence Tillenius, *Sketches from Life 3*. 26 February 1990. Pen and ink, and charcoal on paper. (Courtesy the artist)

sort of pump or lever: when it descends in the next instant's flicking, the bull will explode forward. Thus does the whole hind of the animal not only suggest movement but also confirm the ability to move the hulking mass of hump and head forward rapidly. Almost certainly, these are the lines which Jefferys noted and praised in his letter. Capturing this strong sense of the essential lines of power in the beast demonstrates Tillenius's intimate awareness of the animal. Figures 18 and 19, from the same sketchbook, show in their sum what Tillenius offers from his combination of passion for the life of the wild, and his patient studiousness. It comprehends a much greater variety in the image of the buffalo than that provided by any of his predecessors—occasional students only, by comparison. For all Catlin's wordage about the beast's nobility, he produced only statues stuck on landscapes. Kane could not get the buffalo in motion. Rowan managed shape, and Jefferys the colouring, but the essence, the spirit of the animal, remained elusive to them. The newborn calf, the frolicking cow, the preoccupied, the curious, the panic-stricken, the timid, the gaunt, and the ailing—Tillenius has situated himself to catch their personalities and daily life, but, moreover, in doing so, he has resisted the temptation to personify them. They never take on human attributes. They are beings, the largest of

Fig. 20. Clarence Tillenius and background study for the *Red River Buffalo Hunt* Diorama, Manitoba Museum of Man and Nature, Winnipeg. (Courtesy Penny Morris Photo, Winnipeg)

Fig. 21. Clarence Tillenius preparing the *Red River Buffalo Hunt* Diorama, Manitoba Museum of Man and Nature, Winnipeg. (Courtesy Penny Morris Photo, Winnipeg)

Fig. 22. Clarence Tillenius, *Red River Buffalo Hunt* Diorama, Manitoba Museum of Man and Nature, Winnipeg. (Courtesy Robert R. Taylor Photo, Winnipeg)

North America, but beings that, in Tillenius's renderings of them, remain animals. To the extent that they do, all that is "gone" is only what Tillenius has no opportunity of studying for himself: vast herds roaming free on an open, short grassland prairie.

Or so it would seem. In fact, however, Tillenius has always dedicated himself as a student of wildlife to reading as widely as he can for information pertinent to a particular animal or bird. In his preparing of the historical subject of a Red River buffalo hunt for the diorama at Winnipeg, for example (Figs. 20, and 21, and 22)—one of seventeen done by him—only a portion of the necessary information could be gleaned from his own field studies. Once he exhausted all the possibilities there, including a stampede at him,[72] he applied himself to his library. In his current project, which aims to complete all the partly worked-out compositions that he has made of buffalo over the past five decades (hence the lack of precise dates for the paintings), Tillenius exhibits both contemporary and historical interests in his subject. There is not quite a balance, however; of the four dozen works planned for the series—thirty of which are now completed—the emphasis leans to the contemporary.

The earliest of these paintings in oil, *Buffalo on the Assiniboine Plains* (Fig. 23), from 1954, is perhaps the most stylized of those reproduced here, with a use of colouring that is more dramatic and more typical of landscape painting styles of the 1950s, generally, than is evident in its successors. What the painting demonstrates early on in Tillenius's study, however, is his search for variety of depiction. To situate a bull in the full foreground, tight to the picture plane, but with a sudden cutaway, on the left edge, both to falling ground and to open horizon, is already a considerable achievement in the handling of the task of situating the animal in the landscape's space. That the foreground bull stands at eye level or slightly above, further demonstrates the artist's confidence with its depiction. The chief success, however, is the sureness with which he has displaced the conventional buffalo image to the middle ground's second beast, in order to provide a new image in the immediate foreground animal. This is a bold initiative for it defines the buffalo no longer in terms of that striking feature—remarked on by Catlin in prose, but by all illustrators in pictures—of the eye that seems to be "strained quite open."

What *Buffalo on the Assiniboine Plains* also features may be found in all the paintings shown here, that is, an intimate understanding of scale and proportion, of how the animal relates to terrain, other ani-

Fig. 23. Clarence Tillenius, *Buffalo on the Assiniboine Plains*. 1954. Oil on canvas. (Courtesy the North American Life Assurance Company, Winnipeg)

Fig. 24. Clarence
Tillenius, *Métis Buffalo
Hunt*. Oil on canvas.
(Courtesy the artist)

Fig. 25. Clarence Tillenius, *Counter-Attack*. Oil on canvas. (Courtesy the artist)

Fig. 26. Clarence Tillenius, *Testing of Champions*. Oil on canvas. (Courtesy Mr. and Mrs. George Friesen, Winnipeg)

Fig. 27. Clarence Tillenius, *Range Mothers—Grizzly and Buffalo*. Oil on canvas. (Courtesy the artist)

Fig. 28. Clarence Tillenius, *Wolves and Buffalo at River Crossing*. Oil on canvas. (Courtesy Mr. and Mrs. James Henderson, Edmonton)

mals, and, occasionally, humans. His striking familiarity with them can be felt even in such imagined scenes as the ones depicted in *Métis Buffalo Hunt* (Fig. 24) and *Counter-Attack* (Fig. 25). These are not theatre pieces in the way that Catlin's are. Tillenius's keen understanding of action, as muscles depict it, allows him to assemble particular beasts in a striking variety of contorted forms without exaggerating them and without losing the picture's focus. The essence of the "galloping horde" jumps out at the viewer, whose point of view, like that of the viewer of the diorama in Winnipeg, seems to lie in the path of the pounding hooves.

In several of these paintings, it will be noticed, the picture divides down the centre. Different in other respects, particularly that of colour values, *Testing of Champions* (Fig. 26), *Range Mothers—Grizzly and Buffalo* (Fig. 27), and *Wolves and Buffalo at River Crossing* (Fig. 28) share this feature, which, by emphasizing the territoriality of the terrain, makes the landscape a prominent, rather than an incidental—mere drapery—part of the picture. This is a vital trait in wildlife painting; indeed, what one has with Tillenius's work as not with his predecessors' is his identity as a wildlife painter, not a landscape painter who has found some unique staffage. Verging on exaggeration itself, this distinction nevertheless serves to underscore the important presence in nature that the viewer of Tillenius's paintings automatically feels. That he is no painter-visitor but a Westerner from birth certainly abets, if it does not mark the source of, this discernible quality. The unequal-because-unlevel foreground on which the champions contest their domain (which quality rescues *Testing of Champions* from conventionality), the faint incongruity of a creek's banks by the time of year when its water has all but run dry, and the use of deadwood to emphasize what foci of animal life river edges are—all testify to the wealth of learning that this artist's eye possesses.

The most intimate of these paintings, *At the Waterhole—Frosty Morning* (Fig. 29), consummately captures buffalo in nature: their intimate connection with it impresses the viewer to a remarkable degree. The painting does not deny human participation but suggests that the world of the human is connected in no meaningful way to it. More than any other, this picture attests to that quality, which all wildlife painters must have, of dissociating themselves from the animal life they portray, that is, of refusing the Landseerean gambit of humanizing animals. Partly, this effect is achieved by Tillenius's capturing the ideal time of day for animals—early morning, before man usually begins his interaction with the world. The preceding night lingers in the deep blue water of the pool's right side, where the painting, as the water does the buffalo, lures the viewer's eye. Further, one cannot help feeling, the pocket of natural mystery which is tucked out of view under the foreground bank holds the spell that the frost has cast over the entire landscape. This narrative element (one source of the effect of intimacy) is enhanced by another: the link from animal to animal around the waterhole, crossing the centre axis to the buffalo standing in the early morning sun. Each beast waiting its turn participates in an enthralling dramatic grouping while an almost indeterminable host of others loom out of the frosty bush, which encloses and defines the scene on this magically intimate scale.

This effect works another way in the limitless landscape, *Before the White Man Came* (Fig. 30). In this painting, Tillenius adumbrates the unnumberable herds of life. Instead of adopting a point of view that looks down on a sea of buffalo, however, he has chosen the much more imposing eye-level perspective. The terrain falls away but not before the bosses of the beast which is tight to the picture plane, and of the others immediately behind and to the right of it break the plane of the horizon. This technique strikes the eye somewhat as the three-dimensional figures in a diorama do. Rather than the essential buffalo, then, this painting defines the essential landscape by means of buffalo. The landscape cannot actually contain its numbers; the vision of the prairie on the advent of the white man is not defined by vast space, as it conventionally was, but by vast life, on the move, alive. Kelsey's verse, "This plain affords nothing but Beast and grass," comes to mind, but Jon Whyte's poem, *Homage, Henry Kelsey*, perhaps captures better something of this painting's effect:

> *The one is a black a Buffilo great*
> whose size would call forth titan's tumult
> summoning trumpeted speeches from dumb mouths
> and in his majesty the thunderheads
> roil in his cumulus hulking shoulders' mass . . . . [73]

With the grand achievement of this prodigious series of buffalo paintings, Clarence Tillenius not only deserves, yet again, our notice as western Canada's pre-eminent wildlife painter; he affirms that the buffalo are not gone. In art, they are with us more than ever.

Fig. 29. Clarence Tillenius, *At the Waterhole—Frosty Morning*. Oil on canvas. (Courtesy Mr. and Mrs. James Henderson, Edmonton)

Fig. 30. Clarence Tillenius, *Before the White Man Came*. Oil on canvas. (Courtesy the artist)

I.S. MacLaren is a professor of English and Canadian Studies at the University of Alberta.

note: While Professor MacLaren is Associate Editor of this journal, he took no part in the process of editorial evaluation and independent assessment of this article.

Notes

1. Carl Sandburg, "Buffalo Dusk," *Smoke and Steel* (New York: Harcourt, Brace, 1920), p. 235.
2. Anon., "Saving the Buffalo," *The Beaver*, Outfit 279 (June 1948), pp. 2, 13. A comprehensive map, "Origins of the Park Buffalo," and further details about Canada's restocking schemes are available in Sheilagh C. Ogilvie, *The Park Buffalo*, Robert C. Scace, ed. (Calgary: Calgary-Banff Chapter, National and Provincial Parks Association of Canada, 1979). The map appears at pp. 32–33.
3. Pedro de Castaneda, of Najera, *The Narrative of the Expedition of Coronado by Castaneda*, G.P. Winship, trans. (1896); rpt. in *Spanish Explorers in the Southern United States. 1528–43*, F.W. Hodge and T.H. Lewis, eds. (1907; Austin, Tex.: Texas State Historical Association, 1984), pp. 383–84; qtd. in Robert Thacker, *The Great Prairie Fact and Literary Imagination* (Albuquerque: University of New Mexico Press, 1989), p. 16.
4. See Ingo Krumbiegel and Gunter G. Sehm, "The geographic variability of the Plains Bison. A reconstruction using the earliest European illustrations of both subspecies," *Archives of Natural History* 16 (1989), p. 174. The article's title is misleading, for no reference is made to the López de Gómara illustration (Fig. 1).
5. Rpt. in David A. Dary, *The Buffalo Book: The Full Saga of the American Animal* (1974; rev. ed., n.p.: Sage Books, Swallow Press/Ohio University Press, 1989), p. 7. Another, showing a bison wearing a most doleful expression, is reprinted in Martin S. Garretson, *A Short History of the American Bison* (New York: American Bison Society, 1934), frontispiece.
6. Francisco López de Gómara, *La Historia General delas Indias, con todos los Descubrimientos, y Cosas notables que han acaesido enellas, dende que se ganaron hasta agora* (Saragossa, 1552–53); Thomas Nicholas, trans. and abridged as *The Pleasant Historie of the Conquest of the Weast India, now called new Spayne, atchieved by the worthy Prince Hernando Cortes, Marques of the Valley of Huaxacac, most delectable to read* (London, 1578).
7. See Olive Patricia Dickason, *The Myth of the Savage and the Beginnings of French Colonialism in the Americas* (Edmonton: University of Alberta Press, 1984); Roy Harvey Pearce, *The Savages of America: A Study of the Indian and the Idea of Civilization* (Baltimore: Johns Hopkins University Press, 1953), and *Savagism and Civilization: A Study of the Indian and the American Mind*, 2nd. ed. (Baltimore: Johns Hopkins University Press, 1965); and Robert F. Berkhofer Jr., *The White Man's Indian: Images of the American Indian from Columbus to the Present* (New York: Knopf, 1978).
8. André Thevet, *La Cosmographie Universelle d'André Thevet cosmograph du roy. Illustrée de diverses figures de choses plus remarquables vevès par l'auteur, & incogneuès de noz anciens & modernes*, 2 vols. (Paris: P. L'Huillier; Guillaume Chaudere, 1575). Woodcut rpt. also in Dickason, p. 179; Krumbiegel and Sehm, p. 176. Another woodcut of a buffalo, based on the one in López de Gómara but reversed, had appeared in Thevet's earlier book, *Les Singularitez de la France Antarctique, autrement nommée Amerique: et de plusieurs Terres & Isles decouvertes de notre temps* (Paris: Chez les heritiers de M. de la Port; Antwerp: Christophle Plantin, 1858); rpt. in Dary, p. 8, Krumbiegel and Sehm, p. 175.

9. Dickason's caption reads as follows: "Canadians killing eastern woodland buffalo" (p. 179). Without reference to her work, Krumbiegel and Sehm disagree. Their caption reads: "Hunting the Florida Bison. Seminole Indians are depicted as Germanic warriors hunting the wisent" (p. 176). It is uncertain that Thevet ever travelled to North America, and this uncertainty necessarily calls into question both Krumbiegel and Sehm's ascription of the designation *Bison bison bison* (Southern Plains Bison) to the animals in these early depictions, and their location of them and the hunters in Florida (a much bigger area of southeastern North America than the name now designates), especially as they do not refer to the earliest pictures, in López de Gómara. Finally, they base their argument on pictures that, if custom was followed in these particular publications, were made, not by the books' authors, but by artists who never saw North America or a buffalo.

10. Dary, *The Buffalo Book*, pp. 10–11.

11. Lawrence J. Burpee, ed., "The Journal of Anthony Hendry [*sic*], 1754–55," *Proceedings and Transactions of the Royal Society of Canada*, 3rd ser., sec. II (1907), p. 333.

12. This is the finding of Frank Gilbert Roe, *The North American Buffalo: A Critical Study of the Species in its Wild State* (1951), 2nd ed. (Toronto and Buffalo: University of Toronto Press, 1970), pp. 215–16. Kelsey's journals were not available in published form until 1929.

13. D.M.R. Bentley, "'Set Forth as Plainly May Appear': The Verse Journal of Henry Kelsey," *Ariel: A Review of International English Literature* 21, no. 4 (Oct. 1990), p. 26.

14. *The Kelsey Papers*, Arthur G. Doughty and Chester Martin, ed. and introd. (Ottawa: Public Archives of Canada and The Public Record Office of Northern Ireland, 1929), p. 3. Words that Kelsey spelled with contractions have been expanded to their modern forms.

15. Elliot Coues, ed., *New Light on the Early History of the Greater Northwest, the Manuscript Journals of Alexander Henry, Fur Trader of the Northwest Company, and of David Thompson, Official Geographer and Explorer of the Same Company, 1799–1814*, 3 vols. (New York: Francis P. Harper, 1897) I, 174 n.39.

16. Alexander Henry, in Coues, ed., *New Light*, I, 167.

17. *The Kelsey Papers*, p. 13.

18. Daniel Williams Harmon, *A Journal of Voyages and Travels in the Interiour of North America* (Andover: pr. by Flagg and Gould, 1820), pp. 110–11.

19. Two partial exceptions, by American painters, are the following: John Mix Stanley, *Herd of Bison, Near Lake Jessie*, Taft Collection, Kansas State Historical Society (rpt. in Thacker, *The Great Prairie Fact*, p. 93); and Alfred Jacob Miller, *A Buffalo Rift*, National Archives of Canada (rpt. in colour in *The Canadian Encyclopedia*, 3 vols. [Edmonton: Hurtig, 1985], I, 237; 2nd ed., 4 vols. [Edmonton: Hurtig, 1988], I, 295).

20. Henry Marie Brackenridge, *Journal of a Voyage up the River Missouri: Performed in Eighteen Hundred and Eleven* (1814), 2nd. ed. (Baltimore, 1816), pp. 199–200; rpt. in *Early Western Travels 1748–1846*, Reuben Gold Thwaites, ed., vol. 6 (Cleveland: Arthur H. Clark, 1904), pp. 149–50.

21. The gardened appearance of wooded parts of the prairie may be attributed, in part, to the buffalo itself. The buffalo performed an aesthetic office by trampling down the grasses into the semblance of a lawn. As well, the buffalo's penchant, when wallows were not readily available, for scratching up against clumps of poplars for relief from mosquitoes not only kept such groves clear of underbrush but also trimmed and cleaned the poplar boles. Responding to Henry Kelsey's observation that the northern prairie parkland resembled "fields of about half a Mile over Just as if they had been Artificially made with fine groves of Poplo growing

round them" (*The Kelsey Papers*, p. 11), James W. Whillans suggests that the early travellers "might imagine . . . that everything had been 'Artificially made'." (James W. Whillans, *First in the West: The Story of Henry Kelsey, Discoverer of Canadian Prairies* [Edmonton: Applied Arts Products, 1955], p. 102.)

22. Rindisbacher may not have been the first to paint buffalo in what is today Canadian territory. George Heriot, many of whose North American paintings depict British North American subjects and landscapes, painted at least one picture of buffalo between the years 1800 and 1816. Given that Heriot is not known to have travelled any farther west than the eastern end of Lake Erie, his watercolor likely represents an eastern woodlands buffalo. See Gerald Finley, *George Heriot: Postmaster-Painter of the Canadas* (Toronto, Buffalo, London: University of Toronto Press, 1983), p. 242.

23. See Alvin M. Josephy, Jr., *The Artist was a young Man: The Life Story of Peter Rindisbacher* (Fort Worth, Tex.: Amon Carter Museum of Western Art, 1970), chpts. II, III; and Virginia G. Berry, *A Boundless Horizon: Visual Records of Exploration and Settlement in the Manitoba Region 1624–1874* (Winnipeg: The Winnipeg Art Gallery, 1983), pp. 15–20.

24. *Views in Hudson's Bay, Taken by a Gentleman on the Spot in the Years, 1823 and 1824. Illustrative of the Customs, Manners and Costumes of those Tribes of North American Indians Amongst whom Capt'n. Franklin has passed in his present and former arduous Undertaking*, six lithographs (London: Pr. by W. Day, 1825).

25. Josephy, Jr., *The Artist*, p. 65.

26. The latter watercolour is reproduced in colour in Josephy, Jr., *The Artist*, Plate XXXV, p. 65. *Indian Hunter Killing a Bison* is Plate XXI, p. 39.

27. Qtd. in Josephy, Jr., *The Artist*, p. 37.

28. It is unclear if Robert Hood, the other midshipman-artist on the first Franklin expedition, saw many buffalo but he did paint a picture of them: *Buffalo Bull May 1820: Indian hunters attacking a herd in the plains bordering on the Saskatchewan*. This painting is reproduced in colour as Plate 8 and commented on (pp. 171–72) in *To the Arctic by Canoe 1819–1821: The Journal and Paintings of Robert Hood, Midshipman with Franklin*, C. Stuart Houston, ed. (Montreal and London: McGill-Queen's University Press, The Arctic Institute of Canada, 1974). Back snowshoed from Cumberland House to Fort Chipewyan by way of the prairies and Fort Carlton in the winter of 1820, while Hood remained at Cumberland House.

29. The engraving appears in Captain John Franklin, *Narrative of a Journey to the Shores of the Polar Sea in the Years 1819, 20, 21, and 22* (London: John Murray 1823), facing p. 113.

30. Franklin mentions that the fence is filled in between the stakes only "within fifty or sixty yards from the pound . . . to screen the Indians" (*Narrative of a Journey*, p. 112).

31. Perhaps not entirely new: Franklin suggests that "this species of hunting . . . in fact is very similar to that of taking elephants on the Island of Ceylon, but upon a smaller scale" (*Narrative of a Journey*, p. 113).

32. Thomas Cary, *Abram's Plains: A Poem* (1789), D.M.R. Bentley, ed. and introd. (London, Ont.: Canadian Poetry Press, 1986), ll. 196–211.

33. See Walter Shaw Sparrow, *British Sporting Artists from Barlow to Herring* (1922), 2nd ed. (London: Spring Books, 1965), chpt. 5.

34. William H. Truettner, "For European Audiences: *Catlin's North American Indian Portfolio*," in *Prints of the American West: Papers presented at the Ninth Annual North American Print Conference*, Ron Tyler, ed. (Fort Worth, Tex.: Amon Carter Museum of Western Art, 1983), p. 26.

35. The flying gallop formula used here by Catlin to express motion appears to have been borrowed from conventional representations of horses, but is as fanciful a

creation of their action as of a buffalo's. In a fine essay concerning paintings of horses of the American West, Martin E. Petersen argues that "action paintings are further stylized by the conventions used to express motion in horses. There are four formulas . . . : the canter, the flexed plunge, the extended plunge, and the flying gallop. Only the canter was accurate in terms of the photographic evidence available to artists [only] as early as the 1880s. The flying gallop, or rocking horse pose, was used to point out the horse's legendary swiftness. This pose, in which the horse is depicted with all legs extended off the ground, is traceable to prehistory. . . . Earliest examples . . . may be seen in the Lascaux cave paintings, and the convention endured. . . . Only with the advent of photography . . . was this convention of rapid movement challenged in the name of realism and accuracy. . . ." (Martin E. Petersen, "On the Nature of the Horse of the American West in Nineteenth Century Art," *Great Plains Quarterly* 7 [1986], p. 39.) I am indebted to one of the anonymous assessors of the present essay for drawing Petersen's article to my attention.

36. The Bruce Peel Special Collections Library, University of Alberta, possesses three very different copies of *Catlin's North American Indian Portfolio*. One is uncoloured, while only one of the other two has the horse painted white in Catlin's Plate 5 (Fig. 6). (The copy at the Amon Carter Museum of Western Art, reproduced in Truettner's essay, "For European Audiences," as Fig. 4, has a white horse as well.) The standard authority for study of the various copies of a single Catlin painting is Truettner's thorough book, *The Natural Man Observed: A Study of Catlin's Indian Gallery* (Washington: Smithsonian Institution Press, [1979]). For *The Buffalo Hunt "Chase,"* see esp. p. 258.

37. George Catlin, *Catlin's North American Indian Portfolio. Hunting Scenes and Amusements of the Rocky Mountains and Prairies of America. From Drawings and Notes of the Author, made during Eight Years' Travel amongst Forty-Eight of the Wildest and most remote Tribes of Savages in North America* (London: the author, 1844), p. 6.

38. *Catlin's . . . Indian Portfolio*, pp. 5–6.

39. *Catlin's . . . Indian Portfolio*, p. 8.

40. Truettner, "For European Audiences," pp. 33–34.

41. *Catlin's . . . Indian Portfolio*, pp. 3, 6. The definitive study of Catlin and his ideas is Brian W. Dippie's *Catlin and His Contemporaries: The Politics of Patronage* (Lincoln and London: University of Nebraska Press, 1990), to which the orientation of this portion of the discussion is indebted.

42. Catlin's prose account of the surround appears in his *Letters and Notes on the Manners, Customs, and Condition of the North American Indians*, 2 vols. (London: the author, 1841), I, 199–200. The painting also appears, engraved, in that book, as Plate 79.

43. *Catlin's . . . Indian Portfolio*, p. 3.

44. Interested readers may wish to consult such general studies of the nineteenth-century American plains' painters as Bernard De Voto, *Across the Wide Missouri* (Boston: Houghton Mifflin, 1947); William H. Goetzmann and William N. Goetzmann, *The West of the Imagination* (London and New York: W.W. Norton, 1986); and William H. Goetzmann et al., *The West as Romantic Horizon* (Omaha: Center for Western Studies, Joslyn Art Museum, 1981).

45. C.W. Jefferys was one of the first detractors of Kane's horses: "His western horses in build and action are the ideal Arab steeds of the painters of the Romantic School, and recall those of Delacroix and Géricault" (qtd. by Lawrence J. Burpee in Paul Kane, *Wanderings of An Artist Among the Indians of North America from Canada to Vancouver's Island and Oregon through the Hudson's Bay Company's Territory and Back Again* [1859], rev. ed., John W. Garvin, ed., Lawrence W. Burpee, introd. [Toronto: Radisson Society, 1925]; facs. rpt. of rev. ed., J.G. MacGregor, in-

trod. [Edmonton: Hurtig, 1968], p. xliv). In terms of this particular painting, J. Russell Harper argues convincingly that an Italian print of youths on horse, chasing a bull, served Kane as a model: *Paul Kane's Frontier* (Austin, Tex., and London: University of Texas Press, for the Amon Carter Museum of Western Art, and the National Gallery of Canada, 1971), pp. 37–38, 213, 289. However much Kane learned from the Italian print, he does not attempt to make his buffalo over in the image of the bull that the print shows being chased through an Italian park. As well, see Petersen, "On the Nature of the Horse," pp. 34–43; and Ann Davis and Robert Thacker, "Pictures and Prose: Romantic Sensibility and the Great Plains in Catlin, Kane, and Miller," *Great Plains Quarterly* 6 (1986), p. 11.

46. See Doug Owram, *Promise of Eden: The Canadian Expansionist Movement and the Idea of the West 1856–1900* (Toronto, Buffalo, London: University of Toronto Press, 1981).

47. Harper, *Paul Kane's Frontier*, p. 18.

48. Thacker, *The Great Prairie Fact* (see note 3, above), p. 239n.

49. Kane, *Wanderings of an Artist*, p. 81.

50. See I.S. MacLaren, "'I came to rite thare portraits': Paul Kane's Journal of his Western Travels, 1846–1848," *The American Art Journal* XXI, no. 2 (1989), pp. 6–21.

51. Paul Kane's Journal, Stark Museum of Art, Orange, Texas 11.85/5; qtd. by permission; transcribed in *The American Art Journal* XXI, no. 2 (1989), pp. 23–62, and followed by a Glossary of Common Words used by Kane. This passage appears at p. 30.

52. Harper, *Paul Kane's Frontier*, p. 37.

53. Paul Kane's Journal, *The American Art Journal*, p. 27.

54. Kane, *Wanderings of an Artist*, pp. 260–65. No description of the feast appears in either Kane's field notes (Paul Kane's Journal) or his book's draft manuscript (Stark Museum of Art, 11.85/2 [C]). It is reasonable to conclude, then, that a ghost writer, in the hire either of Kane's English publisher, Longman, Brown, Green, Longmans & Roberts, or of the Hudson's Bay Company's London governors, cooked the account.

55. Kane, *Wanderings of an Artist*, pp. 259–60. The field notes (Paul Kane's Journal) make no mention of this hunt, but the draft manuscript (Stark Museum of Art, 11.85/2 [C] does, and confirms the weight given in the book's account.

56. *Buffalo Grazing* is reproduced in colour in Ronald Rees, *Land of Earth and Sky: Landscape Painting in Western Canada* (Saskatoon: Western Producer Prairie Books, 1984), p. 78.

57. Kootenai Brown; qtd. in William Rodney, *Kootenai Brown: His Life and Times 1839–1916* (Sidney, B.C.: Gray's Publishing, 1969), pp. 103, 104, 105.

58. Charles Mair, "The American Bison," *Proceedings and Transactions of the Royal Society of Canada* VIII, sec. II (1890), pp. 93–108. Species are delineated at p. 95.

59. W. Rowan, Field Notes, vol. VIII (14 Mar.-27 Oct. 1925), Rowan Papers, University of Alberta Archives, 69–16–771, p. 68. Qtd. by permission of the Archivist.

60. W. Rowan, "Canada's Buffalo," *Country Life* (England) 14 Sept. 1929, pp. 358–60. This appears to have been Rowan's only publication on the subject. Although his reply to a letter from D. Soper, dated 30 Oct. 1931, has not turned up, Soper's next letter, dated 3 Dec. 1931, states his regret that Rowan has "written nothing on the osteology of the Wood Bison." Finally, in a letter dated more than three years later, 4 Jan. 1935, Soper requests a copy of the "Canada's Buffalo" essay (Rowan-Soper Correspondence, Rowan Papers, University of Alberta Archives, 69–16–375; qtd. by permission of the Archivist).

61. C.W. Jefferys; qtd. in Robert Stacey, *Western Sunlight: C.W. Jefferys on the Canadian Prairies* (Saskatoon: Mendel Art Gallery, 1986), pp. 47, 58. Jefferys' studies of

buffalo are illustrated in Stacey's work, pp. 90–91. This portion, in particular, of the present essay, and all of it generally have benefitted from my discussion with Mr. Stacey.

62. See Stacey, *Western Sunlight*, p. 24.

63. Clarence Tillenius; qtd. in Lorne Reimer, "Clarence Tillenius welcomed back home," *The Stonewall Argus and Teulon Times*, 12 Nov. 1986, p. 10.

64. See Marilyn Baker, *The Winnipeg School of Art: The Early Years* (Winnipeg: University of Manitoba Press, for Gallery 1.1.1., School of Art, 1984), pp. 29–43.

65. See Roger Billcliffe, *The Glasgow Boys: The Glasgow School of Painting 1875–1895* (London: John Murray, 1985).

66. Nancy E. Dillow, *Alexander J. Musgrove, the Forgotten Innovator* (Winnipeg: Winnipeg Art Gallery, 1985); Virginia Berry, *Vistas of Promise: Manitoba 1874–1919* (Winnipeg: Winnipeg Art Gallery, 1987), pp. 61, 63; and author's conversations with Clarence Tillenius. One of Musgrove's best known paintings, *The Prairie Sentinel*, is featured on the cover, and reproduced on p. 37, of Dick Harrison's *Unnamed Country: The Struggle for a Canadian Prairie Fiction* (Edmonton: University of Alberta Press, 1977).

67. Tillenius, *Clarence Tillenius* (Winnipeg: Agassiz Galleries, 1984), p. 3.

68. Lorne E. Render, *Carl Rungius: An Artist's View of Nature*, Provincial Museum and Archives of Alberta, Publication no. 1 (Edmonton: Provincial Museum and Archives of Alberta, 1969).

69. Tillenius also visited Rungius at his Banff studio in 1944 and 1945. In 1958, a year before the death of the American, Tillenius reviewed the entire Glenbow-Alberta Foundation's collection of paintings by Rungius, one of which depicts buffalo.

70. He sketched them very early in his career. See Clarence Tillenius, *Sketch Pad Out-of-Doors* (Winnipeg: the author, 1956), pp. 44–45, 96–97. Tillenius first saw live buffalo in Winnipeg's Assiniboine Park Zoo, about 1930. He completed his first large buffalo painting (Fig. 29) in 1954 (Ray Torgrud, Television Interview with Clarence Tillenius, CKY-TV Winnipeg, 2 Aug. 1991).

71. Tillenius, *Sketch Pad*, p. 15.

72. See Clarence Tillenius, "An Artist among the Buffalo," elsewhere in this issue of *Alberta*.

73. Jon Whyte, *Homage, Henry Kelsey*, Dennis Burton, illus. (Winnipeg: Turnstone Press, 1981), pp. 23–24.

CLARENCE TILLENIUS

An Artist among the Buffalo

The deep snow around my hide-out was criss-crossed with buffalo tracks: the winter sky was grey and lowering: an expectant hush lay over the landscape.

To these marshes lying between the Great Slave Lake and southward across the Peace River I had come to study and paint the buffalo: here, in one of the last places in North America where one can get a sense of what the great western wilderness was like in the days of the buffalo, those far-off days before the white man came. This time I came in midwinter to spend time among the herds as they forage over the deep snow covering the meadows of the Sweet Grass marshes bordering the river. Curiously, unlike elk or caribou, the buffalo do not seem ever to paw away the snow; they swing their heavy heads from side to side sweeping it aside with their muzzles. The heavy coat of hair cushions the skin, yet, at times, when successive thaws and freezing have left shards of ice in the snow layers, I have seen their muzzles cut and bleeding from the constant shoving against the blade-sharp edges of the ice.

Since I would shortly be commissioned to create and execute a re-creation of the great Red River buffalo hunts of the 1870s, I asked the wardens of Wood Buffalo National Park if I could somehow conceal myself and have a herd stampede towards me so that I could experience being in the very centre of the galloping beasts. The park wardens, who were all enthusiasm when I had explained my project, took me to a piled-up heap of logs and brush, telling me to hide there while they obligingly rounded up a buffalo herd and drove it towards me.

Now I was for it: and with that realization came a disquieting thought. The wardens had said the herd would split when they reached the log pile: but would they? I knew that some of those massive bulls weigh well over a ton: would a few logs be any obstacle to them? The wardens had also cautioned me that a buffalo herd's splitting to either side of me depended on my showing myself in time. The danger lay, they told me, in letting the buffalo get too close before popping up, since a buffalo might then in sudden anger or panic hook me as it ran by. I had faith in the wardens' wealth of experience, but I was concealed in the middle of a log pile heaped helter skelter only some seven or eight feet high, and now was feeling a certain doubt about this fortress halting a single buffalo bull, let alone a stampeding herd, angry or not.

A low muttering sound like distant thunder growing steadily louder warned that the time for second thoughts was past. With the wind blowing crossways suddenly there hove into view above the bushes an undulating brown line—the backs of the oncoming buffalo herd. They thundered down on me, but at the last moment divided as they reached the log pile I was crouched in. Four or five cows caught my scent as they went by: they wheeled and bounded up to the log pile grunting menacingly. Moments later they spun round and followed the vanishing herd. Safe in my log pile, I breathed easier and spent the rest of the afternoon recreating in my mind the impressions and appearance of the oncoming herd and putting those impressions down on paper.

Buffalo, when running hard, even after a comparatively short distance, give a misleading appearance of fatigue. Their tongues seem to hang out a foot; the peculiar rocking gait might lead one to think that they are tiring. Nothing could be farther from the truth: buffalo are fiercely enduring; when in running trim, the cows especially can run all day, so that only the fleetest horses can overtake them. The big bulls, because of their greater bulk, resent being made to run and will eventually stop and turn to give battle to whatever pursues them. The enormous head and fore-shoulders of a full-grown buffalo bull are so imposing and ponderous that it is almost incredible to see the ease with which the big bull whips around to meet a rival or face an enemy. The secret is the almost even balance of his great weight over the short sturdy forelegs: the momentum of the heavy head swinging to the side seems to flip the lighter hind quarters like a top in the opposite direction. Buffalo can be treacherous and it is well not to trust them too far, especially at those dangerous times when the cows are protecting their small calves and when the bulls are in the seasonal rut. While on this tack, the wardens offered a notable distinction. If a bull hooks at you in passing, no matter whether he connects or misses, he will pay no heed but keep right on going. An enraged cow, on the other hand, especially one with a calf, will swing and pursue you singlemindedly, no matter which way you jump. (Did Kipling not say: "the female of the species is more deadly than the male"?)

The uncertain temper of the buffalo cow was brought home to me very early on in my experience. One spring day, I think in 1931, at Manitoba's Assiniboine Park Zoo, I had made some amateurish sketches of a buffalo bull sleeping in one of the enclosures. In a farther pasture were several cows with their calves. I made my way around to that side where a single cow and her calf were grazing near the fence, the cow close to the fence, her calf a little farther away. The fence, double around most of the pens, was single here, since the public did not usually venture to that side. Leaning on the fence, I made several sketches of the cow who finally turned her back. To attract her attention I reached through the fence and flipped a pebble in her direction, but had barely time to leap back from the fence when she struck it with a crash that loosened staples and made the wires hum the length of the barrier. At a second crash I was twenty yards away making a mental resolve never to be so foolhardy again. With such startling speed did she swap ends that nothing could have escaped the sweep of those sharp horns. I invoked a silent blessing on the page-wire fence that had been my shield.

In order to keep a respectful distance, I have conducted much of my study of the buffalo through binoculars or with a tripod-mounted telescope. A man with one hand cannot well sketch while holding either binoculars or telescope: my solution was to set my sketchpad on one tripod and mount a twenty-power telescope on a second tripod. This arrangement also served me well when observing grizzlies in the Rockies and on the Yukon tundra, but I hit upon it first when observing the cow buffalo herd with newborn calves in the Riding Mountain range of Manitoba.

An excellent vantage point from which to observe is a waterhole: here in the early morning or late evening one may see the buffalo, usually led by an old cow, making their way to drink. Another good place is an open hillside where the groups of young calves come together to frolic; in either case, an artist may see all manner of interesting compositions. When the herd is collected in a fairly compact group all is well, but occasionally they may be scattered all around you among the bushes where visibility is restricted. Danger can quickly arise when an inquisitive calf suddenly catches sight of you and comes to investigate. His mother will quite likely follow in order not to let him out of her sight. If the calf does not panic and run (which in itself may cause a sudden stampede of animals all around you—an anxious moment), he may come even closer to investigate. This in turn may well trigger a rush by the buffalo cow to head off her calf, during which you might be trampled or hooked, depending on her mood.

But when a buffalo herd is fleeing a common danger, even deep-laid animosities may be temporarily forgotten. On one occasion, flying with a pilot in a slow plane over the Sweet Grass marshes south of the Peace River, we came upon a herd of perhaps forty buffalo, cows, calves, and two or three bulls. Without hesitation, the herd dashed into a deep, wide creek, the calves swimming frantically beside their mothers, the whole cavalcade looking like a tidal wave going through the water. On the marsh's far shore were several large willow clumps, and as the herd dashed through these they startled a large, brown blackbear who had apparently been having a sleep in a bed he had pawed out in the shade of a willow clump. At this unexpected invasion the bear leaped up. As our low-flying plane caught up with and passed over the galloping herd, to our astonishment we saw the bear bounding along in the midst of cows and calves, seemingly paying no attention to them or they to him. Apparently, the sense of fleeing from a common danger had temporarily erased the normal reaction of buffalo to bear, which is certainly not one of trust.

Later in the day, on that same flight, I saw below us a blackbear in another channel of the marsh eating what I took to be a buffalo calf. I asked the pilot to circle lower since I could see several adult buffalo making a wide detour around to windward of the bear. As we came down lower and directly over him, I saw that what he was feeding on was not a calf but the drowned carcass of an adult bull, which, presumably, had broken through the ice earlier in the winter and perished. During the day we flew over a number of similar drowned carcasses in the marsh, and I realized that such drowning deaths must be a considerable source of buffalo mortality, in that district at least.

I had corroboration of this on another trip to the area—this time in February—when I was being guided by a warden along the marshes and creeks bordering the Peace. I had noticed a number of fox and coyote tracks all converging towards what looked like a muskrat "push-up" on the snowy surface of the frozen creek, but as we came up to it I was surprised to see the rump and part of a backbone protruding above the snow. It was the carcass of a buffalo bull; the foxes had eaten a tunnel through the pelvis and down into the frozen abdominal area. The warden then told me the following story.

I had stopped my pickup truck on the road above the creek when I heard a fearful roaring down on the creek below. It was a very cold night with bright moonlight, snow very deep, sometime in late December or early January. I listened a few minutes: there would be a silence, and then the roaring bellow again. I plowed down through the timber in snow up to my hips and came out on the marsh. What a sight! Two big buffalo bulls, one following the other along the creek, had fallen through the ice a few rods apart. The creek there is about seven feet deep but only a couple of feet of water on top of five feet or so of "loonshit". The bulls could get their muzzles a few inches above the water only by rearing up: each time they did would come that hopeless agonized roar. Their heads were already coated with fifty pounds or more of frozen snow and muck almost too heavy to lift. There was nothing to be done for them: I went back up to my truck, got my rifle, and shot them both.

So, yet another of Nature's tragedies, those countless episodes played out in the wilderness far from the haunts of man, had come to pass. And, of course, except that the warden's sense of pity stirred him to put the bulls out of their suffering with a bullet, the course of nature would not in the end be different. The bison bulls had fed on the marsh grasses to grow the meat that now fed foxes, ravens, eagles, and coyotes, even bears: whose bodies in turn enrich the marsh soil and grow more grass to nourish another generation of buffalo. For us as human beings this eternal unrolling of Nature's cosmic plan provides the stuff of art and theatre even while we as individuals play only bit parts.

The battle between a pair of evenly matched, fully adult buffalo bulls is truly a battle of giants, though battles to the death are comparatively rare. The first such contest that I was privileged to witness I came upon unexpectedly. I had been following a well-beaten

buffalo trail through thickly growing aspen and Balm-of-Gilead poplars around a large lake, heading for a series of open hillsides where
I had earlier seen dozens of buffalo wallows. As I came out of the
sheltering timber I heard a hoarse bellow and then a continuous
roaring with a kind of growling undertone. The sound vibrated
along the ground, not unlike the roaring of African lions. Now I saw
roiling clouds of dust billowing up from a hillside ahead; a couple of
steps farther a pair of huge buffalo bulls came into view, pawing the
ground, throwing dust over themselves, and roaring. As I watched
in fascination, the bigger bull with a sudden sideways lunge and a
swing of his enormous head tried to take his opponent off guard and
crush his ribs. By an adroit manoeuvre, his adversary swung to
meet the thrust and the two massive skulls met head on head with a
resounding thud. Now a mighty struggle ensued: divots of turf flew
through the air as the fiercely clawing back hooves gripped and
strained for purchase. As the battle raged up and down the hillside,
a couple of younger bulls, evidently excited beyond measure, ran
back and forth around the fighting herd-masters, acting as though
they too wanted to join the fight but finding no opening. The two
gladiators had neither eyes nor attention for any but each other.

For almost an hour the duel raged on. Strings of foam dripped
from the open jaws: black tongues protruding and their sides heav-
ing, they gasped heavily for breath as they stood a moment glaring
at each other. It seemed like a truce, and then, just as the younger
bull seemed turning to go, the other with a sudden lunge caught him
unprepared and down he went. I did not see exactly what happened:
the victorious bull must have had his horns below the fallen rival; either he lifted his enemy with a swing of his powerful neck or the fallen bull rolled completely over, regained his feet, and fled the scene.
Whether or not he was badly gored I was not close enough to see,
but as he departed he did not seem lame. Several days later, I saw
two or three larger bulls with rips and bloody gashes in their sides:
perhaps the defeated champion was one of these. As dearly as I
would have liked to watch this battle from very close up, I felt that it
would be foolhardy in the extreme to approach too near such wild-
eyed combat: a move like that might prove one's last.

Another lesson the animal artist in buffalo country quickly learns
is that buffalo are highly conservative creatures: they are distrustful
in the highest degree of anything new or strange appearing in terrain unfamiliar to them. Arriving one summer in Alberta's Elk Island
National Park and impatient to begin painting, I built a rough blind

of stumps, small logs, and dead branches on a hillside a few feet above a buffalo trail skirting the pond and beaver dam below. A site overlooking a beaver dam offers an ideal location since deer, bears, wolves, foxes, lynxes, and other beasts will all use this beaver-built bridge on occasion to avoid the treacherous footing of the flooded marsh. I had spent the day from early dawn in this blind, watching the life of the wild going on all around me, and when I left with night coming on I intended to return early next morning. My paint box, easel, and tripod made a fairly heavy backpack, and I debated whether or not it would be better to leave them overnight in the blind. Long experience in the woods, however, has taught me that one should never leave equipment behind to be retrieved later if there is any chance of its being needed elsewhere, so I gathered all the gear together and slogged the miles back to my overnight camp.

As things turned out, that night and next morning I had an adventure with a pair of battling moose bulls and did not get back to the beaver dam until the day following. I rounded the hillside, came suddenly on the blind I had so carefully dragged together, and there received a rude jolt. Logs, stumps, bushes, and branches had been smashed, tossed, and trampled: even a small bush had been hooked out of the ground by a horn thrust. A buffalo herd had obviously come by and, spotting my blind as something new that did not belong there, proceeded to destroy it. Had my sketching outfit, easel, and brushes been left there they would have been smashed also.

On the other hand, I have spent days at a time in the neighbourhood of a buffalo herd, not spooking them by trying to get too close but simply observing them through binoculars and noting the play of light and shade on their ever-moving shaggy bodies. For so unique and distinctive an animal, it yet takes years of observation and study for an artist to make himself completely familiar with the movements and the shapes of buffalo: observing the bulls with the massive hair boss over the forehead and the heavy golden mantle extending over the withers and down to the knees; contrasting this with the shapes of the lighter-bodied cows. The calves too are deceiving, the hump over the shoulders and the odd conformation of the neck and head being so different from the domestic calf with which one may be familiar.

There is never an end to surprises when working among the buffalo. On my most recent trip to Elk Island National Park, I one night parked my heavy truck with camper studio in an open glade of the aspen woods alongside a trail heavily trodden by elk and buffalo. In the early dawn I was wakened by an odd crunching sound apparently right outside the camper. It was still quite dark: I looked out but saw nothing. The crunching sound continued for some time; suddenly, something definitely brushed against the truck. I spied out the camper's side window only to look down on the back of an enormous buffalo bull pushing his head under the truck to snatch a few mouthfuls of grass. I must have parked on top of the choicest clump of grass the place afforded, and he was not about to be done out of it by anybody or anything.

I was completely willing that he should have it: even setting aside that no one in his right mind would argue with a buffalo bull, or cow, the interaction with the world of the buffalo has throughout my life brought me so much pleasure that whatever a buffalo might claim as his inalienable right I am more than happy to concede. All I ask is that the race of buffalo continue to enrich this land for all the generations to come.

Clarence Tillenius is a Winnipeg artist and the dean of Canadian wildlife painters.

C. GATES
T. CHOWNS
H. REYNOLDS

Wood Buffalo at the Crossroads

Introduction

The saga of the North American bison (*Bison bison*) is chronicled as one of the most tragic abuses of wildlife on this continent.[1] The bison is the largest terrestrial mammal in North America, and in prehistoric and early historic times it was the dominant herbivore on the grasslands of the central plains. It played an important role in grassland and boreal ecosystems and was a principal resource for the indigenous human population inhabiting the interior plains region of the continent. At the close of the nineteenth century, following the onset of European settlement, the bison was nearly driven to extinction. The plains subspecies (*B. b. bison* Linnaeus) was effectively extirpated in Canada by 1885 and only a few hundred wood bison (*B. b. athabascae* Rhoads) remained in northern areas between Lake Athabasca and Great Slave Lake.[2] The chronology of depletion was similar for the two subspecies. In this century, the plains bison has been saved from extinction and presently numbers over 100 000 individuals, largely on commercial ranches. The wood bison has achieved more modest abundance, and further recovery of this subspecies is clearly at a crossroads.

This article deals with the history of the wood bison, tracing it through three distinct periods, the historic period, the early conser-

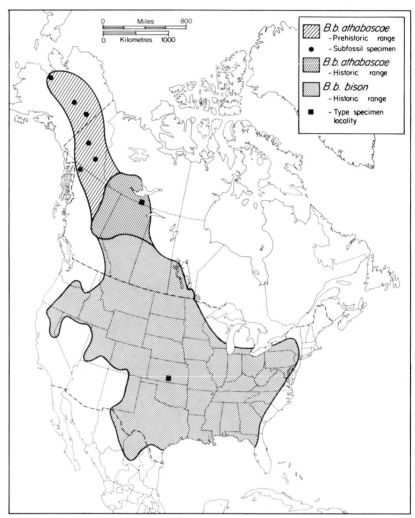

Fig. 1. Historic and prehistoric distribution of wood bison (*Bison bison athabascae*) and historic range of plains bison (*Bison bison bison*), after van Zyll de Jong (1986).

vation period, and the recovery period. Major limiting factors to further recovery are identified and discussed.

The Historic Period

Distribution and Abundance

While the abundance and wide geographic distribution of the plains bison is clearly described in numerous historical accounts of North America,[3] the historical record for wood bison is less well known. This is reflective of its lower abundance in the past, the remoteness of its range, and its shorter period of contact with Europeans. The historic range of the wood bison was reported to have been centred in the north central section of the Interior Plains Physiographic Region of Canada. This region includes northern Alberta, southwestern Northwest Territories (NWT), northeastern British Columbia, and northwestern Saskatchewan (Fig. 1).

Sir John Richardson,[4] who travelled with Franklin in his overland search for the Northwest Passage, published one of the earlier descriptions of the range and habitat of the wood bison in 1829:

> As far as I have been able to ascertain, the limestone and sandstone formations, lying between the Rocky Mountain ridge and the lower eastern chain of primitive rocks, are the only districts in the fur countries frequented by the bison. In these comparatively level tracts there is much prairie land on which they find good grass in summer, and also many marshes overgrown with bulrushes and carices, which furnish them with winter food.

Richardson[5] described the Interior Plains area that lies between the Western Cordillera and the Precambrian Shield regions. In this vast area, where the wood bison once existed as an important element of the boreal forest ecosystem, the land is now largely devoid of their presence.

Hugh M. Raup,[6] a botanist who carried out extensive field research on the phytogeography (biogeography of plants) of the Liard, Peace, Slave, and Athabasca basins and who had developed a special interest in wood bison habitat, stated that the former range seemed to conform to the distribution of semiopen prairies in the Mackenzie Basin. These prairies occurred only on compact soils formed in postglacial lakes. Following the last Ice Age, most of the upper Mackenzie Basin was submerged by expansive glacial lakes whose wave action sorted particulate matter into a gradient from coarse sand to fine clay. As these lakes receded, raised beaches remained where water levels had stabilized, and extensive lacustrine plains remained in deeper sections.[7]

Available historical information (Chowns in prep.) indicates that wood bison were located within the confines of interconnected overlapping glacial lake basins and major river valleys of the interior plain, where soil factors were conducive to sedge-grass meadow development. The distribution of the dynamic semiprairie habitat of wood bison is influenced by plant succession and retrogression. Because these animals roamed through prairieland and intervening woodland, the original wood bison range appeared to have been contiguous. Insular populations probably did not occur until numbers were greatly depleted during the mid to late 1800s.

Richardson[8] reported the northern limit of the historic distribution of the wood bison was Lac la Martre, located northwest of Great Slave Lake, NWT. Other accounts from the historic period noted the occurrence of bison west of Great Slave Lake in the vicinity of what is now the Mackenzie Bison Sanctuary (MBS).[9] The eastern limit of endemism followed the boundary between the Interior Plains and the Precambrian Shield, with recorded observations along the Slave and Athabasca rivers[10] and along the Clearwater River, a tributary of the Athabasca.[11]

The parkland transition zone between the boreal forest region and the prairie region appears to have been the southern limit of wood bison distribution. Hind[12] referred to reports from older hunters which indicated that the wood bison was only found north of the Saskatchewan River, and that it never ventured into the open plains. Roe[13] stated that although there are a number of historic references documenting existence of bison between the Athabasca and North Saskatchewan rivers, including their headwaters in the mountains, there is little indication of large numbers.

The Cordillera provided a natural boundary on the west. During his journey to the Pacific in 1793, Mackenzie[14] reported large numbers of bison along the upper Peace River. Harmon[15] and MacFarlane[16] noted that bison were abundant on the plains near the Rocky Mountains and were present as far north as the Liard River, near the mountains. MacFarlane[17] stated that in the early 1800s "many also roamed to the Liard River," but there is little information to indicate that substantial numbers existed on lower portions of the system.

Decline of Wood Bison

The advent of the fur trade late in the eighteenth century resulted in major changes in patterns of use of wildlife resources in the boreal forest region. The fur trade established a tradition of exploiting fur-bearers for their economic value in barter for European goods. Fire-arms introduced with the fur trade not only facilitated harvesting of large herbivores, but provided the means for provisioning brigades and forts, established as trading centres, with large amounts of meat. Pemmican, a mixture of dried, pounded meat and fat, became an important, lightweight, portable food for the traders and voyagers. Bison hunting was a supporting activity for the fur trade within the historic range of the wood bison and was one of the factors responsible for the near extirpation of the subspecies during the nineteenth century.

The region of the lower Peace and Athabasca rivers, with its rich delta, was an important centre of historic abundance of the wood bison. The Northwest Company established Fort Chipewyan in 1788 at the west end of Lake Athabasca, near the delta. This site became an important centre of trade and exploration for other companies that followed. When Franklin[18] passed through in 1820, he recorded that there were numerous bison tracks seen near the post on Christmas Day. Recordings of bison were made in this area by other travellers including Mackenzie,[19] Fidler,[20] Ross,[21] Turnor,[22] Richardson,[23] Butler,[24] Macoun,[25] and Ogilvie.[26] Richardson[27] stated, "a plain extends from near Athabasca Lake to the Clearwater River, tolerably well wooded and frequented by buffaloes."

During the years of intense competition between fur trading companies, until 1821 when the Northwest Company and Hudson's Bay Company amalgamated, at least nine posts were established around the Peace-Athabasca Delta.[28] It was not until 1820, when George Simpson became Chief Trader at the Hudson's Bay Company's Fort Wedderburn (near present day Fort Chipewyan), that journals with information pertaining to bison were maintained.[29] As a centre of trade and associated hunting activity for over thirty years, the Delta's bison herd showed signs of depletion by this time. According to Simpson's journal, the post consumed ninety pounds of bison meat per day and it was necessary to send pemmican to other Mackenzie District posts, the locations of which changed continuously because of the increasing difficulty in procuring local meat supplies. Simpson commented that although bison were generally plentiful in the area, they were "not now so close as formerly." During the summer of 1821, he encouraged the Natives around the fort and those near outlying posts to "devote themselves entirely to buffalo hunting."

Roderick MacFarlane[30] was a Hudson's Bay Company Factor in the Mackenzie and Athabasca Districts, including fifteen years (1870–1885) at Fort Chipewyan. He proclaimed:

> This variety of the American Bison was fairly numerous when I first went north to Mackenzie River, in 1853, but it has since gradually diminished in numbers in the Athabasca district and its utter extermination is now only a question of time, unless restrictive hunting rules are adopted without delay.

During MacFarlane's residence at Fort Chipewyan, the post was supplied with bison meat every winter, but most of it had to be obtained in remote areas north of the lower Peace and near Birch Mountain. In Raup's view,[31] this indicated that winter hunting for bison at that time was no longer reliable in the delta lowlands near Fort Chipewyan. However, meat hunting to supply the Hudson's Bay Company forts was a factor contributing to the decline of the wood bison, since the Company did not promote trade or export in bison hides.

After mass starvation in the winter of 1886–87 among "Indians who once lived bountifully on the buffalo," Hornaday[32] described a petition sent to the Minister of the Interior, signed by the Bishop of the diocese at Fort Chipewyan, and others, asking for assistance in averting more suffering. The last report of bison in the Clearwater River and Fort McMurray area was in 1888 by Tyrrell.[33] Inspector Jarvis[34] stated that the last bison remaining in the vicinity of Birch Mountain were killed in 1896. Harry Radford was sent to Fort Smith in 1909 by the American Bison Society to study wood bison. He reported: "The range has contracted within 15 years, and at present there are no bison whatever between the lower Athabasca and lower Peace Rivers; they withdrew finally from this area about 1898."[35] The history of the decline was similar in other parts of the historic range. As early as 1858, Hector[36] reported that bison in the upper Peace River area were being depleted. Butler,[37] who travelled the river in 1872, believed that they had almost disappeared by 1870 and Macoun[38] stated that the last ones were killed north of Peace River in 1870. According to Ogilvie,[39] by 1889 one of the few remaining places where bison ranged was at the headwaters of the Hay River. Pike[40] mentioned that bison were occasionally heard of at Fort Nelson in 1892. Wood bison may have lingered in the Fort Nelson lowlands until the turn of the century, as Rhoads[41] quoted H.I. Moberly of the Hudson's Bay Company that bison still existed in the upper Hay River, ranging to the upper Liard and upper Peace. Also, Jarvis[42] thought it was possible that a small band existed in the upper Liard. When, in 1908, R.W. McLeod[43] of the R.C.M.P. made a patrol from Fort Vermilion to Hay River near the present day settlement of Meander River, 100 kilometres northeast of Hay Lake, he could find no knowledge of bison in that district within the previous fifteen years (since 1893).

In the Slave River lowlands, approximately 150–200 kilometres north of the Peace-Athabasca Delta, Peter Fidler[44] reported large numbers of bison in 1791. According to Radford,[45] bison were extirpated east of the Slave River by 1880 and they were diminishing in number throughout the remainder of the area. Camsell[46] observed that by 1916 bison occurred only as far to the northeast as the Little Buffalo River, which was confirmed by Seibert[47] in 1922. Therefore, the Little Buffalo River served as the northeastern boundary for Wood Buffalo National Park (WBNP), when it was established in December 1922. The Park was created to protect the only remaining wood bison by including all of its known habitat.

In 1891, Ogilvie[48] estimated that only 300 wood bison remained in the wilderness area between Great Slave Lake and the Peace-Athabasca Delta, including the area north and west of the Athabasca River, across the Peace to the Liard River, and in the mountains northwest of Fort Liard. The population apparently reached an estimated low of around 250 during 1896–1900.[49] After reaching their lowest number near the turn of the century, small scattered bands of wood bison, mainly in what is now WBNP, formed the nuclei for recovery during a subsequent period of protection.

Early Conservation Period

Conservation efforts began in 1877 with the passing of the Buffalo Protection Act;[50] however, this measure was largely ineffective because of lack of enforcement. Legislation was strengthened in 1893 when the Dominion Government passed a law to save the surviving wood bison.[51] Protection was minimal until 1897 when the enforcement mandate was assigned to the North West Mounted Police. In

1907, the first police outpost was established at Fort Fitzgerald, Alberta, on the Slave River, and the first formal patrol of the region occurred. In 1911, six Buffalo Rangers were appointed to patrol the northern range of the wood bison.

With improved protection, wood bison numbers increased slowly to about 500 by 1914.[52] In an effort to safeguard the wood bison from extinction, Wood Buffalo Park was established in 1922 by an Order-In-Council under the Forest Reserves and Parks Act.[53] The number of wood bison on the entire range at that time was estimated at between 1500 and 2000.[54] The survival of the wood bison seemed secure.

The history of wood and plains bison became inextricably intertwined during the mid-1920s, at a time when the recovery of both subspecies seemed to be certain. In 1905, the largest privately owned herd of plains bison in North America, owned by Michel Pablo in Montana, was threatened by the loss of grazing rights after the Flathead Indian Reservation was opened to public settlement. Following negotiations between the Canadian government and the owner, 410 plains bison were purchased and were shipped to Elk Island National Park (EINP) in 1907.[55] After completion of the newly enclosed Buffalo National Park at Wainwright, Alberta, 325 plains bison from EINP, 218 plains bison from the original herd in Montana, and seventy-seven plains bison from the exhibition herd in Banff were brought to Wainwright during 1909 to establish a core herd of 620 plains bison.[56] Several more shipments of animals over the next five years from three different sources brought the total number of plains bison introduced at Wainwright to 748. A census of the Buffalo National Park herd conducted in 1913 indicated a total of 1188 plains bison, but by 1923 the herd had increased to 6780. The range was being depleted and overcrowding was a problem.

Buffalo National Park administrators announced a proposal for a phased slaughter to control the herd, and 2409 bison were killed between 1922 and 1924. The operation met with such severe public criticism that it was abandoned. A publicly more acceptable solution proposed to ship 2000 plains bison north each year to the recently created Wood Buffalo Park.[57] Maxwell Graham, with the Department of the Interior, made a lame attempt at justifying the project, claiming that a northern segment of the wood bison population would remain isolated from the introduced stock, separated by natural barriers of swamp and muskeg.

The proposed transfer of plains bison into occupied historic wood bison range was seriously challenged by the American Society of

Mammalogists[58] and by individual biologists.[59] They believed that interbreeding would result in the loss of both subspecies of bison and that the wood bison population would become infected with diseases imported with the introduced plains bison. Officials with the Department of the Interior were unmoved and reaffirmed their intention to proceed with the transfer, based on the mistaken belief that there was no contact between separate herds of wood bison occupying northern and southern ranges. The biological advice was simply ignored.

From 1925 to 1928, a total of 6673 plains bison were transported by rail from Wainwright to Waterways (now Fort McMurray), Alberta, the railway terminus, and then by barge down the Athabasca and Slave Rivers to Labutte Landing in Wood Buffalo Park near Hay Camp.[60] The bison were then released at several sites along the west bank of the Slave River, south and north of Hay Camp, into range that was occupied by wood bison.[61]

Bovine tuberculosis (*Mycobacterium bovis*) was identified in the Wainwright herd in 1919. The most probable source of infection was the bison herd transferred from Banff in 1909.[62] In 1923, 76% of the animals slaughtered at Wainwright had tuberculosis-like lesions. This discovery led to a decision, based on the mistaken belief that tuberculosis was a disease of old animals, to transfer only young bison to WBNP. The first occurrence of tuberculosis in bison in WBNP was reported in 1937–38.[63] Brucellosis (*Brucella abortus*) was identified in WBNP bison in 1956[64] and was thought to have been introduced with the plains bison.

The two subspecies of bison interbred as had been predicted. Subsequently, the number of bison in WBNP increased to an estimated 12 000 by 1934.[65] In 1933, Raup[66] reported that the wood buffalo, as a race, was rapidly disappearing but speculated that an intact northern herd still survived. However, by 1940, it was generally believed that the wood bison, as a distinct subspecies, had become extinct as a result of hybridization.

Wood Bison Recovery Period

Rediscovery and Salvage
During the 1950s, some zoologists thought that small groups of wood bison still existed in remote areas of WBNP.[67] In 1957, N. Novakowski observed bison in the Nyarling River and Buffalo Lake area of northwestern WBNP during an aerial survey.[68] He suspected

that they were wood bison. In 1959, five specimens were collected from the herd of about 200 animals. Three adults were photographed and the skulls and skins were sent to the National Museum of Natural Sciences in Ottawa. Pelage characteristics, size, and cranial measurements compared closely to specimens of the original wood bison.[69] The Nyarling River herd was, accordingly, classified as morphologically representative of wood bison. The taxonomic affiliation of other herds in and near WBNP was not studied.

In February 1963, seventy-seven wood bison were captured in northwestern WBNP in the Nyarling River area near Needle Lake with the intention of establishing a captive breeding herd of wood bison. At the capture site, sixty-one animals were tested for tuberculosis and brucellosis. One animal was positive for tuberculosis and 52% were infected with brucellosis. Based on negative test results, twenty-one apparently disease-free wood bison were selected of which nineteen were successfully transported by truck to a large holding corral west of Fort Smith.[70] Three calves were born to this herd in the spring of 1963. During July, these captive bison were tested again for tuberculosis and brucellosis; results of these tests were negative. The Fort Smith corral herd was then declared disease-free by the Health of Animals Branch, Federal Department of Agriculture, and the three calves were inoculated for brucellosis.[71]

After outbreaks of anthrax (*Bacillus anthracis*) occurred in bison in the Slave River lowlands in 1962 and at Grand Detour (located approximately 35 km north of the holding site) in 1963, a decision was made to transfer a herd of wood bison to a suitable area north of Fort Providence, NWT. In August 1963, eighteen of the originally captured wood bison were barged to Fort Providence and then were transported by truck to a release site located approximately twenty-five kilometres north of Fort Providence within the present-day MBS.[72] These bison were vaccinated for anthrax prior to shipment.

A second bison roundup in the Nyarling River area near Needle Lake in WBNP was held in February 1965. Of sixty-nine bison that were discovered, forty-seven were captured in the roundup corrals and seven died from injuries and other causes. Forty of the forty-seven captured animals were subsequently transferred to the holding corrals at Fort Smith.[73] Continued outbreaks of anthrax in the Slave River lowlands precipitated a decision to establish a herd of wood bison out of the region to safeguard the gene pool. After testing negative for brucellosis and tuberculosis, twenty-four animals were transported to EINP in the fall of 1965. One animal died en

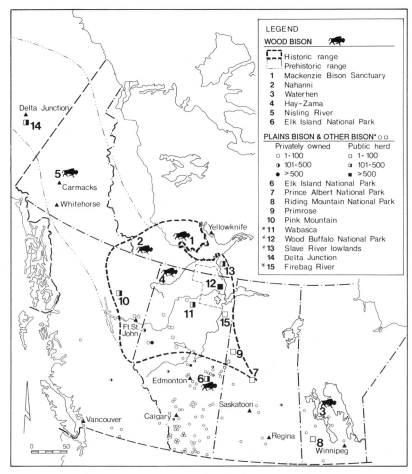

Fig. 2. Distribution of captive and free-roaming herds of bison in western Canada in 1985 (reproduced with the permission of the Wood Bison Recovery Team).

route and two more died in the Park later that year. A total of twenty-one wood bison survived to establish a breeding herd that has provided stock for relocations to the NWT, Yukon, northern Alberta, Manitoba, and to captive breeding herds in zoos and wild animal parks. Three additional calves were shipped from Fort Smith to EINP, one in 1967 and two more in 1968.

In summary, fifty-nine wood bison (nineteen in 1963 and forty in 1965) were removed from the Nyarling River-Needle Lake area of WBNP and were transported to holding corrals near Fort Smith.

From the first group, eighteen animals were transferred to the MBS near Fort Providence in 1963. Sixteen of these wood bison survived to establish the MBS herd. From the second group, twenty-four animals were transferred to EINP, of which twenty-one survived. Three additional calves were shipped from Fort Smith for a total of twenty-four wood bison from the Nyarling River population contributing to the founding herd at EINP. The present day wood bison gene pool has been derived from forty animals salvaged from northwestern WBNP.

Current Status
The Committee on the Status of Endangered Wildlife in Canada (COSEWIC), a standing committee of the Federal-Provincial Wildlife Conference, is responsible for producing the official Canadian Endangered Species list. After reviewing scientific status reports on species, COSEWIC may then assign a species to one of five recognized categories: Extinct, Extirpated, Endangered, Threatened, and Vulnerable. Wood bison were classified by COSEWIC as an endangered subspecies of Canadian wildlife in 1978. This status was downlisted to threatened in June 1988 based on data in a revised status report.

There are four free-ranging herds of wood bison in Canada. Three of these herds are the MBS population and the Nahanni-Liard herd in the southwestern NWT and the Nisling River herd in the southwestern Yukon (Fig. 2, locations 1, 2, 5). The fourth herd was established in the northern Interlake region of Manitoba in April 1991. The eighteen animals moved to the MBS in 1963 have given rise to the world's largest and most successful herd of wood bison, which currently represents about 70% of the total population. During the period 1963 to 1987, the Mackenzie population increased at an average exponential rate of r = 0.215; 1718 were counted in April 1987.[74] As the population increased in size, the area occupied by the herd also increased. The herd now ranges in an area exceeding 8000 square kilometres, including expansion ranges in the Mink Lake area to the northwest of the Sanctuary. In recent years, the growth rate of the herd has declined. Natural limiting factors such as predation have started to exert an effect on the population. The current rate of growth is approximately 10%. In April 1989, the population was estimated to number 2040, representing 86% of all wood bison located within historic and prehistoric range, or 92% of all free-ranging wood bison (Table 1). Based on disease testing results to

Table 1 Status of wood bison in April 1991

	FREE-RANGING	CAPTIVE
Herds in Historic and Prehistoric Range		
Mackenzie, NT	2040	0
Nahanni, NT	60	0
Nisling River, YK	110	0
Hay-Zama, AB	0	31
Hanging Ice Ranch, NT	0	118
Subtotal	**2210**	**149**
Herds Outside the Historic Range		
Elk Island National Park, AB	0	250
Waterhen Wood Bison Ranches Ltd., MB	13	148
Zoos and wild animal parks:		
Canada:		
Valley Zoo, AB	0	4
Alberta Wildlife Park, AB	0	33
Moose Jaw Wild Animal Park, SK	0	5
Metro Zoo, Toronto, ON	0	37
Banff National Park, AB	0	9
Yukon Game Farm, YK	0	11
United States:		
San Diego Zoo, CA	0	6
Lubee Foundation, FL	0	6
Germany:		
Tierpark Berlin	0	6
Zoologisher Garten, Leipzich	0	6
Tierpark Hellabrunn, Munich	0	4
Subtotal	**13**	**525**
Total	**2223**	**674**
GRAND TOTAL	**2897**	

date and the observed rate of growth, this herd is considered to be free of bovine tuberculosis and brucellosis and is comprised of animals in excellent physical condition.

In 1980, twenty-eight wood bison were transported from EINP to a site near Nahanni Butte, located at the edge of the Mackenzie Mountains in southwestern NWT. Upon release to the wild, the herd fragmented and some animals travelled distances exceeding 250 kilometres into British Columbia. Accidental deaths contributed further losses causing the nucleus herd to dwindle to fourteen the following year. Since 1981, the small population has increased steadily at a rate of about 10% annually, to approximately forty bison in 1989. In March of that year, the herd was augmented with another release of twelve wood bison transported north from the Moose Jaw Wild Animal Park in southern Saskatchewan. Four calves were seen accompanying the newly released group in July 1989, a sign that the transfer was successful. The current wild population is estimated to number about sixty animals; however, it is still too soon to predict if this herd will exceed 200 in number and contribute to the minimum objective of the recovery program.

The third free-ranging herd of wood bison is located within the defined prehistoric range.[75] In March 1986, thirty-four wood bison were transported from EINP and released into a five square kilometre fenced area in the flood plain of the Nisling River, located eighty kilometres west of Carmacks, Yukon Territory. The herd prospered under intensive management and twenty-one wood bison were first released from the enclosure in March 1988. More captive animals were released in 1989, bringing the total free-ranging herd to forty-two head. In March 1989, ten calves from Moose Jaw Wild Animal Park were transported to the fenced area. Nineteen wood bison remained in the enclosure as insurance against unforeseen losses within the wild herd. Additional releases to the wild in 1990 and 1991 have now reduced the captive herd to zero. At present, there are approximately 110 wood bison in the wild in the southwestern Yukon. An approved management plan outlines a course of action to import supplementary stock from EINP in March 1992 and for continued annual releases designed to achieve a wild herd of 200 by 1994.

A wood bison reestablishment project was initiated in northwestern Alberta in 1981 by the Canadian Wildlife Service (CWS) and the Alberta Fish and Wildlife Division in cooperation with the Dene Tha Indian Band. A site was selected in the vicinity of Hay-Zama Lakes and a three square kilometre holding corral was constructed. The site is within the historic range of the subspecies. The first shipment of twenty-nine wood bison arrived in February 1984. Flooding conditions and severe winter weather resulted in the need for supplementary feeding within the compound. Problems of poor reproduction and calf survival have limited growth of this herd. In April 1989, there were twenty-nine wood bison in the enclosure. Although the initial plan called for release to the wild in 1988, the reintroduction project has been postponed indefinitely because of the risk of infection with bovine tuberculosis and brucellosis from free-ranging bison found in the region. During the winters of 1989 and 1990 mature bulls were removed from the enclosure, leaving twenty-one females and immature males. Ten calves were born on site in summer 1990. The captive herd of thirty-one animals continues to be maintained in the holding pen, but reintroduction to the wild is unlikely until an acceptable solution to the northern diseased bison problem is implemented.

In 1990 the Government of the NWT entered into an agreement with the Fort Smith Hunters and Trappers Association to establish a wood bison ranch in the Slave River lowlands north of Fort Smith. In March of 1990 and 1991, surplus wood bison from EINP were transferred to the Hanging Ice Bison Ranch. The present herd numbers about 120 animals. The ranch is being developed and managed for commercial production and to provide stock at cost for conservation projects. Once the ranch reaches production capacity it will market bison meat in the NWT, adding to agricultural self-sufficiency in the region.

Several herds of wood bison are held in captivity outside the historic and prehistoric range. The largest is the EINP herd. It has played a crucial role in the recovery of wood bison in Canada by safeguarding the gene pool as well as providing stock for the reintroduction of two wild populations, for a fenced herd intended for release to the wild, for two commercial ranches, for six captive breeding herds, and for two zoos abroad. The wood bison herd at EINP was declared free of bovine brucellosis and tuberculosis in 1971 after a four-year intensive disease eradication program, which included slaughter of all parent stock, rigorous testing, and slaughter of all reactors. In April 1991, the population was approximately 250 head. It is a semiwild fenced population that, basically, interacts with a full complement of natural environmental factors, excepting natural predation. The herd receives supplemental feed only during annual round-up activities in winter.

In February 1984, thirty-four wood bison that were surplus to the captive breeding program were transferred into a twenty-three square kilometre enclosure near Waterhen in the northern Interlake region of Manitoba. By April 1989, the enclosure had been increased to thirty-nine square kilometres and the herd had increased to approximately 200 animals as a result of subsequent shipments and births within the enclosure. All wood bison transferred to Manitoba originated from captive breeding herds in Canada and EINP. The success of the Waterhen project can be attributed to the keen interest and sustained effort of the Waterhen Indian Band and the support of government and nongovernment agencies. In June 1989, wood bison were sold for the first time to private bison breeders and two bulls were slaughtered for the commercial meat market. As a result of subsequent live sales, culling of bulls for local consumption, and meat sales, the Waterhen captive herd presently numbers about 150 wood bison. The captive herd is being managed by the Waterhen First Nation for commercial production. An introduction of thirteen wood bison to the wild in the Chitek Lake area north of the enclosure occurred in April 1991.

With the rapid growth of the EINP herd during the early 1970s, the need to broaden the geographic distribution of captive breeding herds was recognized as a measure to reduce the risk of inadvertent loss of the gene pool. In 1976, the Calgary Zoo received four calves, the first transfer of wood bison from EINP to establish a captive breeding herd under the cooperative lease program. Between 1976 and 1982, successful transfers of wood bison were made to seven zoos and wild animal parks, including five in Canada and two abroad. The captive breeding herd lease program was terminated by the CWS in 1990 with management responsibility of current stocks being relinquished to those zoos and parks housing the animals. In April 1991, eight facilities within North America held approximately 110 wood bison in captivity (Table 1).

Recovery Potential

Human activities and development that are incompatible with the existence of large free-roaming wood bison herds continue to increase within the historic range of the wood bison. This results in a continuing loss of available habitat for this threatened subspecies and further diminishes the potential for its recovery. Approximately 3% of the historic range is presently occupied by healthy wood bison herds while an additional 21% is potentially available under current constraints, though little favourable bison habitat remains within this zone (Fig. 3). Approximately 34% of the historic range is unavailable owing to human activities and development, including a

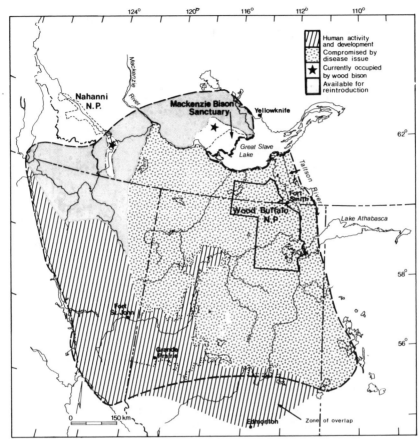

Fig. 3. The availability of range for wood bison recovery within the historic range of the subspecies.

portion of this area that is occupied by an introduced herd of plains bison in northeastern British Columbia.

Plains Bison Ranching and Introductions
In recent years, a renewed interest in game ranching in western Canada has resulted from growing consumer interest in leaner meats, recognition of the high productivity of wild herbivores, a need for landscape conservation, and the declining profitability of conventional agriculture. Although the concept has been practised for nearly two decades, the industry is still in its infancy and enabling legislation is presently being developed. In 1987 there were 251 com-

mercial game ranches and farms in Alberta, Saskatchewan, and Manitoba, holding 5100 plains bison and 2900 wapiti.[76] The number of farms and ranches is increasing rapidly as the industry continues to exhibit expansion growth. There are at least forty plains bison ranches or farms and one free-ranging herd of plains bison within the historic range of the wood bison.[77]

Presently, the plains bison is the predominant species being commercially produced. It is classified as a domestic species in the prairie provinces, but is designated as wildlife in British Columbia. The wood bison is designated as wildlife in all western provinces and territories, except in Manitoba where it shares the same legal status as plains bison. The establishment and operation of plains bison ranches within the historic range of wood bison constitutes a potential problem for wood bison recovery because existing legislation and policies are inadequate to remove the risk of escape of plains bison stock.

The potential impact of this problem is exemplified by an actual situation in northeastern British Columbia. In 1971, forty-eight plains bison were purchased from EINP at a tender sale and were transferred to a private ranch at Pink Mountain, near Fort Nelson. The British Columbia government issued a permit to transport and import bison on the condition that the animals and their offspring be maintained on the rancher's property "within the confines of an adequate fence of such materials and dimensions to preclude the escape of the animals." Nevertheless, the herd escaped within a short time after arrival and established a free-ranging herd in the area. By 1979 the wild herd had grown to approximately 150 head, and by 1989 had increased to at least 600 animals,[78] and occupied an area exceeding 500 square kilometres.

The ownership of this herd of plains bison has been the subject of litigation, with a private rancher claiming ownership and indicating the desire to capture and remove the entire herd. A settlement was announced in December 1989 in a press release issued by the Ministry of Environment, British Columbia, which allowed the rancher to remove 200 head from the free-roaming herd. The remainder of the herd is to continue to be managed as a wild herd under the authority of the government of British Columbia.

Under existing constraints, the potential to replace the Pink Mountain plains bison herd with wood bison offers an excellent opportunity for enhancing the status and distribution of wood bison within its historic range. Given the availability of wood bison to stock the area, the willingness of the rancher to remove the plains bison, and a desire on the part of government, the replacement of the plains bison herd could be achieved. If this is not done, the risk of plains bison dispersing into adjacent unoccupied range in the Hay River basin and possibly the Liard River basin is sufficiently high to jeopardize reestablishment of wood bison in those areas of historic range.

The Pink Mountain controversy has significant implications for endangered species and spaces management and recovery in Canada. The conservation principle involved was clearly reviewed in 1987 by the International Union for the Conservation of Nature (IUCN) in a publication entitled "The IUCN Position Statement on Translocation of Living Organisms." It described precautions needed to avoid the negative consequences of poorly planned translocations. Regarding alien species, the document stated, "the conservation of the native flora and fauna should always take precedence." The IUCN further implored that in general, introductions that have a negative effect on native flora or fauna should be removed. Furthermore, the IUCN position is consistent with conservation principles outlined in the World Conservation Strategy[79] and the recently published Wildlife Policy for Canada.[80]

Diseased Bison Herds
The greatest single factor affecting the availability of historic range and the potential for further recovery of the wood bison is the existence of diseased herds of bison in and around WBNP. Bison herds located in and around WBNP and in the Slave River lowlands are infected with bovine brucellosis and bovine tuberculosis. These diseases are widely distributed throughout the region, from outside the southwestern border of the park near Fort Vermilion, to the Buffalo Lake area in the northwest section of the Park, to the bison herds found on the east side of the Slave River in the NWT.[81] The prevalence of tuberculosis was reported in 1988 by the Bison Disease Task Force to be 36% based on 2977 bison subjected to postmortem examination in thirteen different sample periods taken in WBNP between 1950 and 1974.[82] The prevalence of brucellosis was also determined to be 36% based on blood tests of 1999 bison taken in WBNP during ten different sample periods between 1956 and 1974. A more recent study[83] reported a combined prevalence rate of 43% for both diseases on postmortem analysis of fifty-six bison killed by Native hunters near WBNP during 1982–84. Based on fifty-eight blood samples

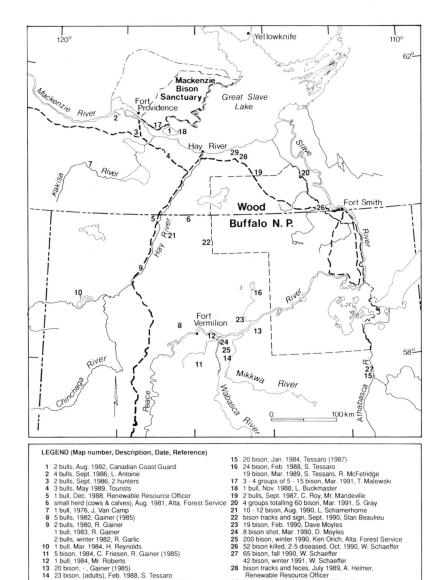

LEGEND (Map number, Description, Date, Reference)

1 2 bulls, Aug. 1982, Canadian Coast Guard
2 4 bulls, Sept. 1986, L. Antoine
3 2 bulls, Sept. 1986, 2 hunters
4 3 bulls, May 1989, Tourists
5 1 bull, Dec. 1988, Renewable Resource Officer
6 small herd (cows & calves), Aug. 1981, Alta. Forest Service
7 1 bull, 1976, J. Van Camp
8 5 bulls, 1982, Gainer (1985)
9 2 bulls, 1980, R. Gainer
   1 bull, 1983, R. Gainer
   2 bulls, winter 1984, R. Garlic
10 1 bull, Mar. 1984, H. Reynolds
11 5 bison, 1984, C. Friesen, R. Gainer (1985)
12 1 bull, 1984, Mr. Roberts
13 20 bison, - , Gainer (1985)
14 23 bison, (adults), Feb. 1988, S. Tessaro
    17 bison, Mar. 1989, S. Tessaro, R. McFetridge

15 20 bison, Jan. 1984, Tessaro (1987)
16 24 bison, Feb. 1988, S. Tessaro
    19 bison, Mar. 1989, S. Tessaro, R. McFetridge
17 3 - 4 groups of 5 - 15 bison, Mar. 1991, T. Malewski
18 1 bull, Nov. 1988, L. Buckmaster
19 2 bulls, Sept. 1987, C. Roy, Mr. Mandeville
20 4 groups totalling 60 bison, Mar. 1991, S. Gray
21 10 - 12 bison, Aug. 1990, L. Schamerhorne
22 bison tracks and sign, Sept. 1990, Stan Beaulieu
23 19 bison, Feb. 1990, Dave Moyles
24 8 bison shot, Mar. 1990, D. Moyles
25 200 bison, winter 1990, Ken Orich, Alta. Forest Service
26 52 bison killed, 2-5 diseased, Oct. 1990, W. Schaeffer
27 65 bison, fall 1990, W. Schaeffer
    42 bison, winter 1991, W. Schaeffer
28 bison tracks and feces, July 1989, A. Helmer,
    Renewable Resource Officer
29 bison tracks and feces, July 1990, A. Helmer

Fig. 4. Distribution of bison sightings reported since
1976 in the region west of Wood Buffalo National Park
and south of the Mackenzie River.

taken from bison in four different geographic locations within the Park during the summer of 1990, forty-seven were positive reactors to brucella tests indicating a prevalence rate of 81% for brucellosis.

The existence of the reservoir of these two bovine diseases threatens the recovery of wood bison in a number of ways. First, wildlife and agricultural management agencies discourage the establishment of free-ranging bison herds in areas adjacent to WBNP because such herds would inevitably become infected, thereby increasing the size of the enzootic, or infected zone. Consequently, 42% of the historic range of the wood bison (Fig. 3), lying largely in northern Alberta and southern NWT, including WBNP, is not available for establishing healthy wild herds of bison. Second, these diseases could be transmitted to healthy herds of wood bison, in particular, to the Mackenzie and Nahanni herds.

These bovine diseases affect population dynamics by causing morbidity, increasing mortality, reducing fecundity, and increasing the vulnerability of infected individuals to predation.[84] The most important transmission of these two diseases involves direct or indirect contact between infected and noninfected bison, or with contaminated feed and water. The present wide distribution of these diseases among bison in the WBNP region illustrates that the diseases have dispersed widely from the original focus of introduction since 1925.

Conditions currently exist that favour transmission of these bovine diseases between infected and healthy herds. Bison of uncertain origin and disease status are scattered at low density throughout northern Alberta[85] and southwestern NWT (Fig. 4). The largest herds are located near WBNP, east of Fort Vermilion, at Wentzel Lake (site 16, Fig. 4), in the area between the Wabasca and Mikkwa rivers (sites 14, 24, 25, Fig. 4) and along the Firebag River south of the Park (sites 15, 27, Fig. 4). Disease testing has been undertaken[86] at only three locations (sites 13, 14, 16, Fig. 4). One of two bison collected near site 13 in February 1985 tested culture-positive for brucella. One of four bison collected near site 14 in March 1989, at postmortem, had lesions in bronchiolar lymph nodes that were consistent with tuberculosis; in addition acid-fast organisms (a characteristic of *Mycobacterium bovis*) were identified. In February 1988, six bison were collected at Wentzel Lake, site 16. One showed a suspicious serologic reaction for brucellosis. While sample sizes were too small to determine actual prevalence of disease, the existence of these two bovine diseases in bison outside of WBNP has been clearly demonstrated.

The issue of diseased bison has been formally reviewed by an Environmental Assessment Panel for the federal departments of Environment and Agriculture. The Panel conducted a public review and completed its task with the release of a final report in August 1990.[87] The Panel concluded that removal of the existing bison population and replacement with disease-free wood bison is the only method of eliminating the risk of transmission of bovine brucellosis and tuberculosis from bison in and around the Park to domestic cattle, wood bison, and humans. The Panel also concluded that formation of a Northern Bison Stakeholder's Group with representatives of Aboriginal People, government agencies, and nongovernment groups was essential to the design and implementation of their proposal. On 20 June 1991, the Government of Canada announced the formation of a Northern Buffalo Management Board (NBMB) to deal with the diseased bison issue. The NBMB has been asked to develop a management plan during the next year for the eradication of bovine tuberculosis and brucellosis in the buffalo herd and at the same time, it must ensure the continuing presence of healthy, free-roaming bison herds in northern Canada. While the plan is being developed, interim measures to prevent the spread of diseases will continue. This action will support the existing national program conducted in northern Canada by the federal, provincial, and territorial governments to reestablish the wood bison.

Factors Limiting Existing Herds

The EINP herd has attained the desired maximum size and further growth will be managed by removing bison for other recovery projects.[88]

The growth rate of the Mackenzie herd has slowed in recent years, as a result of natural factors. The scope for further growth of this herd is unknown, but with occupation of the last large area of suitable habitat near Mills Lake expected in the near future,[89] it is anticipated that additional population growth will be limited. While the herd is naturally regulated at the present time (a hunting quota is restricted to forty males), maintenance of moderate to high productivity will depend on active management. Further geographic expansion of breeding herds is expected to be limited by habitat availability.

It is still too soon to predict if the Nahanni and Yukon herds will contribute substantially to the recovery of wood bison although both herds were originally intended to contribute to recovery objectives. These populations are using habitats that were not evaluated during initial assessments and forecasts of range capability,[90] and the potential for each herd to increase to 200 or more bison is unknown.

Clearly, additional free-roaming herds are required to assure the recovery of the wood bison within its historic range and to secure the subspecies against catastrophic events such as drownings, wildfire, and disease.

Crossroads

During the past twenty-eight years, the wood bison has only recovered in the wild to the numerical status that it had achieved in 1925, when the introduction of diseased plains bison into its range nearly caused its extinction. Under present circumstances, the scope for further recovery of the wood bison within its historic range without disease eradication is severely limited, because of the presence of diseased bison herds. On the other hand, disease eradication would increase the potential for reestablishing healthy wood bison herds in at least an additional 42% of their historic range thereby significantly increasing the scope for further recovery of the wood bison.

Wood bison are a keystone species in those sections of the boreal forest where suitable habitat exists. They occupy a niche—meadows dominated by coarse grasses and sedges—that no other native herbivore can exploit. They are a key element in the dynamic interplay among other indigenous large mammals, serving as major prey for wolves and indirectly influencing the abundance of other large herbivores. Outside WBNP and the Slave River lowlands wood bison have been largely absent since the end of the last century. Presently, the potential exists to bring about changes in public policy that can result in the restoration of wood bison to near their former status in a healthy, productive, and intact ecosystem within a large portion of the boreal forest region, but only with elimination of these two bovine diseases. This can only be achieved with the support of the public and scientific communities. After nearly three decades of effort and modest success, wood bison recovery is now clearly at a crossroads.

C. Gates is the Bison Ecologist with the Department of Renewable Resources, Government of the Northwest Territories.
T. Chowns is a District Superintendent with the Department of Renewable Resources, Government of the Northwest Territories.
H. Reynolds is a Wildlife Biologist with the Canadian Wildlife Service, Western and Northern Region.

Notes

1. F.G. Roe, *The North American Buffalo: A Critical Study of the Species in Its Wild State*, second ed. (Toronto: The University of Toronto Press, 1970); and T. McHugh, *The Time of the Buffalo* (New York: Alfred A. Knopf, 1972).
2. Gordon C. Hewitt, *The Conservation of the Wild Life of Canada* (New York: C. Scribners Sons, 1921).
3. Roe, *The North American Buffalo*.
4. John Richardson, *Fauna Boreali-Americana*. Part I. 1829.
5. John Richardson, *Arctic searching expedition: A journal of a boat-voyage Rupert's Land and the arctic seas* (London: 2 vols., 1851), pp. 413–26.
6. H.M. Raup, "Phytogeographic Studies in the Athabaska-Great Slave Lake Region I. Catalogue of the Vascular Plants," *Journal. Arnold Arboretum*. 17 (1936), pp. 180–315; H.M. Raup, "Range conditions in the Wood Buffalo Park of western Canada with notes on the history of the Wood Bison" *Special Publication American Committee for International Wild Life Protection* Vol. I No. 2 (1933); and H.M. Raup, "Phytogeographic Studies in the Peace and Upper Liard River Regions, Canada. Catalogue of the Vascular Plants," *Journal. Arnold Arboretum*. 6 (1934), pp. 1–252.
7. J.H. Day, *Soils of the upper Mackenzie River Area, NWT* (Ottawa: Research Branch, Canada Department of Agriculture, 1968).
8. Richardson, *Fauna Boreali-Americana*.
9. Alexander Mackenzie, *Voyages from Montreal, on the River St. Laurence, through the continent of North American to the Frozen and Pacific Oceans: in the years 1789 and 1793* (London: 1801); Sir John Franklin, *Narrative of a journey to the shores of the Polar Sea in the years, 1819, 1820, 1821, and 1822* (London: 1823); Frank Russell, *Explorations in the far North* (University of Iowa: 1898); Harry V. Radford, "Preliminary report on the condition of the wild Wood Bison of Northwestern Canada," unpublished manuscript dated 20 June, 1911, at Fort Smith, NWT, and directed to Prof. Franklin W. Hooper, Pres. American Bison Society, 17 pp; and Samuel Hearne, *A journey from Prince of Wale's Fort in Hudson's Bay to the Northern Ocean, 1769, 1770, 1771, and 1772*, edited with an introduction by Richard Glover (Toronto: MacMillan, 1985).
10. Alexander Mackenzie, *Voyages from Montreal*; Sir John Franklin, *Narrative of a journey to the shores of the Polar Sea*; Richard King, *Narrative of a journal to the shores of the Arctic Ocean* (London: 1836); Thomas Simpson, *Narrative of the discoveries on the north coast of America effected by the officers of the Hudson's Bay Company during the years 1836–39* (London: 1843); and J.B. Tyrrell, ed., *Journals of Samuel Hearne and Philip Turnor* (Toronto: Champlain Society, Publication 21, 1934).
11. E. Rich, ed., *Simpson's Athabaska Journal, 1820–21* (Toronto: Champlain Society, Hudson's Bay Company Series, No. 1, 1938); Thomas Simpson, *Narrative of the discoveries...during the years 1836–39* (London: 1843); and John McLean, cited by F.G. Roe, *The North American Buffalo*.
12. H.Y. Hind, *Narrative of the Canadian Red River Exploring Expedition of 1857 and of the Assiniboine and Saskatchewan exploring Expedition of 1858* (London: 1860).
13. Roe, *The North American Buffalo*.
14. Mackenzie, *Voyages from Montreal*.

15. D.W. Harmon, *A Journal of Voyages and Travels in the Interior of North America* (Andover: 1820).
16. R. MacFarlane, "Notes on mammals collected and observed in the Northern Mackenzie River District, Northwest Territories of Canada," *Proceedings U.S. National Museum*, 28 (1908), pp. 673–764.
17. Ibid.
18. Franklin, *Narrative of a Journey*.
19. Mackenzie, *Voyages from Montreal*.
20. Tyrrell, *Journals of Hearne and Turnor*.
21. Ibid.
22. Ibid.
23. Richardson, *Fauna Boreali-Americana*.
24. Capt. W.F. Butler, *The Wild North Land* (London: 1874).
25. John Macoun, *Manitoba and the Great Northwest* (London: 1883).
26. W. Ogilvie, "Report on the Peace River and tributaries in 1891," *Annual Report Department Interior of Canada for 1892* (1893).
27. Richardson, *Arctic Searching Expedition*.
28. *National Atlas of Canada* (New York: Macmillan Publishing Company, 1974).
29. Rich, ed., *Simpson's Athabaska Journal*.
30. MacFarlane, "Notes on mammals."
31. Raup, "Range conditions."
32. W.T. Hornaday, *The Extermination of the American Bison*. Report of the U.S. National Museum for 1887 (1889), pp. 367–548.
33. J.B. Tyrrell, "Catalogue of the mammalia of Canada exclusive of the Cetacea," *Proceedings Canadian Institute* No. 24 (1888), pp. 70–71.
34. Insp. A.M. Jarvis, "Annual reports of the Royal Northwest Mounted Police, 1897–1907" (Ottawa: 1907).
35. Radford, ". . . the condition of the wild wood bison . . ."
36. Hector, Dr. (1863) *Upper North Saskatchewan River, September 1858, Journals, reports, etc., of the Palliser expedition, 1857–1860*, p. 111.
37. Butler, *The Wild Northland*.
38. Macoun, *Manitoba and the Great Northwest*.
39. W. Ogilvie, *Exploratory Survey of Park of the Lewes, Tat-on-Duc, Porcupine, Bell, Trout, Peel, and Mackenzie Rivers* (*Annual Report Department Interior Canada for 1889*) (1890).
40. Warburton Pike, *The Barren Ground of Northern Canada* (London: 1892).
41. S.M. Rhoads, "Notes on living and extinct species of North American Bovidae," *Proceedings Academy Natural Science of Philadelphia* (1897), pp. 483–502.
42. Jarvis, "Annual reports of the N.W. Mounted Police."
43. Serg. R.W. McLeod, *Annual Report Northwest Mounted Police, 1908*.
44. Tyrrell, *Journals of Hearne and Turnor*.
45. Radford, ". . . the condition of the wild wood bison . . ."
46. Charles Camsell, *Salt and Gypsum Deposits of the Region Between Peace and Slave Rivers, Northern Alberta*, Summary Report Canadian Geographic Society (1916), pp. 135–36.
47. F.V. Seibert, "Some notes on Canada's so called wood buffalo," *Canadian Field-Naturalist* 39 (1925), pp. 204–6.
48. Ogilvie, "Report on the Peace River and tributaries in 1891."
49. J.D. Soper, "History range, and home life of the northern bison," *Ecological Monographs* 11 (4) (1941), pp. 349–412.
50. Hewitt, *The Conservation of the Wild Life of Canada*.
51. Soper, "History and home life."
52. A.W.F. Banfield and N.S. Novakowski, "The survival of the wood bison (*Bison bi-*

son athabascae Rhoads) in the Northwest Territories," *National Museum Canada, Natural History Paper* 8 (1960).

53. Soper, "History and home life"; and W.F. Lothian, *A history of Canada's national parks.* Vol. 1 (Parks Canada, Indian and Northern Affairs, Ottawa, 1976), Cat. No. QS-7034–010–EE-A1.

54. Seibert, "Some notes on Canada's so-called wood buffalo"; and Soper, "History and home life."

55. McHugh, *The Time of the Buffalo.*

56. W.F. Lothian, *A history of Canada's national parks,* Vol. 4, (Ottawa: Parks Canada, Supply and Serv. Canada, 1981), Cat. No. R62–110/4–1981E.

57. M. Graham, "Finding a range for Canada's buffalo," *Canadian Field-Naturalist 38* (1924), p. 189.

58. A.B. Howell, "Letter to the editor of the Canadian Field-Naturalist from the Corresponding Secretary of the American Society of Mammalogists," 13 April 1925, *Canadian Field-Naturalist* 39 (1925), p. 118.

59. F. Harper, "Letter to the editor of the Canadian Field-Naturalist." *Canadian Field-Naturalist* 39 (1925), p. 45; and W.E. Saunders, "Letter to the editor of the Canadian Field-Naturalist," *Canadian Field-Naturalist* 39 (1925), p. 118.

60. Lothian, *A history of national parks,* Vol. 4.

61. Soper, "History and home life."

62. S. Hadwen, "Tuberculosis in the buffalo," *Journal American Veterinary Medicine Assoc.* 100 (1942), pp. 19–22.

63. R.B. Mitchell, "A review of bison management, Wood Buffalo National Park 1922–1976," in J.G. Stelfox, ed., *Wood Buffalo National Park Bison Research: 1972–76.* 1976 Annual Report prep. for Parks Canada by Canadian Wildlife Service, Edmonton, Section B: pp. 1–43.

64. L.P.E. Choquette, E. Broughton, J.G. Cousineau and N.S. Novakowski, "Parasites and diseases of bison in Canada IV. Serologic survey for brucellosis in bison in northern Canada," *Journal of Wildlife Diseases* 14 (1978), pp. 329–32.

65. Soper, "History and home life."

66. Raup, "Range conditions in the Wood Buffalo Park. . . ."

67. W.A. Fuller, "The biology and management of the bison of Wood Buffalo National Park," *Canadian Wildlife Service Wildlife Management Bulletin Series* 1, no. 16 (1962), pp. 52; and N.S. Novakowski and W.E. Stevens, "Survival of the wood bison (*Bison bison athabascae* Rhoads) in Canada," (Paper delivered at the 45th meeting of the American Society of Mammalogists, Winnipeg, 21 June 1965).

68. Ibid.

69. Banfield and Novakowski, "Survival of the wood bison."

70. N.S. Novakowski, "Report on the transfer of wood bison" (Canadian Wildlife Service, Edmonton, Unpublished Report, CWS-37–63, 1963). 5 pp.

71. ——, "Wood bison transfer-completion report" (Canadian Wildlife Service, Edmonton, Unpublished Report, CWS-35–63, 1963). 4 pp.

72. Ibid.

73. Novakowski and Stevens, "Survival of the wood bison."

74. C.C. Gates and N.C. Larter, "Growth and dispersal of an erupting large herbivore population in northern Canada: the Mackenzie wood bison (*Bison bison athabascae*)," *Arctic* 43 (1990), pp. 231–38.

75. C.G. van Zyll de Jong, "A systematic study of recent bison, with particular consideration of the wood bison (*Bison bison athabascae* Rhoads 1898)," *National Museum of Natural Sciences* Publication in *Natural Sciences* 6 (1986).

76. L.A. Renecker, C.B. Blyth and C.C. Gates, "Game production in western Canada," in *Wildlife Production Systems: Economic Utilization of Wild Ungulates,* Robert

J. Hudson, K.R. Drew and L.M. Baskin, eds. (Cambridge University Press, 1989), pp. 248–67.

77. D. Patten, vice-president, Canadian Buffalo Association, personal communication, 1990.

78. Ibid.

79. D.F. Pollard and M.R. McKechnie, *World Conservation Strategy—Canada. A Report on Achievements in Conservation*, Conservation and Protection, Environment Canada. Ottawa 1986. Minister of Supply and Services, 1986. Cat. No. EN 40–337/1986E. 61 pp.

80. Environment Canada, *A Wildlife Policy for Canada*, Environment Canada, Canadian Wildlife Service, for Wildlife Ministers' Council of Canada, 1990. Cat. No. CW66–59/1990E.

81. E. Broughton, "Diseases affecting bison," in *Bison ecology in relation to agricultural development in the Slave River lowlands, NWT*, H.W. Reynolds and A.W. Hawley, eds, Occ. Pap. No. 63. Canadian Wildlife Service, Minister of Supply and Services, Canada 1987. Cat. No. CW69–1/63E, 1987, pp. 34–38; and S. Tessaro, "A descriptive and epizootiologic study of brucellosis and tuberculosis in bison in northern Canada" (Ph.D. Thesis, University of Saskatchewan, 1988).

82. Bison Disease Task Force, *Evaluation of brucellosis and tuberculosis in bison in northern Canada* (Ottawa: Agriculture Canada, 1988).

83. Tessaro, "Brucellosis and tuberculosis in bison."

84. Broughton, "Diseases affecting bison"; and Tessaro, "Brucellosis and tuberculosis in bison."

85. B. Gainer, "Free-roaming bison in northern Alberta," *Alberta Naturalist* 15 (1985), pp. 86–87.

86. S. Tessaro, Agriculture Canada, Saskatoon, personal communication.

87. Northern Diseased Bison Environmental Assessment Panel, "Northern Diseased Bison," Report of the Environmental Assessment Panel. Federal Environmental Assessment and Review Office. August 1990. Minister of Supply and Services Canada 1990. Cat. no. EN 106–16/1990. 42 pp.

88. F. Bamber, Superintendent, Elk Island National Park, personal communication.

89. Gates and Larter, "Growth and dispersal."

90. H.W. Reynolds, J.R. McGillis and R.D. Glaholt, "Range assessment of the Liard-South Nahanni Rivers region, NWT as habitat for wood bison" (Canadian Wildlife Service, Edmonton, unpublished report, 1982); and H.W. Reynolds, J.R. McGillis, and R.D. Glaholt, "Range assessment of the Nisling River valley, Yukon Territory as habitat for wood bison" (Canadian Wildlife Service, Edmonton, unpublished report, 1982).

L.N. CARBYN

Wolves and Bison

Wood Buffalo National Park—
Past, Present and Future

The steady drone of the small airplane was ringing in my ears as we circled over the large meadows near the Hornaday River. Stretched below us, as far as the eye could see, was the endless wilderness landscape of Wood Buffalo National Park. Somewhere down below was a pack of wolves that had been radio-collared. The steady beep of the signal from the collar indicated that the animals were not far off. Suddenly, black spots on a small lake caught our eyes—a herd of bison. Scattered tracks in the snow indicated that they had been feeding on the sedges bordering the shores. The herd of about ninety were in a tight defensive formation when we spotted them. Such behaviour was a sure sign that wolves were nearby. It did not take long for us to spot the predators, eight wolves resting. Over a period of a week, we were to continue our daily surveillance of this pack.

When we returned the next day, it was obvious from the tracks in the snow that the pack had repeatedly tested the herd without making a kill. However, within several days, they killed a cow and then, shortly thereafter, a calf. Snow conditions were ideal to discern the circumstances under which the calf was killed: the wolves had chased the herd through open meadows for 4.3 kilometres; not until the bison ran through forest cover did the pack kill the calf. It is conceivable that the calf was killed in the forest and not out in the open because the vegetation had hindered the calf's progress more than the adult bisons'.[1] In a sense, the vegetation acted as a "filter," making it easier for the wolves to kill stragglers when these were calves and not bulls. Normally, in open areas, bulls tend to form the rear of herds that are in full flight, while calves are found somewhere in the middle or near the lead of the herds. Once the pack had killed the calf, it stopped to feed on it while the herd continued to flee, in a tight formation, at least initially, and without any signs of stopping to feed. One could tell when the herd slowed down because the tracks became more spread out. After travelling for twenty kilometres through the bush, the herd continued on for another sixty-two kilometres along a snow plowed road. The total distance travelled as a result of the attack by the wolf pack was eighty-six kilometres, all in less than twenty-four hours.

Many times I have wondered what the adaptive advantages of such behaviour could be? I first visited the area years ago as a graduate student, but over the years kept coming back, because for me Wood Buffalo National Park is one of the most fascinating places on earth. It is a rugged place—in summer the days are long, hot, and often oppressively humid; in winter they are short, dark, and cold. Yet, for those who have the patience and the right frame of mind to get to know it, the land possesses a fascinating vitality. The incident of the stampeding bison herd is but one example of nature's secrets that is special to Wood Buffalo National Park. Would it not have been more adaptive for the herd to cut its losses once the calf was killed and to have resumed feeding immediately? As it was, the area where the herd ended up was a very poor bison range, and there was a good possibility that another hungry wolf pack was waiting nearby. On the other side of the question stand many other possibilities. Was it possible that a single calf, even in winter, provides an insufficient meal for all the pack's members? Instead of leaving that herd the wolves could simply start the attack over again. Or, would a fresh herd be less defensive than one in which an animal has already been taken? These possibilities tantalize and spur the imagination of anyone who studies such relationships in nature.

Wood Buffalo is not only Canada's largest national park, but also one of the best places still to witness and observe the interaction between the largest canid and the largest prey on the North American continent. The park still contains the world's largest free-roaming bison herds. These ungulates thrive on its aquatic systems. Huge basins carved out by glaciers some 10 000 years ago have evolved and changed into what is now a unique ecosystem. The Peace-Atha-basca Delta and the Slave River, with its associated creeks and low-lands, provide the necessary sedge meadows and habitats for the survival of bison. Such a landscape, of forest, karst topography, delta meadows and rivers, even without its wildlife, is spectacular.

The bison of the park have a long history of persecution and inter-ference by man. Their struggle to survive, as described below, has been remarkable, but in recent years (1970–90) their numbers have declined dramatically, probably as a consequence of a combination of factors.

Wolves too have experienced a great deal of persecution by man, but, unlike bison, they still occupy approximately 80% of their for-mer range.[2] That these two species are found together within the na-tional park makes a study of their interrelationship possible. Early in this century, predation by wolves on bison in the area was the subject of comment by two very well known naturalists. Ernest Thompson Seton travelled through the area in the company of local guides. His publication, *Arctic Prairies*, describes his trips.[3] Dewey Soper, another well known naturalist, first conducted field work from 1932 to 1934. Unlike Seton, Soper remained in the area for longer periods. Travelling by dog team and boat, he covered most of the region, from the vicinity of Birch Mountain north to the Nyarling River and Great Slave Lake, and west, to Buffalo Lake, the upper wa-ters of Buffalo and Little Buffalo rivers, Thultue Lake, and the Jack-fish River drainage. As well, he made shorter trips into the park in 1937, 1939, and 1944, making more detailed investigations in 1945. In that year, his official instructions were to study the interrelationship of timber wolves and bison. Upon his return from the field, he sub-mitted a report to Ottawa.[4]

The report dealt at length with wolf predation on bison. He con-cluded that the predator was too numerous and posed a real threat to the bison herds:

having correctly reached the conclusion that wolves are every-where on the increase across the North and that it is desirable to reduce their number for certain specific and justifiable reasons, the fundamental objective, then, is to get rid of a goodly percent-age of them. At the moment nothing else matters. It is a question of killing wolves. No other issue should obscure this proposi-tion...three dead wolves are better than none and the three are dead, incontestably dead. They are beyond the powers of reproduction and destruction. If we want to kill wolves, does it much matter within reason how they become defunct? The point, as I see it, under the circumstances is to momentarily set aside some of the disputations of the situation and go straight to the objective—reduction of the wolf population. The answer is comparatively simple—"kill them."[5]

The next major study of wolves and wolf predation in the park was conducted between 1978 and 1981 by Sebastian Oosenbrug. Oosenbrug's methods moved the research into the modern world—he radio-collared forty-three wolves and monitored their activities from the air.[6] His three-year study described numerical relationships between wolves and bison. Tim Trottier, a student at the time, and I continued observational work after Oosenbrug left in 1982. Initially, the work was carried out from a 2.5 metre high tower (Fig. 1), which was located at Lake One, an area north of the Peace River.[7] After 1985, the approach was to follow herds and observe bison and wolves at close range (Fig. 2). These "naturalistic" studies were most interesting for their largely inconspicuous placement of the human observer amongst the predator and its prey.

All the studies have shown that wolves regularly and successfully prey on bison. Wolves' territories in winter are large,[8] and most of their time is spent travelling from one bison concentration to another.[9] Kill rates in winter vary, but a pack of ten will kill an adult bison every five to ten days. Summer predation on calves is heavy, and at low bison densities may account for 50% or more of the calves before they reach one year of age.[10] Moose, white-tailed deer, and Woodland Caribou are the other ungulates in the system, but their distribution is scattered and their densities are generally low.

There is some question as to how bison numbers have been influenced in the past by wolf predation. A brief review of the historical relationships is important for an understanding of how the current decline in numbers of bison can be accounted for. Samuel Hearne, the first European to discover bison in the region, referred to the species as "very plentiful."[11] From 1772 to 1907, fur traders, explorers, scientists, and adventurers passed through the area but little was known of the actual numbers of bison and of wolves. Indications, however, were that bison numbers declined after 1840.[12] From 1840 to 1893, hunting by man, severe winters, and, possibly, predation resulted in a precipitous drop in numbers of Wood Bison to critically low levels. At its lowest point during the late nineteenth

Fig. 1. In the background, wolves follow the herd.
(Carbyn)

Fig. 2. Following a pack of wolves at close range.
(Carbyn)

century, the population was estimated at 500 or 600 animals.[13] Legal protection was granted for bison in 1893, but the laws were not enforced until 1897. With protection came a slow recovery. But the most dramatic event, and in hindsight a very unfortunate happening, was the introduction of some 6673 plains bison into the local system.

Between 1925 and 1928, 6673 Plains Bison (4826 yearlings, 1515 two-year-olds, and 332 three-year-olds) were introduced in the Hay Camp area. In all "consignments," females were in the majority.[14] By 1926, some of the introduced bison had crossed the Peace River onto the Peace-Athabasca Delta and used that area from then on. To protect these bison, the federal government added approximately 17 408 square kilometres to the original Wood Buffalo National Park. Many of the transferred bison probably did not survive through the first year. E.G. Oldham stated that "there is a wide difference of opinion as to the actual numbers that survived the trip. Also, no accurate information is available as to the number of animals that succumbed shortly after arrival."[15] At any rate, since young breeding stock was introduced into an area with an apparent abundance of food, the conditions were ideal for a rapid increase. By 1928, the total bison population was estimated at 7500; it increased to 10 000—12 000 by 1934.[16] Introduced and established herds mixed. It is not unlikely that mature Wood Bison bulls in the park played a major role in breeding during the first years that Plains Bison were introduced. Numbers increased, reaching their peak sometime in the 1950s and 1960s. By the late 1960s or early 1970s, a decline began which continues in 1991.

One major consequence of the 1925–28 introductions of the Plains Bison was the likelihood that two bovine diseases were also introduced into the area. These bacterial diseases are bovine tuberculosis (caused by *Mycobacterium bovis*) and brucellosis (caused by *Brucella abortus*). Despite the introduction of these diseases, the combined Wood Bison/Plains Bison herds increased. Therefore, the diseases were present in the bison not only when their numbers increased (1925 to mid-1960s) but also when they decreased (1970s-90).

Meanwhile, wolf populations were considered "low" during the 1920s;[17] they were on the rise around 1925, and by 1932–34, wolves were numerous in the park.[18] The increase was generally considered as part of what appeared to be a circumboreal trend that extended from Alaska to Ontario. Soper, believing that wolf predation on bison was a significant mortality factor, recommended, as seen above, that wolves be controlled. Fuller and Novakowski referred to the wolf numbers as a "menace" and followed up on Soper's recommendation by conducting wolf control operations.

However, sometime after 1935, or ten years before Soper filed his report, Buffalo rangers had already started to poison wolves.[19] Little information is available on how many wolves died; however, the program was probably effective in reducing the pressure of predation on bison. Predator control continued at various levels of intensity until the late 1960s, although it is not clear exactly when a program of poisoning was terminated. During that decade, control became more of a secretive unofficial operation because the environmental concerns regarding predator control had increased. Some kills in the 1960s went unrecorded because systematic control of predators was not sanctioned by park authorities. It is believed that between the early 1940s and the mid-1960s, a range of twenty to one hundred wolves were killed per year. The largest numbers were killed during the three-year period between 1951 and 1953, when at least 186 wolves were taken. After poisoning programs were stopped, wolves continued to be killed, either as part of deliberate efforts to obtain fur, or as a result of casual encounters with trappers. Official predator control was replaced by trappers killing wolves as part of their regular trapping activities. This altered policy resulted in a less systematic reduction in numbers. In 1967, local residents requested that wolf control be continued, but were refused by the park superintendent. Throughout the 1970s and 1980s, aerial surveys conducted by the warden in the park indicated that wolf numbers were high. Based on number of sightings per hour flown, these records indicated that the wolf population was particularly high from 1970 to 1974.

Drowning is another factor of potential importance to the population dynamics of the bison. A very major component of the herds was lost in the 1974 spring floods (park files), when, it is thought, some 3000 bison were lost. Drowning was also reported during the spring of 1958 (approximately 500 animals[20]) and the winter of 1960/61 (between 1100 and 3000 animals.)[21] Bison may drown during the "shoulder" periods primarily—just after freeze-up and just before break-up—(for example, during spring or fall, when crossing thin ice on flooded meadows and rivers) because, unlike moose, they become trapped when they cannot haul their large bodies out onto ice.

Disease, wolf predation, and drowning were probably all responsible, to some extent, for the observed decline of the bison in Wood Buffalo National Park. It would be foolhardy to single out one factor, and to state categorically that it is the only reason for the observed change in bison numbers. More important is to evaluate the sequence of changes and to discuss the synergistic effects of various forces acting in sequence or simultaneously.

Brucellosis, a disease that affects reproduction in cattle, likely affects bison similarly. From 1952 to 1974, the average pregnancy rates of adult female bison in the park (greater than two years old at age of conception) was 46% as compared to six—82% for disease-free populations.[22] However, we do know that in the presence of disease and low wolf numbers, the bison population increased from the 1930s to the 1950s. Unless the effects of the disease on the herds has changed, it would be difficult to attribute the observed 1970–90 decline solely to the presence of disease. Possibly more revealing is the sequencing of events associated with wolf control from the mid 1930s to the late 1960s.

Mass drowning is a stochastic event, in the wake of which normal reproduction should not be affected significantly. Wolf predation results in a steady year-round loss of numbers to the population. Bison carcasses that become available to wolves as a result of drowning, because they may be scavenged, temporarily reduce predation on bison. This effect is considered of very minor consequence; the impact that wolves would have on a population after it has been reduced is much greater than the impact on numbers prior to a bison herd's drowning. A hypothetical example follows. If 400 calves are killed by wolves each year, then the removal of that many from a total population of 600 calves would have a much greater consequence than if 400 young are removed from a population of 900 calves. If recruitment is to offset losses of adults to the population, then a survival of 500 calves to year one is much more significant than a survival of only 200 calves to year one. The decades of the 1970s and 1980s, unlike the 1940s and 1950s, were ones in which wolf control was not carried out in the park. The losses of about one-third of the bison in the spring floods of 1974 were undoubtedly magnified subsequently by predation from a wolf population that also suffered losses from flooding of dens, but that rebounded more quickly than bison, because of the latter's lower fecundity. To some extent, disease may be predisposing bison to wolf predation, which could well result in higher than normal killing rates and higher wolf densities than one could expect to find in a system lacking the bovine diseases.

A three-fold decrease over two decades raises the question: how low must the bison herds decline before wolf numbers follow? That no answer is currently available indicates the importance of long term research and monitoring to document changes. Concentration of bison in herds makes them more conspicuous therefore vulnerable to predator detection than is the case when comparable numbers are more evenly distributed over large areas. Therefore, wolves are probably less directly influenced by bison declines if the number of herds remains constant while the numbers within the herds decline. Wolves preying on bison would be more immune to prey decline than wolves preying on both bison and moose, because moose are more widely spaced across wolf territories. Density-dependent mortality in wolves would certainly be important when their numbers increase. Mange, caused by an ectoparasite, is one agent of mortality that can be expected to increase with greater contact between wolves when numbers increase.[23] Wolves with mange have been frequently seen in the park. Similarly, the incidence of parvovirus and distemper would increase with higher wolf densities. Such interactions evolve over time, and the effects are variable.

A major long term consideration in the ultimate fate of the Wood Buffalo National Park predator/prey system arises from changes brought about by man's actions well removed from the park itself: the construction in 1968 of the W.A.C. Bennett Hydro-Electric Dam on the Peace River. The dam has changed the natural seasonal pattern of spring runoff in the river system, and the domino effect on many components of the park's ecosystem is of direct consequence to the wolf/bison system.

Sedge meadows and reed grass communities, for example, are the most important sources of food for bison, providing from 70–92% of their annual diet and almost 100% of their winter diet.[24] Sedge meadows, which require periodic flooding to remain viable, occur primarily in delta areas used by approximately 75% of the bison in the park during some part of the year. In the delta, two main components—open delta areas and perched basins—are important, as they support delicately balanced plant communities dependent on surface and groundwater regimes that have been affected by man-made changes. The optimum bison range occurs on open delta land, primarily in the interval between contour elevations of 209.25 metres and 209.85 metres;[25] significant flooding of these ranges occur when the water level reaches 209.5 metres. Land/water interfaces of perched basins are also important as bison range. Perched basins usually begin flooding at 209.85 metres, and approximately 78% are flooded at 210.3 metres. Since they are usually located at higher elevations than open delta and are not connected to the main drainage system by water channels, they are not generally flooded every year. However, major floods of perched basins did occur during seven of the twenty years immediately prior to construction of the Bennett Dam, six of these during the 1960s. In the two decades since the construction of the dam, such flooding has occurred only once; in 1972, a flood at 209.83 metres resulted in the recharging of some perched basins.[26]

While the drying of the delta from 1968 to 1990 coincides with the period in which bison numbers declined, it has probably not had an immediate impact on their numbers. Existing habitat is still more than adequate for the present population. The effects of the drying will be long term, and could have very significant implications for the predator/prey system. If, for example, the area of bison range is significantly reduced, will the greater concentration of the herds make them more vulnerable to predation? Or, if factors in predation are changed so that more calves survive, it is possible that bison numbers will increase. The question then is, can the system that once supported 12 000 bison before habitat deterioration began provide enough range to support similar densities of bison? Only time and circumstances will tell.

Wood Buffalo National Park is a jewel in the Canadian national park system, an area of great aesthetic, cultural, and scientific importance to society. The dynamics of its ecosystem have been influenced both by natural events and by human interference and manipulation. The current decline in bison numbers may be part of a natural process, a response to physical and biological constraints placed on the system, in which the whole must be seen as more than the sum of the parts. It is quite possible that the system will adjust itself to a new level where the former abundance of bison may not be reached. Wolf/bison relationships will also continue to evolve over time, and the process can only survive if it is adaptive on both sides. If, on the other hand, it can be proven that human interference threatens the future of the system, alarm bells should go off. If the long term effects of the Bennett Dam could lead to the ecological collapse of the delta system, remedial actions must be taken.

L.N. *Carbyn* is a research scientist with the Canadian Wildlife Service and an adjunct researcher with the Canadian Circumpolar Institute.

Notes
1. L.N. Carbyn and T. Trottier, "Descriptions of Wolf Attacks on Bison Calves in Wood Buffalo National Park," *Arctic* 41 (Ottawa: National Research Council, 1988), pp. 297–302.
2. L.N. Carbyn, "Management of non-endangered wolf populations in Canada," *Acta Zoologica Fennica* 174, p. 2.
3. Ernest T. Seton, *The Arctic Prairies; A Canoe Journey of 2,000 Miles in Search of the Caribou: Being the Account of a Voyage to the Region North of Aylmer Lake* (New York: Scribner and Sons, 1911), p. 14.
4. D. Soper, "Report on Wildlife Investigation in Wood Buffalo National Park and Vicinity, Alberta and NWT, Canada," *Canadian Wildlife Service Report 252* (1945), p. 240.
5. Ibid., p. 38.
6. S. Oosenbrug and L.N. Carbyn, "Wolf Predation on Bison in Wood Buffalo National Park," *Canadian Wildlife Service Final Report* (1985), 264 pp.
7. L.N. Carbyn and T. Trottier, "Responses of Bison on their Calving Grounds to Predation by Wolves in Wood Buffalo National Park," *Canadian Journal of Zoology* 65 (1987), pp. 2072–78.
8. Ibid., p. 70.
9. Ibid., p. 209.
10. L.N. Carbyn (in prep.).
11. Samuel Hearne, *A Journey from Prince of Wales' Fort in Hudson's Bay to the Northern Ocean* (1795; reprint, N. Israel/Amsterdam, 1968), p. 250.
12. H.M. Raup, "Range Conditions in the Wood Buffalo National Park of Western Canada with Notes on the History of the Wood Bison," *Special Publication of the American Committee for International Wildlife Protection* 1, no. 2 (1933), p. 9.
13. W.T. Hornaday, *The extermination of the American Bison*, Smithsonian Report Part II (Washington 1889), p. 523.
14. S. van Zyll de Jong, *A systematic study of recent Bison with particular consideration of the Wood Bison (Bison bison* athabascae Rhoads 1898), *National Museums of Canada*, no. 6, Ottawa, nd. p. 56.
15. E.G. Oldham, "Buffalo Counts in Wood Buffalo National Park, December 1946 and January 1947," *Parks Canada Memo.*
16. D. Soper, "History, Range and Home of the Northern Bison," *Ecological Monographs* 11 (1941), p. 347–412.
17. W.A. Fuller and N. Novakowski, "Wolf Control Operations, Wood Buffalo National Park 1951–52," *Northern Affairs and National Resources Wildlife Management Bulletin* 1, no. 11, p. 1.
18. D. Soper, "Report on Wildlife Investigation," p. 22.
19. R. Mitchell, "A Review of Bison Management, Wood Buffalo National Park, 1922–76," In J.G. Stelfox, ed., *Wood Buffalo National Park: Bison Research 1972–76: CWS/Parks Canada 1976 Annual Report* (Ottawa: CWS/Parks Canada, 1976), p. B16.
20. W.A. Fuller, "The Biology and Management of Bison of Wood Buffalo National Park," *Wildlife Management Bulletin* 1, no. 16 (1966), p. 38.
21. N. Novakowski, "Estimates of the Bison Population in Wood Buffalo National Park and the NWT based on Transect and Total Counts, 1961," *CWS/Parks Canada Report, 1961* (Fort Smith, 1961).
22. H. Reynolds, R.D. Glaholt and A.W.L. Hawley, "Bison," in J.A. Chapman and G.A. Feldhamer, eds, *Wild Mammals of North America: Biology, Management, and Economics* (Baltimore: Johns Hopkins University Press, 1982), p. 981.
23. A.W. Todd, J.R. Gunson and W.M. Samuel "Sarcoptic Mange, Important Diseases of Coyotes and Wolves of Alberta," in J. Chapman and D. Pursley, eds, *Pro-*

ceedings of the First Worldwide Furbearer Conference 1980 (Fosberg, MA: Fosberg College, 1980).

24. H.W. Reynolds, R.M. Hansen and D.G. Peden, "Diets of the Slave River Lowlands Bison Herd, Northwest Territories, Canada," *Journal of Wildlife Management* 42, no. 3 (1978), p. 586.

25. L.D. Cordes, "Vegetation Change in the Peace-Athabasca Delta, 1970–74," *Parks Canada Report*, 1975 (Ottawa: Canadian Wildlife Service and Parks Canada, 1975), p. C 37.

26. Townsend, personal communication.

GARY WOBESER

Disease in Northern Bison: What to Do?

A Personal Perspective

The presence of bovine brucellosis and tuberculosis among bison in and around Wood Buffalo National Park is one of the few facts about the current situation that is not disputed. The degree of controversy and the nature of some arguments presented in the debate associated with this problem, have convinced me to discuss factors that led me to the conclusion that the solution proposed by the environmental assessment panel, of which I was a member, is the correct one.

The occurrence of the diseases among this group of bison is not a recent phenomenon. Tuberculosis was present among the plains bison moved to the Park during the 1920s and brucellosis probably arrived via the same route. However, changes in several other factors have altered the significance of the diseases recently. The first such event was the elimination of both diseases from cattle in Canada. This required several decades and millions of dollars to accomplish and caused major disruption to many farmers, across Canada, who lost their herds in the effort. While the diseases occurred widely in cattle, any threat of spread of disease from infected bison to cattle was minor, compared to the risk of spread from infected to uninfected cattle. However, when the diseases were eliminated from cattle, any source from which disease might be *reintroduced* assumed new importance. Because the range of infected bison overlaps that of cattle in northern Alberta, and because the diseases can spread from bison to cattle, the bison represent such a risk. The same principle of removing potential sources of reinfection is being employed in the current campaign to eliminate elk that have been exposed to bovine tuberculosis on game farms across Canada.

A second major change has been the successful reestablishment of disease-free wood bison in western and northern Canada, through the Wood Bison Recovery Program. Until recently, the animals in the Wood Buffalo National Park area constituted the only large free-roaming herd of bison in Canada. That is no longer true. The reintroduced herd in the Mackenzie Bison Sanctuary now contains more than 2000 wood bison, and two smaller free-ranging herds of wood bison also exist. These herds occupy only about 2% of the historic range of the wood bison. Those involved in the recovery program estimate that about 73% of the historic range has habitat that is still suitable for bison, so there is a great potential for further reintroductions.[1] Unfortunately, Wood Buffalo National Park is located in the core of the historic range, and about three-quarters of the range that might be repopulated is judged to be unavailable because of the presence of the diseases. (It makes no sense to repopulate an area with disease-free bison, in the certain knowledge that they will become infected and increase the size of the current problem.) The herd of disease-free bison in the Mackenzie Sanctuary has expanded in size and range to such an extent that the separation between these bison and disease-exposed bison in the Park area is within the distance a single bison has been known to roam. It is considered inevitable that contact and disease transmission will occur between the two groups, without intervention.[2] Thus, the conservation initiative to return wood bison to their historic range has stalled, and the major herd that has been established is at risk, because of the diseased bison.

A third change has been the decline of the bison herd in the Park area from about 11 000 animals in 1971 to approximately 3200 in 1990. This decline in population is in sharp contrast to the thirty-six fold increase that occurred in the disease-free herd in the nearby Mackenzie Sanctuary over the same period. That herd increased from only fifty-six animals in 1969 to 2040 in 1990. The relative role of brucellosis and tuberculosis, predation by wolves and humans, natural accidents, and habitat change, in causing the population decline is controversial. The diseases are unlikely to have been solely responsible but may have been very important in conjunction with other factors. Diseased individuals are more susceptible than healthy animals to predation, thus providing more food for wolves and supporting a large wolf population in the area. Disease also reduces the fitness of individuals to deal with rigours of weather and other stressors. The depressing effect of disease, particularly brucellosis, on reproduction has likely also been important in making the population less able to compensate for, and recover from, losses to natural factors, such as drowning. Although the precise nature of the relationship between diseases and the population decline is unclear, the startling contrast between the diseased and disease-free herds indicates that disease has had a role in the population decline. The future of the herd is impossible to predict, but no evidence points to a reversal of the downward trend of the past two decades.

The risk of transmission of these diseases to humans has also changed. The decline in the number of bison has meant that Native hunters have less access to bison outside the Park, fewer bison are killed, and there is less exposure to infected animals, than occurred when bison were plentiful.

In summary, the current situation is that of a herd of diseased bison that has been declining in numbers for twenty years and that poses a risk to cattle, humans and to a major conservation effort to restore wood bison to their historic range.

During meetings held in and around the Park it was stated by many people that, if it could be accomplished instantaneously, the ideal situation would be to have a larger, disease-free herd of bison in the area. This would serve Native people, who have a legitimate claim to use bison, it would enhance the Park, it would increase the potential for eco-tourism in the area, and it would remove the threat of disease transmission to humans and to other animals. Thus, elimination of the diseases appears to be a desirable objective but, obviously, it cannot be done overnight. The suggested routes that might be taken to accomplish this objective range from doing nothing, in the hope the situation will resolve itself, through a series of actions to reduce the effects of disease, to the elimination of disease by one or more methods. The choice among these methods, even if it is to do nothing, must be based on its probability of success, its feasibility, and an assessment of all the costs.

Some have argued that nothing should be done to tamper with the current situation because humans should not disturb the "balance of Nature" between bison and diseases, particularly in a Park. Others believe that the diseases will disappear spontaneously, if the situation is left alone. In considering the question of balance, it is important to remember that the presence of these diseases is not a natural condition. The diseases were knowingly introduced into the Park with plains bison, despite vigorous opposition from knowledgeable biologists at the time. The diseases now not only affect the bison in the Park adversely, but also have ramifications beyond the Park. Those who believe that the diseases will disappear, without intervention, suggest that the herd will continue its current decline in size until some undefined point is reached, at which time there will be too few bison to maintain disease transmission and the diseases will die out. Wolves would be willing cooperators in the scheme by weeding out the unhealthy. However, consideration of the evidence makes this scenario seem improbable. The current population has declined to less than one-third of its former size, with the benefit of intense wolf predation, without any evidence of a decrease in the rate of infection among bison. In the most recent tests available, 81% of a sample of fifty-eight adult bison captured by Park staff throughout the Park, in the summer of 1990, reacted in tests for brucellosis.[3] This rate is higher than those reported in the past when the population was much larger.[4] These animals were not tested for tuberculosis. Had that been done, the combined infection rate would likely have been even higher. Similarly, the Hook Lake herd in the Slave River Lowlands has declined to less than 200 animals, but the diseases have not disappeared from that herd. Both brucellosis and tuberculosis are chronic insidious diseases in which individual animals may remain infected and infectious for years, without having obvious illness. Bison are long-lived, gregarious animals, so that, even if the population were to fall to a very low level, animals would still come together and disease transmission could occur. Thus, it is highly unlikely that the diseases will disappear spontaneously, at least at any level of population where bison would still be a significant feature of the Park area. The costs of a do-nothing approach involve accepting the risks and consequences of disease transmission to wood bison, cattle, and humans, while the bison herd appears likely to continue the decline begun twenty years ago.

A second group of approaches involve methods to reduce the risk of disease transmission to cattle and wood bison, through the use of fencing or buffer zones. (These would not address the effects of disease on the infected bison.) Fences could be used to keep diseased bison either in, or out, of a prescribed area. The risk of disease transmission to cattle could be reduced substantially by construction of bison-proof fences around cattle, and this was suggested as a possible interim measure by the panel. However, fences are not infallible, so a fence would not completely eliminate all risk to cattle. Fences around cattle also would do nothing to prevent contact between diseased and disease-free bison. To accomplish that, bison-proof fences would have to be constructed to completely separate the two groups. Such a fence would have to be double, with a space between, to prevent nose-to-nose contact. A cleared area, of a width equal to the height of the tallest tree, would have to be maintained on either side of the fence, so that wind-falls would not destroy the integrity of the fence. The length of fence required would be immense if all diseased bison, or even only those in the Park, were to be enclosed. (If only the Park was fenced, then all free-ranging diseased bison outside the fence would have to be eliminated.) The costs of fencing would include millions of dollars for construction, maintenance, and replacement, the environmental costs associated with clearing and construction, and the costs associated with the disruption of movement of humans and animals, other than bison. The feasibility of constructing and maintaining fences across the Peace, Athabasca, and Slave rivers, and around large lakes is unknown.

Buffer zones between cattle and diseased bison, and between diseased and disease-free bison, have also been proposed. To be effective, such a buffer zone must be maintained devoid of cattle and bison in perpetuity. The buffer zone would have to be at least one hundred kilometres wide, as individual bison in the area are known to travel that far. Bison in such a zone could be found and removed during winter, through very intensive aerial searching when tracks and feeding sites are visible from the air, but movement into a buffer area during the rest of the year would go undetected.

Fencing or buffer zones might reduce but would not eliminate the risk from disease. They would require massive input on an ongoing basis, and would cause major environmental disruption, as well as disruption to Native people through interference with movement, by fences, and absence of bison from a buffer zone outside the Park.

The other group of options available consists of methods to eliminate disease from the area. These can be grouped into three types: (1) treatment or immunization (2) selective removal of diseased animals and (3) removal of all disease-exposed animals.

Mass treatment or immunization seem attractive because we are accustomed to these as the usual methods of dealing with infectious diseases in humans. The basic requirements for such a program are (a) an effective drug or vaccine and (b) some method of delivering it to the population. There are no satisfactory treatments available for either brucellosis or tuberculosis and there is no vaccine for bovine tuberculosis. A vaccine was used in the control of brucellosis in cattle. Use of the vaccine helped to reduce the prevalence of disease in the cattle population but vaccination was discontinued when it was found to be ineffective as a method to eliminate the disease. The vaccine may be even less effective in bison than in cattle. Thus, the first basic requirement for such a program is not available. Even if a suitable drug or vaccine was available, it would be necessary to capture and hold bison for individual treatment, on a continuing basis. Attempts were made to capture bison in the Park for vaccination against another disease, anthrax, during the years 1965 to 1977. In the most *successful* year during that period, only one-third of the population was actually captured.[5] The roundups of bison for vaccination were accompanied by high losses of animals. This was remembered vividly, with obvious distaste, by local people who took part in the roundups. About 1100 bison were known to have died of anthrax, while more than 600 died of injuries associated with capture and restraint for vaccination. Such losses would not be acceptable. Because neither of the requirements for a successful treatment/immunization program is available, this option for eliminating the diseases must be discarded.

Selective removal of diseased animals, with salvage of all non-diseased animals, also seems to be an attractive alternative, as no one wants to kill healthy animals. Such a program has certain basic requirements. The first is the ability to capture every single bison for testing, as often as is required. The second is a test that will reliably differentiate between infected and uninfected animals. The third requirement is the ability to isolate all of the animals that tested negative, until every single individual in the population is *known* to be free of the disease. (It would be useless to test an animal and then release it back into the wild where it could mingle with infected animals and become infected.)

Unfortunately, each of these requirements presents a problem when considering the bison. The problems in capturing every animal in the area for testing are similar to those described in the discussion of treatment/immunization. Added to this is the fact that the animals would have to be held for repeated testing. The fenced pastures, corrals, and handling facilities required for such a program would involve massive construction and environmental disruption. Brucellosis and tuberculosis are chronic diseases in which animals may be infected, and infectious to others, for years, without appearing to be ill. Infected animals cannot be recognized by visual inspection and various tests on blood, or reaction to injections, are needed to detect infected individuals. The best tests available for detecting brucellosis and tuberculosis were developed for use in cattle and, while they are relatively accurate, they do not detect every individual infected with either disease. (No biological test of any type is 100% accurate.) Animals that became infected shortly before being tested do not react; chronically infected and debilitated individuals have depressed immune function and may not react to the tests; and some individuals fail to react, for no apparent reason. This lack of sensitivity to the tests means that infected animals will be missed by the tests, even under ideal circumstances. Some of these "false-negative" animals will be detected eventually, if testing is repeated regularly over several months or years but, in the meantime, these individuals will have mingled with the animals that actually were disease-free. Transmission of diseases to these uninfected animals is likely and "new" cases may continue to occur among the test-negative animals. No animal could be released back into the wild until it was absolutely certain that it was not infected and that no potentially-diseased animals remained free. This would necessitate holding all animals that were test-negative, together with their offspring, in captivity for at least several years for repeated testing. The close contact during this period would facilitate transmission of disease, from any animal missed during the testing, to many others. Each new discovery of a diseased animal within the group would necessitate starting the entire testing protocol again.

Selective removal or "test and slaughter" was used as part of the program to eliminate these diseases from cattle but it resulted in many failures, even on small farms, because of the inability to identify all infected animals. An example may illustrate this point. One small herd, that contained from eighteen to eighty-seven cattle at various times during the program, was tested twenty-two times over a two-and-one-half year period. Every animal that tested positive for brucellosis was removed immediately following each test. One or more positive animals were discovered during nineteen of the tests and, eventually, when diseased animals were still found on the twenty-second test, the entire herd was depopulated.[6] Because of failures, such as this, the test and slaughter program was replaced by a program of total herd depopulation for eliminating the diseases from cattle.

Consideration of selective removal of diseased animals, with salvage of all test-negative animals, as the technique to deal with the diseases in the Park area must include the realization that the area would be without free-roaming bison for many years, while testing went on, and that there would be a high probability of failure. If test and slaughter were to be used, the most likely scenario, in my opinion, would include a protracted period of several years to capture the bison, massive construction of holding and handling facilities for the bison and their offspring (perhaps one square kilometre of corral for each ten bison), high losses associated with repeated capture and restraint for testing, continued discovery of new cases among the test-negative animals, and eventual admission of failure and depopulation of the entire herd after several years.

In spite of the problems described above, the panel recognized that it might be possible to salvage a very limited number of animals, or reproductive products from some animals, to enlarge the genetic diversity of the bison used for repopulation. The risks of failure would be similar, but by having only a very small number of individuals, and subdividing these into even smaller groups for the testing period, the process could be more tightly controlled and if disease were to reoccur, only part of the group would be lost.

The other option, and the one advocated by the panel, is to remove all bison that have been exposed to the diseases and to replace them with disease-free animals. This would accomplish the objective of eliminating the diseases. Bison for repopulation of the area are available. An important part of the panel's recommendation was that the breeding herds for repopulation of the Park and area should be established before any depopulation occurs, to minimize the period that the area is without bison.

The feasibility of removing every bison from such a large area must be addressed. Several factors should be considered in answering this question. The first is that the bison are not uniformly distributed over the area; most are concentrated in one area in the Park. Most of these animals could be captured by trapping in winter, using bait and corrals, eliminating the need for roundups. Small concentrations of bison in other areas could also be trapped, using smaller corrals. Trapping would not be feasible for small isolated groups or individuals and it would be difficult, and likely inhumane, to attempt to round them up for capture. (Experience in the

Park and elsewhere[7] indicates that it is extremely difficult to move bison where they do not want to go.) Isolated animals would have to be killed where they are found, by careful experienced hunters working on the ground in winter. A second factor to consider is the visibility of bison during various times of the year. During summer, it would be impossible to find individual, or groups of, bison; however, during winter, bison and their characteristic trails and feeding craters are highly visible from the air. Intensive aerial searches could be used to locate bison and to guide hunters to isolated animals. Searches would have to be continued over several winters to ensure that all bison have been removed. The process would require a careful and intensive effort, but the bison can be removed.

Although I have discussed a number of measures that might be partial solutions, such as fencing and buffer zones, in reality, there are only two actual options for dealing with this situation. One is to decide that nothing should be done, the other is to eliminate the diseases. To do nothing is to accept a declining herd of diseased bison that will continue to be a risk to cattle, to disease-free bison, and to humans. If, for any reason, the population of diseased bison should begin to increase in number in future, the risk to all these groups will also increase. When wood bison in the Mackenzie Sanctuary become infected, as seems inevitable, there will be an even larger problem. The continued presence of diseased animals will also mean an end to attempts to reintroduce wood bison to northern Canada. These problems could be eliminated if the diseases were removed from the area. Environment Canada's official spokesman stated, at hearings in Edmonton, that "... the important thing is that there is a herd of disease-free animals roaming free in Wood Buffalo Park."[8] Although there is great disagreement as to how this could be done, most people agree that a herd of disease-free bison would be better than the present situation. The only feasible method of accomplishing this goal is through removal of all the disease-exposed bison and starting anew. The costs for depopulation and restocking will be high in terms of dollars and effort required; the area will be without free-ranging bison for several years; there will be effects on the ecosystem; and the process will be unpopular with many people. These costs must not be trivialized and every effort must be made to reduce and mitigate the effects. Careful planning and implementation of the program by a stakeholders group, as recommended by the panel, should ensure that this happens.

Gary Wobeser is a professor of Veterinary Pathology, specializing in diseases of wild animals, at the University of Saskatchewan. He was a member of the Northern Diseased Bison Environmental Assessment Panel.

Notes

1. S. Price, *Proceedings, Technical Hearing, Northern Diseased Bison Environmental Assessment Panel* Vol. B. (Edmonton: January 26, 1990), pp. 420–26.
2. Ibid.
3. E. Broughton, Agriculture Canada, Ottawa, personal communication, 1990.
4. S.V. Tessaro, "A Descriptive And Epizootiologic Study Of Brucellosis And Tuberculosis In Bison in Northern Canada," Ph.D thesis (Saskatoon: University of Saskatchewan 1987), 320p.
5. Ibid.
6. Agriculture Canada, Health of Animals Branch, *The Alternative Of Herd Depopulation Evaluation Study*, October 1977, supplied to the Panel, February, 1990.
7. M. Meagher, "Evaluation of boundary control for bison of Yellowstone National Park," *Wildlife Society Bulletin* 17 (1989), pp. 15–19.
8. D. Harper, *Proceedings, Technical Hearing, Northern Diseased Bison Environmental Assessment Panel* Vol. B (Edmonton: January 26, 1990), p. 400.

THERESA A. FERGUSON
CLAYTON BURKE

Aboriginal Communities and the Northern Buffalo Controversy

We are meeting here today to discuss important matters so we ask our Creator to guide our deliberations that we may decide wisely.... [1]

The Chipewyan words of Elder Adeline Mandeville opened the Fort Resolution public hearing on the northern bison issue. Community members and outsiders alike rose to their feet and bowed their heads in respect as these words were spoken—but the prayer was not interpreted into English nor does any transcript of it appear in the official records of the hearings. For those members of the Environmental Assessment Panel and other participants who were not Chipewyan speakers, standing with bowed heads was a matter of protocol, a formal show of respect for an elder and for another culture; nonetheless, for them the essence of the prayer remained unheard.

The unheard prayer symbolizes the greatest fears of the communities. Is the environmental assessment process only a formal show of respect for local needs? Will the government make an effort to truly understand and respond to the statements from local aboriginal peoples about the significance of the buffalo to their culture and lifestyle? Are the land agreement guarantees of decision-making powers for aboriginal people in wildlife management going to be sidestepped in this review process?

On 19 January 1990 the people of Fort Resolution gathered at the Antoine Beaulieu Memorial Hall to present their views to a FEARO (Federal Environmental Assessment and Review Office) Panel on the question of what to do about the northern bison. More specifically, the people were responding to a proposal spearheaded by Agriculture Canada to replace all the existing free-roaming bison in the area in and around Wood Buffalo National Park (WBNP) with a "disease-free" and "genetically pure" wood bison herd. As the afternoon lengthened, a succession of people came up to the microphones to face the panel. Elders, the Chief, council members, schoolchildren, hunter/trappers—they all spoke in defense of a resource basic to their lifestyle and in defense of their right to make the decisions about that resource.

With quiet, sustained urgency, they spoke of the past, the present, and the future. They spoke of the clauses protecting their hunting and trapping lifestyle in the Treaty Eight Agreement between their Nation and the Canadian Government; and of the past sacrifices that had been made to conserve buffalo. They spoke of the importance of buffalo in their diet today, of their pleasure in knowing buffalo and in teaching their children to know buffalo, of their conviction that wild meat is the best meat and that subsistence hunting is a valuable and balanced way of life. They spoke of the difficulties of countering all the threats to their land and their resources, threats which have come crowding in upon them in the past few years— pulp mills, mines, dams, extensive forest fires. They spoke of their frustrations in making appearances before panels knowing that, without funds and time, they could never be as prepared as the agency or corporation proposing the project. They spoke of their fears for the future of their culture if the land to which it is so closely tied is irrevocably damaged—and they demanded to be heard.[2]

The Issue

At the heart of this controversy over northern bison is the matter not simply of disease nor of genetic purity but of the role of aboriginal harvesters in managing the wildlife resources on which they depend. The term, "wildlife management," may, at first hearing, seem to be mostly about biology and the use of biological concepts and techniques to reach certain goals. But when we ask the question, "Who sets the goals?," the definition of wildlife management becomes a profoundly political concept. Who has the right to manage wildlife for their own purposes? Is it primarily the right of local harvesters who use the resource? Is it primarily the right of a centralized agency whose goals are derived from a national agenda? If there is joint management, how are these different interests to be balanced?

From the local Native perspective, this concern for the right to manage wildlife is of long standing. Native spokespersons stressed the point strongly in the Treaty Eight negotiations. As a result, the Treaty included a clause which guaranteed that Native people had "the right to pursue their usual vocations of hunting, trapping and fishing" with the proviso that this was "subject to such regulations as may from time to time be made by the Government of the country."[3] The intent of this proviso is clarified in the written comments on the negotiations by the Treaty Commissioners. These comments indicate that the Treaty Commissioners had assured the people that "only such laws as to hunting and fishing as were in the interest of the Indians and were found necessary in order to protect the fish and fur-bearing animals would be made, and that they would be free to hunt and fish after the treaty as they would be if they never entered into it."[4]

Subsequent events make it clear that the fatherly interest displayed by the government representatives was little more than a negotiating stance. It is also clear that the Euro-Canadian law-makers had a very limited interpretation of what was involved in the "usual vocation" of hunting and trapping. Whereas harvesters had been managers, making decisions about conservation and the appropriate use and handling of resources, government policy, once imposed, strove to separate the harvester from the management function. In this view, harvesters merely used the resource; only the formally educated managers had the knowledge and vision necessary to conserve the resource.

In the case of bison management, this process of alienating harvesters from management actually started prior to the signing of the Treaty with the 1896 enforcement of the law banning the hunting of the bison.[5] Fort Fitzgerald/Fort Smith people, in agreement with the goal of conserving bison, agreed to this ban but on the understanding that it was to be for only five years. Fort Resolution people signed the Treaty after the Commissioner agreed that the ban would not be enforced.[6] After the signing of the Treaty, the ban on hunting buffalo was extended and more overt arguments separating the harvesters from management were made.[7] Eventually, what was originally intended as a short-term ban on hunting buffalo lasted for some sixty years.

A reversal in this general trend in wildlife management has occurred with the rapid evolution in the past twenty years of the concept of aboriginal rights. The government has recognized that aboriginal rights exist and that these rights must be addressed through mechanisms to support aboriginal values and lifestyles. The need for aboriginal peoples to have meaningful roles in wildlife management has been particularly stressed.[8] Both the Fort Chipewyan Cree Band Land Claim Agreement and the Dene-Metis Agreement in Principle stipulated joint aboriginal-government agency management of wildlife.[9] These agreements were landmarks in that the aboriginal rights in wildlife were specified to involve the right to make decisions, not just the right to be consulted by a governmental decision-making body. This is a significant difference.

Even as negotiations based on these agreements proceeded to establish an appropriate structure and process for wildlife management in the designated areas in and around the park, this proposal to slaughter the park area bison came forward from a government task force and was further developed by Agriculture Canada. In fact, the chief representative of Agriculture Canada at the FEARO Panel's technical hearings stated that he had no knowledge of these land agreements.[10] This proposal was designed without any input from local harvesters; the proposed project management committee was to consist of government agencies, with aboriginal people having only a consultative role;[11] and once the proposal was developed, the input of aboriginal people was sought only as part of the public review. This equation of the harvesters' input with that of the general public denies the special status conferred on them by the land agreements and previously recognized by the federal government.

Small wonder that a senior negotiator for the Dene-Metis, George Kurszewski, characterized the proposal as a return to the Dark Ages:

I'm really, really appalled at Agriculture Canada for coming out with this kind of proposal without recognizing that their own Prime Minister has recognized back in September the 7th, 1988 that the Dene/Metis have an Aboriginal right to be joint managers, and I'm not saying consultation, I'm saying managers of the resources of this area, and you come to us with a proposal that

says you're going to manage this project and you're going to consult with the local people....We're not going to let you get away
with it.[12]

The Slaughter and Replacement Proposal

The proposal to eliminate the free roaming bison herds in the area in
and around WBNP and replace them with other bison was first formally suggested in a 1989 report of the intergovernmental Bison Disease Task Force. This report, entitled "Evaluation of Brucellosis and
Tuberculosis in Bison in Northern Canada" suggested a number of
other options but settled upon the "elimination and replacement
with wood bison" plan as the most efficient way to remove these
two diseases and at the same time further the Canadian Wildlife Service's goal of reintroducing the wood bison to all of its historic
range.[13] This particular option was expanded upon by Agriculture
Canada in its response to the Information Requirements procedure
of the FEARO Panel set up to look into the issue. This expanded proposal is thus simply entitled, "Agriculture Canada's Submission to
the Northern Diseased Bison Assessment Panel."[14] In the public
hearings held subsequent to the Information Requirement stage,
Agriculture Canada took the role of proponent and presented their
proposal in each of the communities visited by the FEARO Panel.

The slaughter and replacement plan is a response to a situation
which government agencies characterize as critical with national
economic implications. It has been known for some decades that the
bison in WBNP area are infected with tuberculosis and brucellosis,
diseases generally thought to have been introduced to the area with
the plains bison in 1926–28. Vaccination and slaughter programs in
the 1950s attempted to address this problem but were unsuccessful.[15]

As Canada's national cattle herd achieved a "brucellosis-free" status and progressed toward achieving a "tuberculosis-free" state as
well, diseases in the WBNP area herd were perceived once again as a
problem. The disease-free status is important in maintaining Canadian cattle and cattle products as desirable items on the international
market. A reservoir of these diseases in a wildlife population is seen
as very threatening to this status and increasingly so as more cattle
are pastured in northern Alberta on grazing leases.[16]

The problem, as defined in the Task Force report and in the Agriculture Canada proposal, is that the WBNP area bison are heavily

diseased, with roughly 35.8% of the bison having tuberculosis and 35.6% of them having brucellosis. Such levels are viewed as a threat not only to the health of the domestic cattle in the Fort Vermilion area and by extension to all other herds to which these cattle are transferred, but also to the health of bison users and to the health of other wildlife in the area including the wood bison of the Mackenzie Bison Sanctuary. The proposal to slaughter and replace the WBNP area bison parallels the strategy followed when brucellosis is detected in any cattle herd in Canada.[17]

In this paper we are identifying this proposal with Agriculture Canada, but a number of government agencies were involved with the original formulation of the plan. Prominent among these is the Canadian Wildlife Service. The interests of the Canadian Wildlife Service in this proposal are linked to the activities of the Wood Bison Recovery Team and the RENEW (Recovery of Nationally Endangered Wildlife) Committee. The objectives of RENEW are essentially to preserve species from any depletions of populations such that there is a possibility of the species entering any of the defined categories of "rare," "threatened," "endangered," or "extinct"; and for those species already in these categories to undertake programs to augment their population to the point where they are removed from these categories.

The Wood Bison Recovery Team, appointed by the RENEW Committee, has identified a minimum population requirement of four herds of 200 wood bison each in order that the wood bison survive as a wild subspecies. A yet larger population is seen as very desirable. This recovery is to involve a reintroduction of wood bison into its original historic and prehistoric range. Related goals are the maintenance of the genetic integrity of wood bison populations and their protection from serious diseases.[18]

The major free roaming herd of wood bison is now located in the Mackenzie Bison Sanctuary. This herd has experienced swift growth since its re-introduction there and represents a success story for this type of conservation work. The Recovery Team feels that its continued health and genetic integrity is threatened by the proximity of the WBNP area herd.

The Buffalo Resource: Its Definition

Critical in the design of a management plan for any particular resource is how that resource is defined. Defining an environmental feature as a resource involves more than some "objective" assessment of its nutritional or energetics potential. To be defined as a resource, environmental features must first be defined as fulfilling some need of a social group. This definition of a use value is a cultural act, a subjective act. A social group places an arbitrary value on an environmental feature and that value stems first from the particular needs, political, economic, social, or religious, of the social group. The goals and means of subsequent management derive from the assigned values.

Significant differences in value are attributed to bison by, on the one hand, the proponents of the slaughter and replacement plan, and on the other, by local Native peoples. The Agriculture Canada proposal develops its argument for the valuation of the WBNP area bison by contrasting the narrowly defined values it assigns to those bison with the much more broadly defined values that it attributes to the national cattle herd and the wood bison. The thrust of many of the statements of aboriginal people in the hearings was to reject a narrow and negative definition of the WBNP area bison and to explain the positive values these animals embody for them.

The WBNP area bison herds are primarily defined by Agriculture Canada as "transmitters of disease." These "transmitters" are contrasted with the "brucellosis-free" and soon to be "tuberculosis-free" national cattle herd and the disease-free wood bison herds of the Mackenzie Bison Sanctuary and Elk Island National Park. A secondary value, equally negative, is also attributed to the WBNP area bison, that of the "transmitter of genetic impurity." The definition of these herds as genetically contaminated refers to their origins in the mixing of herds from two subspecies, the plains bison (*Bison bison bison*) and the wood bison (*Bison bison athabascae*). This intermixing resulted from a management decision in the 1920s to transport plains bison into the area of the then new Wood Buffalo Park, the same decision, incidentally, that resulted in the introduction of these diseases into the area.[19] The Agriculture Canada arguments contrast these "genetically contaminated" herds with the "pure" wood bison herd. These latter herds are the ones placed at risk of genetic contamination and are the herds from which the replacement animals would be drawn.

Actually, the relativity of the use of these terms of purity has been made quite clear. The national cattle herd is "brucellosis-free" only in the sense that brucellosis outbreaks have been reduced to a very low incidence.[20] There are still occasional outbreaks—none of which has actually been traced to the northern bison. Similarly, the "genetic purity" of the wood bison is relative, since these animals are the descendants of a wood bison herd which did have some contact with the plains bison herds.[21] These animals, when captured, did prove to have some incidence of these diseases. Their current, apparent disease-free status was achieved by vaccination programs and the separation of calves from diseased cows for several bison generations.[22]

Aboriginal people strongly object to the assignment to bison of these negative values of "disease transmitters" and "transmitters of genetic pollution." The latter definition they find particularly offensive, arguing that so far from being an objective, scientific evaluation, such ideas are at the heart of racism.[23] The fallacy on which this concept of "genetic pollution" is based also became apparent at the technical hearings. There are as yet known no distinctive genetic markers for wood bison population. There is no discrete trait that declares unequivocally "here is a pure wood bison." The differences between wood bison and plains bison have been defined on the basis of phenotypes, not genotypes, and there is considerable variability of phenotypes within these populations.[24]

The assignment to the WBNP area buffalo herds of the value of "disease transmitter" local people qualify rather than reject. Many local people recognize that disease is a problem in certain groups of bison in the area and they agree that a healthy bison herd is a desirable goal. Their definition of a healthy herd allows, however, for some incidence of disease. The overall figures for disease incidence in the bison that Agriculture Canada provides are, moreover, questioned. In their view, sampling has been inadequate and the use of an overall percentage masks extreme variability in disease incidence between herds. Given the values attributed to the bison by Native people, slaughtering healthy bison is an appalling idea. Furthermore, local people argue that the proponents of the slaughter and replacement plan have overstated the risks of disease transmission to the Fort Vermilion cattle herds, to the Mackenzie Bison Sanctuary wood bison, and to the bison harvesters. This exaggerated depiction of the risk has intensified public pressure from elsewhere in Canada but is not based on any documented cases.[25]

Indeed, Agriculture Canada's assignment of values to the bison and their arguments concerning the need for such a drastic management measure appear so unconvincing to most local people that they question the real motivation behind such a proposal:

[Agriculture Canada] would have us believe that because wild buffalo within the Park and in northern Alberta outside the Park have been exposed to two diseases, brucellosis and bovine tuberculosis...that it is necessary to hunt down and kill every buffalo, even if the buffalo is not sick.

We have been told today that in the world today it is somehow all right to kill these buffalo to protect the Canadian cattle market. White experts have told us that the buffalo who have been exposed to these diseases aren't the kind of buffalo that white conservationists are interested in protecting. That the disease-exposed buffalo are somehow less worthy than other buffalo. These so-called experts would have us believe that by calling some buffalo "hybrids"....that we can somehow justify the slaughter.

We believe that the northern buffalo that Agriculture Canada proposes to slaughter will be killed because white agricultural interests want to use these lands for grazing leases and because the white government wants to sell the trees on these lands to foreign pulp mills. As the Indian people of this area, we oppose these uses of the land and this unwarranted slaughter of wildlife.[26]

What values do local aboriginal people place on the buffalo? The statements they made to the panel contained much on what the buffalo means to them and the cultural values to which the buffalo contributes. These were strong, well-integrated statements linking economic self-sufficiency to the integrity of the ecosystem and to cultural identity and survival. These connections are grounded in the spiritual value of the land and its resources. For the purpose of this discussion we can tease out three aspects of these presentations: the economic, the ecosystemic, and the spiritual importance of the buffalo.

To understand the economic importance of the buffalo, one must understand the vision of northern people for northern economic development. This vision was well articulated by community residents in the Mackenzie Valley Pipeline Hearings and first made accessible to southern Canadians through the transcripts and reports from those hearings.[27] This vision rejects the idea that a stable northern economy can be based on an ever expanding nonrenewable resource development strategy—at least, as the latter is conventionally organized. The economically and socially destructive impacts of such development are well documented. In contrast, the northern vision of economic development stresses the priority of the requirements of the renewable resources sector. A mixed cash-subsistence economy combining cash-producing activities and production of bush foods is seen as a means of economic self-sufficiency for a major sector of the northern population. Such an economy is *not* seen as an intermediate step to industrial development and universal full-time wage employment. On the contrary, the mixed cash-subsistence economy is valued for the flexibility it offers this generation and future generations; for the opportunity to maintain traditional links with the land; and for the possibilities it offers for sustainable development.

In the park area, the buffalo is viewed as an integral part of this plan for self-sufficiency, as a source of both food and cash. The buffalo produces meat which is both nutritious and relatively inexpensive. Local people stress that wild meat is healthy food for people, produced by animals which themselves eat natural and therefore healthy foods. Furthermore, the cost of the labour involved and the equipment needed to secure a harvest is low compared to the prices paid to obtain "imported" beef at a store. Buffalo is the focus of a tourist industry as well. Guiding and outfitting operations benefit from the attractiveness of buffalo to photographers and others in search of a northern wilderness experience. Big game hunting is also a possible economic venture as is some form of bison ranching.[28]

The number of years that would elapse before buffalo would again be available for hunting under the Agriculture Canada plan was thus a major concern. Local people placed no confidence in the proposed seven to eight year time frame for slaughtering all the buffalo in such a large area, nor did they believe that it was likely that a huntable population could be developed in eight to ten years, given the environmental factors of anthrax, drownings, and wolf predation which affect the buffalo herds today. Speakers speculated that there might well be a chance that the younger generation would not have the opportunity to hunt buffalo at all.[29]

Buffalo and the existence of Wood Buffalo National Park are also closely linked in this argument. Conservation of bison was the reason for the establishment of the park. Although Parks Canada's view of the park as an area for wildlife conservation has often conflicted with the aboriginal view of the park as an aboriginal hunting and trapping preserve, local hunters and trappers recognize that the existence of the park has been beneficial in excluding many (but not all) industrial development activities and in serving as a nursery area for wildlife which then stocks the surrounding area. The possibility that the park might disappear or become smaller in size with the elimination of the buffalo is a very real fear.[30]

Local people base this fear mainly on two points: historical precedent and a perception that the government will not have the will to follow through on the replacement plan after the current bison herds are eliminated.

Even if the proponents of this plan do not specifically hold the intention of opening up more land in Northern Alberta to agricultural and forestry development, the greater value placed by Euro-Canadian society on agricultural and industrial rather than wildlife economies has historically fostered such events. Local people are very much aware that actions taken now may open the door to all sorts of unintended and disastrous consequences in the future. Aboriginal people are not unsympathetic to the concerns of owners of cattle operations but they note that the profits of the beef industry do not benefit northern communities. To forego the benefits of economic self-sufficiency in their own area in order to benefit another social group in another geographical area is not a sacrifice that should ever be asked of them again.

The fear of a lack of political commitment is exacerbated by the perception that the time frame and the budget outlined in the Agriculture Canada plan are grossly inadequate. As Jackson Whiteknife pointed out:

> Members of the [Wildlife Advisory] Board questioned the ability of government to make and keep commitments to long-term projects such as this proposal. They remember well-intentioned projects sponsored by some level of government which withered and died before completion due to changing priorities, changing personnel and changes in government. Can government stick it out for the duration of a long potentially unpopular project that will almost certainly require a lot of monitoring and redesign?[31]

Economic self-sufficiency is closely linked to the integrity of the ecosystem. During the community hearing, concerns for the broader ecosystem were voiced time and again. Buffalo were represented not as a species in isolation but as part of a broader network. Local people were alarmed at the lack of consideration given in the Agriculture Canada plan to environmental ramifications; and they were alarmed at the possibility of such a drastic decision being made when the basic data needed to determine the ramifications were not available.[32]

Bison are seen as the heart of the herbivore community and thus the heart of the carnivore community as well. This balance in the relationship of different species in the ecosystem was felt to be important. This perspective led to critical questions about the impact of eliminating the buffalo.

> All of these animals are related in terms of dependence and inter-dependence with each other and how they function within . . . the bush. Every animal has a role in the whole development of the bush. The wolf has a reason for being there, the wood buffalo has a reason for being there, the moose has a reason for being there.[33]

A particular concern is the impact of wolf predation on other prey species, once the bison are removed. One scientific report states that without the bison as a food supply, wolves would sharply decrease in number and that a new balance would be quickly achieved.[34] Local people felt, however, that wolves would first utilize other sources of food resulting in a dramatic and destructive increase in predation on furbearers caught in traps and on moose. Populations with a very low density in the area such as woodland caribou, mule deer, and whitetailed deer would be severely affected.[35]

The extermination of bison would have an impact on plant communities as well. Bison help to maintain grassland by knocking down young trees and by disturbing and fertilizing ground, making it more suitable for plants such as grasses. The major bison trails act as firebreaks, checking the spread of summer prairie fires. The prevention of such destructive fires is seen as particularly important in the maintenance of prairie wetlands, by preventing soil erosion and the excessive evaporation of water that occurs when soils are denuded of plants. These wetland areas, in turn, support many important species, such as waterfowl.

The health of the ecosystem, rather than just simply the health of cattle or of bison, people see as a particularly critical issue. Many people pointed to the impact of the Bennett Dam on the health of the deltas of the Peace-Athabasca and the Slave rivers, on the Slave River Lowlands in general, and even on the water regime in the karst area of the park.[36] These impacts have never been fully addressed by the scientific establishment but are felt to be of considerable importance by the local people. With the AlPac hearings preceding the northern bison hearings by mere weeks, local people feel that their environment is under siege.

The local aboriginal people have a sound background in interrelationships in nature based on a long history of living in the area and managing the resources. The local harvesters base their management decisions on extensive field information and an intimate knowledge of the habits and needs of each wildlife species. Traditional knowledge about the resources and environment have been passed on from generation to generation by the elders, providing a longitudinal data base. One aspect of the Agriculture Canada plan that local people found particularly offensive was that this local knowledge base was ignored.

Economic self-sufficiency and environmental integrity have tremendous implications for other aspects of the culture. Hunting is not just an economic activity. It is the context in which persons can renew their spiritual links with wildlife and the land, hone their skills and deepen their knowledge of the world around them, affirm their social relationships with their hunting partners and with those with whom they share their harvest, and pass on their knowledge and skills to the younger generation. This activity may be seen as essential to their cultural identity.

Roy Fabien, Chief of the Hay River Dene, spoke directly to this point when he commented on Agriculture Canada's plan to compensate local communities with bison meat while the buffalo were being exterminated and before the replacement herds were in place:

> The eating of it is just a small part of it. The survival is just a small part of it. The whole idea of a Native person in going and hunting and doing what he knows best is what one is proud of.... So what's going to happen to these people that are now independent, that are now living off the bison? You're going to take all their pride, you're going to take everything away from them and you're going to hand them meat.[37]

Many speakers emphasized the spiritual importance of the land and its resources, including the buffalo, to the local aboriginal people. The land and its resources are the gifts of the Creator and symbolize the covenant between the Creator and his people. They are to be used for subsistence but not to be manipulated as objects for profit. Fred Dawson, an elder at Fort Resolution, said:

> It breaks my heart to hear you talk about the buffalo like this. We have always used them for food, and you cannot take them away from us. The good Lord put the animals on earth for us to use the way we need. I don't see how you can play God and come here and annihilate our buffalo.[38]

In the Amerindian view of the environment, all entities are imbued with souls and because of this, humans can enter into social relationships with them. As in all social relationships, these are based on mutual obligations. Plants, animals, and other natural entities provide humans with the means of subsistence. Humans in return offer respect towards such entities in acknowledgement of the gift and of their spiritual power.

The buffalo, as a major species in the environment, is perceived as spiritually very powerful, as holding the highest position among the four-legged animals. In contrast, domesticated cattle, disease-free or not, are perceived as having lost their self-awareness or spirituality. The details involved in any mass slaughter and the reality of the numbers of healthy animals which will be slaughtered along with sick abrogates the relationship between humans and animals and between humans and the Creator.

In summary, although the goal of a healthy and growing bison herd is one which is shared by aboriginal people, the goal of "genetic integrity" is little valued and even the concept of "disease-free" wildlife herd is thought unrealistic. Achieving the goal of a healthy herd through a massive slaughter and replacement program is considered an extreme strategy, given the lack of firm data on the risks involved. This solution is further viewed as untenable because of the potential disruption of the ecosystem, of the mixed cash-subsistence economy and of other aspects of the relationship between the people, the land, and the bison. The duration and extent of such a disruption will depend on factors which cannot be reliably predicted. Local people fear that like other disruptive periods in their history, this period of disruption may have such effects and be of such duration that the regional economy and ecosystem will be transformed and aboriginal people further alienated from their resources and their land. The failure of the government agencies to include aboriginal peoples in the process of defining the problem and the options for a solution has not created any confidence in their easy assurances that certain impacts are not intended and will not occur.

Postscript: Working on Co-Management

This paper was intended to convey to the general public the values basic to any northern bison management plan, as argued by aboriginal peoples in the community hearings on the northern buffalo issue. In the year or more since this paper was first written, events have moved swiftly and the values outlined above are now active in a new forum, the Northern Buffalo Management Board. The existence of the board is an indication that prayers can be heard! Before we discuss the activities of the board to date, we would like to refer to the report of the FEARO Panel.

In August 1990 the FEARO Panel released its report, "Northern Diseased Bison"[39] which attempted to address the concerns of both the national cattle industry and the aboriginal people. This compromise accepted the overall strategy of slaughter and replacement as necessary but attempted to mitigate specific impacts as identified in the community hearings. Recommendations were made to deal with the matters of wolf predation and of continued funding. Local people and businesses were to be given priority for employment and economic opportunities in the implementation of the project. Most importantly, aboriginal people were to be part of a Bison Stakeholders Group which would design the project and then submit their design to a further environmental assessment and review process.

Furthermore, the report commented on the lack of consultation with aboriginal people prior to the presentation of the slaughter and replacement proposal as well as on the lack of intervenor funding which so seriously hampered the presentation of aboriginal counterproposals.

While the report attempted to deal with the specific impacts identified in the community hearings, it made less of an effort to deal with the unforeseen factors which local people feared the most. The report provided optimistic figures on the growth of wood bison populations in breeding stations but it could not provide an estimate of how long it would take to first depopulate the WBNP area before these wood bison were freed. Aboriginal participation was stipulated in the design of the project but the activities of the Bison Stake-holders Group would have ended before implementation. There was no formal mechanism specified whereby aboriginal people could contribute to the ongoing management of the implementation and thus ensure their input when the unexpected happened.

The panel's recommendations were set aside by the Minister of the Environment, due, undoubtedly, to continued lobbying on the part of aboriginal and other groups. The alternative, the Northern Buffalo Management Board, embodies a suggestion originally made to the panel in the submission of the joint Treaty Eight and Métis leaders.[40] In its present form, the board consists of representatives from nine communities, five government agencies, and three non-governmental organizations. There are two co-chairmen, one an aboriginal representative and the other, a government appointee.

Currently the board is hammering out the terms of reference which will guide their management plan. Prominent among these is a community-based planning component which will permit the values discussed in the foregoing to be developed into management strategies. Aboriginal leaders express a cautious optimism:

> This is a victory for us. We stopped the slaughter. We're a majority in this management board. We have the right of veto. Now we have to sit down and work out together a plan to address the issue. It will not be an easy process but it is now one in which the rights of the aboriginal people are recognized.[41]

Theresa A. Ferguson is a sessional lecturer, School of Native Studies, University of Alberta.
Clayton Burke is an instructor at Arctic College, Fort Smith, NWT.

Notes
1. We would like to thank Leona Poitras for interpreting this portion of Mrs. Mandeville's prayer.
2. Northern Diseased Bison Environmental Assessment Panel, Community and Technical Sessions, 1990 Transcripts. Vol. A, pp. 95–126.
3. Treaty No. Eight, made 21 June 1899, and Adhesions, Reports etc. (Ottawa: Queen's Printer, 1966), p. 12.
4. Ibid., p. 6.
5. Statutes of Canada. Chap. 31, 57–58 VIC. "Act for the preservation of game in the unorganized part of the North-West Territories of Canada."
6. "The Evidence of Johnny Jean Marie Beaulieu of Fort Resolution, NWT, before Mr. Justice Morrow of the Supreme Court of the NWT re: *Paulette et al.*, July 17, 1973," in Dene Rights: Supporting Research and Documents, vol. 1, Legal and Constitu-

tional Basis for Dene Rights (Yellowknife: Indian Brotherhood of the Northwest Territories), pp. 2–13.

7. A.M. Jarvis, "Report of Inspector A.M. Jarvis, C.M.G. on Wood Buffalo in the Mackenzie District," Appendix N; Report of the Royal Northwest Mounted Police. Sessional Paper for 1907 (Ottawa: King's Printer, 1908).

8. Department of Indian Affairs and Northern Development, *In All Fairness: A Native Claims Policy* (Ottawa: Queen's Printer, 1981).

9. Comprehensive Land Claim Agreement in Principle between Canada and the Dene Nation and the Metis Association of the Northwest Territories, September 1988; and Agreement, 1986, 23 Dec. between Canada and Alberta (Fort Chipewyan Cree Band Land Settlement).

10. William Bulmer, Transcripts, Vol. A, p. 151.

11. Ibid., p. 133.

12. George Kurszewski, Transcripts, Vol. B, p. 224.

13. Bison Disease Task Force, Evaluation of Brucellosis and Tuberculosis in Bison in Northern Canada. Prepared for the Bison Disease Steering Committee, 1988.

14. Agriculture Canada, Agriculture Canada's Submission to the Northern Diseased Bison Assessment Panel, 17 November 1989.

15. Bison Disease Task Force, Evaluation pp. 3–4.

16. Ibid., p. vii.

17. Ibid., pp. 4–12.

18. Wood Bison Recovery Team, "Implications of Diseased Bison Populations in Northern Canada for the Recovery of Wood Bison." Northern Diseased Bison Environmental Assessment Panel. Compendium of Supplementary Submissions, 1990, pp. 89, 94–95.

19. Bison Disease Task Force, Evaluation, p. 8.

20. Ibid., pp. 4–13.

21. Frank Laviolette and Hal Reynolds, Transcripts, Vol. B, p. 310.

22. Bison Disease Task Force, Evaluation, pp. 4–51.

23. George Kurszewski, Transcripts, Vol. A, p. 150.

24. Roy Berg, Transcripts, Vol. B, p. 274.

25. Rex Coupland, Transcripts, Vol. A, p. 19.

26. Johnson Sewepegaham, Transcripts, Vol. A, p. 4.

27. Thomas R. Berger, Northern Frontier, Northern Homeland, The Report of the Mackenzie Valley Pipeline, Vol. 1 (Toronto: James Lorimer and Co., 1977).

28. Jackson Whiteknife, Transcripts, Vol. B, pp. 301–4.

29. Danny Beaulieu, Transcripts, Vol. A, p. 104; Chief Henry Beaver, Transcripts, Vol. B, p. 231.

30. For example, Daniel Sonfrere, Transcripts, Vol. A, p. 69.

31. Jackson Whiteknife, Transcripts, Vol. B, p. 302.

32. For example, Chief Unka, Transcripts, Vol. A, p. 112.

33. Johnson Sewepegaham, Transcripts, Vol. A, p. 13.

34. Francois Messier, Effects of Bison Population Changes on Wolf-Prey Dynamics in and around Wood Buffalo National Park, in Compendium of Government Submissions and Technical Specialist Reports in response to the Panel Information Requirements Document, October 1989.

35. George Kurszewski, Transcripts, Vol. B, p. 220.

36. Clayton Burke, Transcripts, Vol. B, p. 272–73; Pat Marcel, Transcripts, Vol. B, p. 311.

37. Roy Fabien, Transcripts, Vol. A, p. 63.

38. Fred Dawson, Transcripts, Vol. A, p. 123.

39. Federal Environmental Assessment and Review Office, 1990. Northern Diseased

Bison Report of the Environmental Assessment Panel, Ottawa: Minister of Supply and Services Canada.
40. Submission of Treaty Eight and Métis Leaders to the Northern Diseased Bison Assessment Panel. Compendium of Submissions, March 1990.
41. George Kurszewski, Co-chairman of the Northern Buffalo Management Board, pers. comm. 18 July 1991.

STACY V. TESSARO

Bovine Tuberculosis and Brucellosis in Animals, Including Man

Introduction

Bovine brucellosis and bovine tuberculosis are caused by two different species of bacteria, *Brucella abortus* and *Mycobacterium bovis*, respectively. The adjective "bovine" is used because the preferred, or primary, hosts of these specific bacteria are cattle and cattlelike animals. Hence, by convention, the diseases are referred to as "bovine" brucellosis and tuberculosis even when they occur in animals other than cattle. There are numerous other species of micro-bacteria that normally occur in the environment, and some of these micro-bacteria can occasionally cause opportunistic infections in animals and humans, particularly under conditions of reduced immunity.

Both diseases are of considerable significance throughout the world because of their effects on the health of animals, including humans, and their impact on agricultural trade and economics. All developed countries, and many developing nations, have policies to eradicate or control bovine brucellosis and tuberculosis, and to prevent the importation of these diseases. Efforts to control the diseases by simple test and slaughter methods, or by calfhood vaccination with brucellosis strain 19 vaccine, have lowered the prevalence of the diseases but have generally failed to eradicate them from cattle populations. Because there is no reliable vaccine or curative treatment for animals, and because test systems cannot detect every individual that is carrying the disease in an infected population, the eradication of bovine brucellosis and tuberculosis in Canada and other developed countries is based on depopulating infected herds of cattle and other primary hosts.

In Canada, programs designed to control bovine tuberculosis and brucellosis were established in 1907 and 1929, respectively. The national cattle population was declared free of brucellosis in 1985, and bovine tuberculosis is expected to be eradicated from the cattle population by 1992. Nearly one million cattle have been sent to slaughter in order to free the population from these two diseases. Despite the immediate hardship of destroying cattle, the eradication effort has been supported by the Canadian livestock industry, government, veterinary profession, and human medical profession. The long-term benefits to animal and human health, and the resulting economic gains, have increasingly offset the cost of the lengthy campaigns. In 1978, it was estimated that failure to control and eradicate both diseases from the cattle population would result in a cumulative economic loss to Canada of one billion dollars in the following twenty years because of the combined negative effects on the health of cattle and loss of important international markets for Canadian cattle.

The Epidemiology of Bovine Tuberculosis

Historically, tuberculosis has been documented as a distinctive clinical disease of humans and other animals for 4000 years, and prehistoric evidence of the disease has been found in human skeletal remains.[1] However, the cause of the disease was not known until 1882, when Robert Koch reported his discovery of the "tubercle bacillus."[2] In 1898, Theobald Smith detected slight differences in morphological characteristics between the "human tubercle bacillus" and the "bovine tubercle bacillus," subsequently named *Mycobacterium tuberculosis* and *M. bovis*, respectively.[3] Recent detailed comparisons indicate that the two are so very similar that they should be reunited as a single species, *M. tuberculosis*.[4] Other important pathogens within the genus include *M. leprae*, which causes leprosy, *M. paratuberculosis*, which causes Johne's disease (paratuberculosis) in animals, and *M. avium*, which causes tuberculosis in birds.

Although all species of mammals are potentially susceptible to infection with *M. bovis*, the disease has a relatively narrow range of primary, or preferred, hosts. A primary host population consists of a species that is susceptible to infection and which will maintain and propagate the disease indefinitely under natural circumstances. Primary hosts for bovine tuberculosis are cattle and cattlelike species including bison, water buffalo, Cape buffalo, and yak. The European badger (*Meles meles*) in Britain, and the brush-tailed possum (*Trichosuris vulpecula*) in New Zealand are nonbovine exceptions, having also been identified as primary hosts.

Secondary or "satellite" hosts are those animals which contract bovine tuberculosis from infected primary hosts, but which would not normally perpetuate the disease under natural conditions. Bovine tuberculosis has been reported in a variety of secondary hosts under two types of circumstances. Sporadic cases may occur in other species that share habitat with, prey upon, or scavenge on, infected primary hosts. For example, on rare occasions, wild deer have contracted tuberculosis by sharing range with infected cattle. Because secondary hosts are relatively resistant to the disease, bovine tuberculosis usually disappears once the disease is eliminated from the primary host population.[5]

The other circumstance where secondary host species may contract and maintain the disease is when they are held in captivity, as in zoos, fur farms, game farms, or animal research colonies.[6] Under these conditions, transmission and maintenance of the disease are facilitated by crowding, reduced levels of hygiene, and stressors such as concurrent disease, social and behavioral manipulation, and alterations in diet. Hence, the disease can be artificially maintained in species that have never been known to contract the disease in the wild. For example, bovine tuberculosis has never been found in wild, free-ranging elk in North America, but it has occurred in captive elk in zoos and on game farms.[7]

In North America, the bison is the only native species of wildlife that can act as a true primary host for *M. bovis*. In bison and cattle, the pathogenesis and epidemiology of bovine tuberculosis are the same.[8] Historical evidence indicates that the disease did not occur in bison prior to contact with infected cattle.[9] Today, among the 140 000 bison on the continent, there is fortunately only one population of bison infected with bovine tuberculosis: the estimated 3500 hybrid bison in and around Wood Buffalo National Park and in the Slave River Lowlands.[10] It is the last uncontrolled reservoir of the disease in Canada.

The disease has not become established in other species of free-ranging wildlife in Canada or the United States, despite prior decades of contact with infected range cattle. During the past fifty years, the disease has only been reported in seven free-ranging wild animals, other than bison, in Canada and the United States: four deer,[11] two wolves,[12] and one raccoon.[13] In the 1930s, the disease was found in a small percentage of elk, moose, and mule deer that shared the enclosure with the heavily infected herd of bison in Buffalo National Park near Wainwright, Alberta,[14] but the disease did not spread beyond the captive populations. Bovine tuberculosis has not been found in other species of wildlife that interact with the diseased population of bison in Wood Buffalo National Park.[15]

The main routes of transmission are by inhalation and ingestion of *M. bovis*. Congenital, venereal, and cutaneous infections occur infrequently. Depending on the route of infection, a primary lesion often develops at the site of infection—this can be in the lungs if the organism is inhaled, or in the intestinal tract if ingested. The infection usually spreads to the adjacent lymph node(s), forming a "primary complex." At this point, the disease may remain dormant for a highly variable period, or it may continue to spread throughout the body.

An infected individual contaminates the environment by exhaling, and coughing up, *M. bovis* from its lungs into the air and onto the pasture. The bacteria can also be shed in feces and urine. When bovine tuberculosis becomes established in the udder, bacteria are shed in milk. Occasionally, fistulous tracts will form between affected lymph nodes and the surface of the skin, allowing infective pus to drain into the environment. The length of time between infection with, and shedding of, *M. bovis* varies among individuals. There is not necessarily a correlation between number of bacteria shed and severity of illness; some infected animals can be shedding large numbers of *M. bovis* despite looking clinically normal.

Herd-mates and other herbivores contract the disease by inhalation or by eating contaminated forage on pasture. Calves can become infected by drinking milk from an infected cow. Predators and scavengers may become infected by eating raw meat and offal from infected primary hosts.

Mycobacterium bovis must enter a mammalian host in order to maintain itself and replicate. The bacterium can survive in the environment for up to two years under ideal circumstances. However, under most conditions, the environmental lifespan of *M. bovis* is only a few weeks because the bacterium does not tolerate lengthy exposure to desiccation, heat, and direct sunlight.[16]

Effects of Bovine Tuberculosis in Animals

A lesion is a site of injury or damage within the tissues of a living animal. The classic lesion of tuberculosis is called a granuloma or granulomatous inflammation, which results from the interaction of the bacterium and the host's leukocytes (white blood cells). By itself, *M. bovis* is a relatively innocuous micro-organism. It is the reaction of the host's own defense mechanisms that causes the damage. Macrophages, which are scavenger cells that develop from leukocytes, attempt to engulf and digest the bacteria. If they fail, and die in the effort, these macrophages release the bacteria, bacterial components, and lytic enzymes and chemical transmitters which destroy host tissue and attract more white blood cells to the site. This cycle exacerbates the damage. Modified macrophages called epithelioid cells and giant cells, and fibrous scar tissue, begin to form around the lesion in an attempt to contain the damage and wall it off from the rest of the body. It is this pattern of cellular response that is referred to as granulomatous inflammation or granuloma formation.

Other white blood cells, including lymphocytes and pus-producing neutrophils, also become involved to variable extent. The dead tissue in the center of the granulomas may become mineralized, or it may undergo liquefaction and cavitation. The lesions often grow to be very large and conspicuous, destroying extensive portions of organs. Historically, these pale, bulging masses of dead tissue, with their ring of inflammatory cells and scar tissue, were called "tubercles." The name of the disease was derived from the word "tubercle."

The course of the disease is highly variable. In some cases, large numbers of the bacteria from a primary focus may enter the bloodstream and be widely dispersed throughout the body. The animal usually dies in a short period of time. This form of the disease is called miliary tuberculosis. At the other end of the spectrum, some hosts are successful in containing the initial infection by encapsulating the lesion in scar tissue. These individuals can eliminate the infection or, at least, remain clinically normal. However, the bacteria can remain dormant within these lesions for variable periods (up to decades in long-lived hosts) and become reactivated, resulting in the renewed progression of the disease and shedding of bacteria into the environment. That the disease can undergo periods of latency is a major reason why tuberculosis is so tenacious in populations of primary hosts. The number of animals showing clinical signs of tuberculosis does not reflect the true extent of the disease in an infected population; a larger proportion of the population will be carrying or incubating the disease without showing overt signs of illness.

Other variations in the course of the disease exist between these two extremes. In some individuals the disease has a waxing and waning pattern, while in others it is slowly and relentlessly progressive. It may primarily damage one organ system, such as the respiratory tract, or it may spread with variable speed to many organs. The latter course is called "generalized" tuberculosis. Although tuberculosis is often thought of as a disease of the lungs, it can attack any organ system in the body. In addition to spread via the lymphatics and bloodstream, the disease can also extend along natural body passages and cavities. Examples of this include: spread throughout the lung via the bronchial tree; spread along the pleura of the lungs, peritoneal lining of the abdomen, and meninges of the brain; spread along the ureter from the kidney to the urinary bladder; and spread to the gastrointestinal tract as a result of swallowing bacteria coughed up from the lungs. The clinical signs of the disease and cause of death vary, depending on which organ systems are affected and the extent of the tissue damage. The debilitating course of the disease also renders the host susceptible to death from secondary causes such as other diseases, predators, and starvation.

Besides having a highly variable clinical course among hosts of the same species, tuberculosis can manifest itself differently among different species of hosts. This variability is often referred to as the "spectrum" of tuberculosis.[17] Secondary hosts are relatively resistant to infection by *M. bovis* and can often limit, or eliminate, the infection. Other species, such as European badgers and brush-tailed possums, appear to have difficulty in coping with the infection and readily succumb to fulminating tuberculosis.

The physiological status of an animal also influences the behavior of the disease. Old age, pregnancy, and other concomitant diseases can allow increased severity of tuberculosis. External factors such as poor nutrition, crowding, and behavioral stress can also enhance the severity and transmission of tuberculosis. Under optimal environmental conditions a primary host population will remain infected, but illness will usually be less evident than when the animals live under poor conditions.

Bovine Tuberculosis in Man

There have been numerous synonyms for tuberculosis in humans, including: consumption, phthisis, scrofula, the white plague, lupus (tuberculosis of the skin), and Pott's disease (tuberculosis of the spine). During the nineteenth century, and first half of this century, tuberculosis surpassed all other infectious diseases in causing human debilitation and death.[18] While *M. tuberculosis* is the more common cause of tuberculosis in humans, *M. bovis* can be a significant health problem for persons exposed to infected animals, or products from infected animals.[19]

Both *M. tuberculosis* and *M. bovis* can produce the same, indistinguishable spectrum of clinical disease in humans.[20] However, *M. tuberculosis* more often causes pulmonary disease, while *M. bovis* more frequently causes extra-pulmonary disease, including cervical lymphadenitis, osteomyelitis, arthritis, meningitis, and abdominal tuberculosis. Unlike *M. tuberculosis*, *M. bovis* has occurred much more frequently in children than in adults, and more often in rural populations than in urban communities. Circumstantial evidence of human-to-human, and human-to-animal, transmission of *M. bovis* has been documented, but appears to be uncommon. Where the disease was eliminated from cattle populations, it soon disappeared from the human population. Humans are typical secondary hosts of *M. bovis*.

Bovine tuberculosis was a serious problem in western developed countries until a few decades ago. In the 1930s, in a survey of 18 000 mycobacterial isolates, it was estimated that 10% of all human cases of tuberculosis were caused by *M. bovis*.[21] Similar survey figures were obtained in individual countries: 12% of 5476 human cases in Denmark;[22] 12% of 714 human cases in the Netherlands;[23] 15% of 2278 human cases in Germany;[24] 12% of 1200 human cases in the United States;[25] 10% of 320 human cases in Canada.[26] In Scotland during the 1940s, 3000 to 4000 cases of "surgical tuberculosis," caused by *M. bovis*, were reported annually.[27] In Britain in 1939, approximately 25–30% of deaths due to extra-pulmonary tuberculosis, and 1–2% of deaths due to pulmonary tuberculosis, were attributed to

M. bovis[28] infection. Wilson[29] estimated that bovine tuberculosis killed 2000 people, mainly children, annually in Great Britain. In a prospective study published in 1942, Hedvall[30] reported that 42% of sixty-seven patients suffering from bovine tuberculosis died of the disease.

Most human infections have resulted from the consumption of raw milk from infected cattle.[31] Concern over bovine tuberculosis was a major impetus for mandatory pasteurization of milk in most western countries. The medical profession recognized that pasteurization of milk would reduce the magnitude of the problem, but would not eliminate it for those people who were occupationally exposed to *M. bovis* through direct contact with infected cattle. Farmers, livestock workers, dairy processors, abattoir workers, rendering plant employees, meat inspectors, butchers, veterinarians, and laboratory workers were exposed by inhalation, ingestion, and cutaneous infection by *M. bovis*. Compliance with pasteurization requirements could not be guaranteed, especially in farm families and rural communities, when there was a high incidence of bovine tuberculosis in cattle. Subsequently, the double approach—pasteurization and implementation of animal health programs—led to a dramatic and rapid decline in the incidence of bovine tuberculosis in the human populations of western developed nations.

Sporadic human cases of *M. bovis* infection still occur in developed countries. Wigle et al.[32] summarized findings from thirty-one active cases of the disease in people who were detected between 1964 and 1970 in Ontario. These and another thirty human cases discovered between 1964 and 1976 in Ontario and British Columbia have been discussed by Enarson et al.[33] Between 1977 and 1987, 1.2–1.4% of human cases of tuberculosis reported in England were attributable to *M. bovis* infection.[34] Where the disease has been controlled or eliminated from cattle, sporadic human cases of bovine tuberculosis are usually attributable to recrudescence of infection acquired years earlier during childhood, or to infection acquired overseas.

Human infections caused by *M. tuberculosis* and *M. bovis* are detected and treated similarly. This convenience has often resulted in failure to attempt to differentiate the two causes of human tuberculosis.[35] Bacteriological identification of isolates is essential in determining the source and epidemiological significance of the infection. Cases of mixed infection have been reported. Some isolates of *M. bovis* from humans have shown resistance to one or more of the commonly used antituberculosis drugs.[36]

The Epidemiology of Bovine Brucellosis

In 1887, Sir David Bruce reported his discovery of the bacterium that caused the human disease known as Mediterranean fever, Malta fever, or undulant fever.[37] The pathogen was later named *Brucella melitensis*. In 1897, Bernhard Bang reported his discovery of the cause of contagious, or epidemic, abortion in cattle.[38] The latter disease became known as "Bang's disease," and the causative bacterium was named *Brucella abortus* because of its close taxonomic relationship with the agent of Mediterranean fever. Today, there are six species within the genus *Brucella*, each species having its own range of primary hosts.

In terms of suitable hosts, much of what has been said about bovine tuberculosis is also true for bovine brucellosis. Under special circumstances, any species of mammal can be, at least temporarily, infected with *B. abortus*. However, in nature, the primary hosts of the bacterium are cattle and cattlelike animals. Other mammals, including man, can become secondary, or satellite, hosts when they have contact with a population of primary hosts. However, they usually play no major role in the perpetuation or spread of bovine brucellosis. Once the disease is eliminated from a reservoir of primary hosts, it also disappears from the secondary hosts in the region. The disease may become established, and maintain itself, in some populations of secondary hosts under unnatural conditions of captivity or management, but such occurrences have been rare.

In North America, numerous surveys have been conducted to determine if there has been any significant spill-over of bovine brucellosis from cattle into wildlife populations. The disease has become established in bison herds but, because of eradication programs, bovine brucellosis is now limited to the free-ranging bison populations in and around Yellowstone and Wood Buffalo National parks, and to a small number of captive bison herds in the United States.[39] All other publicly and privately owned bison herds in North America are now free of the disease. As primary hosts of *B. abortus*, bison and cattle exhibit the same characteristic features of bovine brucellosis.

The disease also occurs in the population of 20 000 elk that are intensively managed on twenty-two winter feeding grounds in western Wyoming.[40] Bovine brucellosis has not been detected in surveys of free-ranging elk elsewhere in North America, despite past opportunities for contact with infected range cattle. The unique situation in Wyoming has been attributed to the extremely high density of elk which can only be maintained by the use of winter feeding stations. Elk have been seen aborting directly onto the feed that is distributed to them. Hence, the transmission and maintenance of the disease are facilitated by this management system. A small percentage of elk that lived within the enclosure with the infected bison population at Elk Island National Park had serological evidence of exposure to bovine brucellosis.[41] However, when the disease was eradicated from the bison, it also disappeared from the elk population.

Serological evidence of exposure to B. *abortus* has only been found in thirty-five (0.18%) of 19 629 wild deer tested in North America, and bacteriological evidence of infection has only been reported once, in a white-tailed deer in the United States.[42] Serological surveys of moose populations have failed to find any evidence of exposure. Severe, clinical brucellosis has been reported in five wild moose: three that were in contact with infected bison,[43] and two that were in the vicinity of infected cattle.[44] These cases, and a recent experimental study,[45] indicate that brucellosis is a severe, usually fatal, disease in moose.

Serological, and limited bacteriological, evidence of infection has been found in domestic dogs and wild carnivores (coyotes, foxes, wolves) that have scavenged on infected cattle or bison.[46] When bovine brucellosis has been eliminated from cattle and bison populations, the disease has spontaneously disappeared from the local carnivores, and there have been no instances of reinfection of the new herds of cattle or bison as a result of contact with the local carnivore populations.

Most animals become infected by oral exposure to B. *abortus*. Herd-mates and other herbivores contract bovine brucellosis by eating contaminated forage on pasture, and calves can get the disease by suckling infected cows. A small number of calves are infected *in utero* and are born with latent infections. Less common routes of infection include inhalation, contact with the skin or conjunctiva, and sexual transmission. Carnivores can become infected by eating raw tissues of infected herbivores. Once ingested, the bacteria spread to regional lymph nodes, and then to many organs via the bloodstream.

In primary hosts, B. *abortus* will selectively colonize the gravid uterus and placenta. This affinity for the female reproductive tract has been partially explained by the presence of a chemical called erythritol which is produced by the uterus during pregnancy. The disease will often become dormant for various periods in nonpregnant females and most other members of the population. The bacteria are adapted to survive within white blood cells, impervious to attack by host antibodies. Primary hosts usually remain infected for years, often for life. Secondary hosts are often able to overcome the infection, unless they are continuously exposed to *B. abortus* through contact with infected primary hosts. When infected females abort or calve, huge numbers of *B. abortus* are passed in the fetus, placenta, and birth fluids. This is the major source of environmental contamination.

Brucella abortus can survive in the environment for several months, under optimal conditions.[47] However, it does not tolerate desiccation, heat, or direct sunlight for very long, and generally lasts only a few weeks or less under most conditions. In order to maintain itself and reproduce, *B. abortus* must infect a suitable mammalian host.

Effects of Bovine Brucellosis in Animals

The major effect of *B. abortus* in primary hosts is reproductive failure. This can be manifest in the form of abortion, stillbirths, and weak, nonviable calves. Some females may become infertile as a result of endometritis and salpingitis. In recently infected herds, the disease can spread rapidly through the population causing many of the females to abort. This is often referred to as an "abortion storm." Once established in a primary host population, the incidence of abortion usually declines, but the disease continues to manifest itself as periodic cycles of herd abortions, sporadic abortions, reduced fertility, and delivery of weak or nonviable calves. Because the reproductive cycle of infected cows can be asynchronous, breeding and calving seasons often become broader, and calves are born at unusual times of the year when they are less likely to survive. Infected cows also produce less milk.

The disease affects the reproductive tract of some bulls, causing inflammation of the testes, epididymides, and accessory sex glands. This can result in reduced fertility and infertility. Some animals with chronic brucellosis will develop arthritis and infection of the tendons and tendon sheaths surrounding the joints. A variety of joints can be involved, but those of the limbs, especially the stifle ("knee") and carpal joint ("wrist"), are most frequently affected. Hygromas, which are large fluctuant swellings, may develop over the diseased joints. The large volume of fluid within hygromas often contains many bacteria, and can be a source of infection for other animals if the hygroma is ruptured. Brucellar arthritis often causes severe crippling, with secondary loss of body condition. Affected animals are markedly lame and are often slow or reluctant to move. Affected bison have difficulty keeping up with the herd and are prone to predation and starvation.[48]

Only a small percentage of secondary hosts develops significant signs of clinical disease when infected with B. abortus. Moose are exceptional in their apparent inability to cope with bovine brucellosis. When brucellosis has caused disease in secondary hosts, it has usually been manifest as sporadic reproductive tract infections and arthritis.

Bovine Brucellosis in Man

Humans are a notable secondary host of B. abortus. Human infection is often called "undulant fever." Bovine brucellosis is a public health problem in developing and third world nations, but is now rare in human populations in developed countries. A high percentage of human infections is subclinical (unapparent).[49] Most clinical cases exhibit nonspecific symptoms: fever, chills, sweats, headache, muscle pains, joint pains, and general malaise.[50] A small percentage of cases develops more serious illness: heart disease, especially endocarditis;[51] osteoarticular disease, especially of the spine, hip, and knee;[52] central nervous system disease, including meningitis and meningoencephalitis;[53] liver disease;[54] orchitis and epididymitis;[55] and empyema.[56] Abortion caused by B. abortus is extremely rare in humans.[57] Prior to the 1960s, the overall case fatality rate for bovine brucellosis in humans was estimated to be 1–2%.[58] Acute brucellosis in humans can be cured by appropriate antibiotic therapy, but chronic brucellosis can be more difficult to treat, and illness may periodically recur for years after the initial infection.[59] There are no reported cases of human-to-human, or human-to-animal, transmission of the disease.

Serological surveys done in Canada between 1937 and 1951 indicated that 8.6–19.4% of people in rural areas were exposed to B. abortus.[60] Although the incidence of chronic brucellosis in Canada was never measured, it was suggested that, "a very considerable volume of undiagnosed illness of a chronic type may be due to *Brucella* infections."[61] Over 6,000 human cases of brucellosis were reported annually in the United States during the 1940s,[62] and research indicated that only 3.5–10% of all cases were officially recorded.[63] Other American studies suggested that the number of chronic cases was ten to twenty-five times greater than the number of acute cases reported to health authorities.[64] Brucellosis in humans has been misdiagnosed and under-reported because of the extreme variability of clinical signs,[65] the unreliability of serological tests, and the difficulty of isolating *B. abortus* from infected persons.[66]

Unpasteurized milk and dairy products from infected cattle were once common sources of *B. abortus* for humans.[67] The number of cutaneous, aerosol, and conjunctival infections has superseded foodborne infections since pasteurization of milk became mandatory.[68] Brucellosis is a well recognized occupational disease of people working with infected animals.[69] Like bovine tuberculosis, bovine brucellosis has become an extremely rare disease in Canada and other countries that have markedly reduced opportunities for human exposure by pasteurizing milk and implementing a rigorous animal health program.

Summary and Conclusions

Bovine tuberculosis and brucellosis are chronic, insidious diseases that are characterized by their ability to persist indefinitely in populations of primary hosts, such as cattle and bison. Rather than causing spectacular outbreaks of clinical disease, bovine tuberculosis and brucellosis tend to smoulder within a population—infecting many individuals, but only debilitating and killing a small proportion of them at any one time. Over a period of years, the cumulative loss, in terms of valuable individuals and overall productivity, is significant.

Under optimal environmental conditions, when there is little pressure for high productivity, infected herds will persist in spite of the diseases. Under less than optimal conditions, the diseases work synergistically with other causes of morbidity and mortality to depress the viability of the population.

The diseases cause considerable pain and disability in affected individuals. Tuberculosis and brucellosis can take weeks, months, or even years to kill an animal. The experiences of, and descriptions by, veterinarians and human physicians attest to the amount of suffering caused by *M. bovis* and *B. abortus*. In addition to affecting primary hosts, both diseases can spill over into other species, including man, resulting in sporadic cases of illness or death in these animals as well.

Towards the end of a long disease eradication campaign, people often take for granted the progress and benefits of the effort, and their conviction to complete the task may wane. The national and international effort to eradicate bovine tuberculosis and brucellosis has played a major role in reducing animal and human suffering and hardship. Hopefully, the campaign to free Canada of these diseases will not falter when the goal is clearly in sight.

Stacy Tessaro is a Researcher at the Health of Animals Laboratory, Agriculture Canada, Saskatoon.

Notes

1. R. Dubos and J. Dubos, *The White Plague: Tuberculosis, Man, and Society* (Boston: Little, Brown, and Company, 1952), p. 5.
2. R. Koch, "Die Aetiologie der Tuberkulose" (The etiology of tuberculosis), *Berliner Klinische Wochenschrift* 19 (1882), pp. 221–30.
3. T. Smith, "A Comparative Study of Bovine Tubercle Bacilli and of Human Bacilli from Sputum," *Journal of Experimental Medicine* 3 (1898), pp. 451–511.
4. M. Tsukamura, S. Mizuno, and H. Toyama, "Taxonomic Studies of the *Mycobacterium tuberculosis* Series," *Microbiology and Immunology* 29 (1985), pp. 285–99.
5. S.V. Tessaro, "A Descriptive and Epizootiologic Study of Brucellosis and Tuberculosis in Bison in Northern Canada" Ph.D. thesis (Saskatoon: University of Saskatchewan, 1987), pp. 44–55.
6. Ibid., p. 45.
7. C.D. Stumpff, "Epidemiological Study of the Outbreak of Bovine TB in Confined Elk Herds," *Proceedings of the Annual Meeting of the United States Animal Health Association* 86 (1982), pp. 524–27.
8. S.V. Tessaro, "Review of the Diseases, Parasites, and Miscellaneous Pathological Conditions of North American Bison," *Canadian Veterinary Journal* 30 (1989), pp. 416–22.
9. E.T. Seton, *Hoofed Animals*, Vol. 3, Part 2 of *Lives of Game Animals* (Boston: Charles T. Branford Company, 1909), p. 676.
10. Federal Environmental Assessment Review Office, *Northern Diseased Bison: Report of the Environmental Assessment Panel* (Ottawa: Ministry of Supply and Services Canada, 1990), pp. 1–47.
11. P.P. Levine, "A Report on Tuberculosis in Wild Deer (*Odocoileus virginianus*)," *Cornell Veterinarian* 24 (1934), pp. 264–66; L.B. Belli, "Bovine Tuberculosis in a White-tailed Deer (*Odocoileus virginianus*)," *Canadian Veterinary Journal* 3 (1962), pp. 356–58; and M. Friend, E. Kroll, and H. Grust, "Tuberculosis in a Wild White-tailed Deer," *New York Fish and Game Journal* 10 (1963), pp. 118–23.
12. L.N. Carbyn, "Incidence of Disease and Its Potential Role in the Population Dynamics of Wolves in Riding Mountain National Park, Manitoba," in *Wolves of the World: Perspective of Behavior, Ecology, and Conservation*, F. Harrington and P. Paquet, eds. (New Jersey: Noyes Publication, 1982), pp. 106–16.

13. M.H. Brown, "Tuberculosis in the Canada Raccoon," *Transactions of the Royal Society of Canada* 25 (1931), pp. 159–62.
14. S. Hadwen, "Tuberculosis in the Buffalo," *Journal of the American Veterinary Medical Association* 100 (1942), pp. 19–22.
15. Tessaro, "A Descriptive," pp. 213–32.
16. C. Wray, "Survival and Spread of Pathogenic Bacteria of Veterinary Importance within the Environment," *Veterinary Bulletin* 45 (1975), pp. 543–50; and B.J. Duffield and D.A. Young, "Survival of *Mycobacterium bovis* in defined environmental conditions," *Veterinary Microbiology* 10 (1984/85), pp. 193–97.
17. C.J. Thorns and J.A. Morris, "The Immune Spectrum of *Mycobacterium bovis* in Some Mammalian Species: A Review," *Veterinary Bulletin* 53 (1983), pp. 543–50.
18. F.B. Smith, *The Retreat of Tuberculosis 1859–1950* (London: Croom Helm, 1988), pp. 1–24.
19. G.S. Wilson, J.W.S. Blacklock, and L.V. Reilly, *Non-pulmonary Tuberculosis of Bovine Origin in Great Britain and Northern Ireland* (London: National Association for the Prevention of Tuberculosis, 1952), pp. 1–108; and J. Francis, *Tuberculosis in Animals and Man: A Study in Comparative Pathology* (London: Cassell and Company, 1958), pp. 83–100.
20. A.S. Griffith, "Bovine Tuberculosis in Man," *Tubercle* 18 (1937), pp. 529–43.
21. R.M. Price, "The Bovine Tubercle Bacillus in Human Tuberculosis," *American Journal of Medical Science* 197 (1939), pp. 411–27.
22. K.A. Jensen, V. Lester, and K. Tolderlund, "Frequency of Bovine Infection Among Tuberculous Patients in Denmark," *Acta Tuberculosea Scandinavica* 14 (1940), pp. 125–57.
23. A.C. Ruys, "On Tuberculosis in Man Due to the Bovine Type of the Tubercle Bacillus in the Netherlands," *Tubercle* 20 (1939), pp. 556–60.
24. G. Meissner and K.H. Schroder, "Bovine Tuberculosis in Man and Its Correlation with Bovine Cattle Tuberculosis," *Bulletin of the International Union Against Tuberculosis* 49 (1974), pp. 145–48.
25. H.H. Kleeberg, "Tuberculosis and Other Mycobacterioses," in *Diseases Transmitted From Animals to Man*, W.T. Hubbert, W.F. McCulloch, and P.R. Schnurrenberger, eds. (Springfield: Charles C. Thomas, 1975), pp. 303–60.
26. R.M. Price, "Types of Tubercle Bacilli in Human Tuberculosis," *Canadian Journal of Research* 7 (1932), pp. 606–16.
27. Wilson, *Non-pulmonary Tuberculosis*, pp. 1–108.
28. B.R. Clarke, *Causes and Prevention of Tuberculosis* (Edinburgh: E. and S. Livingstone, 1952), pp. 187–202.
29. G.S. Wilson, *The Pasteurization of Milk* (London: Arnold, 1942), p. 212.
30. E. Hedvall, "Bovine Tuberculosis in Man: A Clinical Study of Bovine Tuberculosis, Especially Pulmonary Tuberculosis in the Southernmost Part of Sweden," *Acta Medica Scandinavica, Supplement* 35, 1942, pp. 1–196.
31. N.S. Galbraith and J.J. Pusey, "Milk-borne Infectious Diseases in England and Wales, 1938–1982," in *Health Hazards of Milk*, D.L.J. Freed, ed. (London: Bailliere Tindall, 1984), pp. 27–59.
32. W.D. Wigle, M.J. Ashley, E.M. Killough, and M. Cosens, "Bovine Tuberculosis in Humans in Ontario: the Epidemiologic Features of 31 Active Cases Occurring Between 1964 and 1970," *American Review of Respiratory Disease* 106 (1972), pp. 528–34.
33. D.H. Enarson, M.J. Ashley, S. Grzybowski, E. Ostapkowicz, and E. Dorken, "Non-respiratory Tuberculosis in Canada: Epidemiology and Bacteriologic Features," *American Journal of Epidemiology* 112 (1980), pp. 341–51.
34. M.D. Yates and J.M. Grange, "Incidence and Nature of Human Tuberculosis Due to Bovine Tubercle Bacilli in South-east England," *Epidemiology and Infection* 101 (1988), pp. 225–29.

35. C.H. Collins and J.M. Grange, "Zoonotic Implications of *Mycobacterium bovis* Infection," *Irish Veterinary Journal* 41 (1987), pp. 363–66; and D.G. Pritchard, "A Century of Bovine Tuberculosis, 1888–1988: Conquest and Controversy," *Journal of Comparative Pathology* 99 (1988), pp. 357–99.

36. N.I. Habib and F.D. Warring, "A Fatal Case of Infection Due to *Mycobacterium bovis*," *American Review of Respiratory Disease* 93 (1966), pp. 804–10; Y.P. Kataria, "Observations on Human Infection with *Mycobacterium bovis*," *Tubercle* 50 (1969), pp. 14–21; P.G. Jones and J. Silva, "*Mycobacterium bovis* Meningitis," *Journal of the American Medical Association* 247 (1982), pp. 2270–71; and J.M. Grange and C.H. Collins, "Bovine Tubercle Bacilli and Disease in Animals and Man," *Epidemiology and Infection* 92 (1987), pp. 221–34.

37. D. Bruce, "Note on the Discovery of a Microorganism in Malta Fever," *Practitioner* 39 (1887), pp. 161–70.

38. B. Bang, "Die Aetiologie des seuchenhaften ('infektiosen') Verwerfens" (The Etiology of Contagious Abortion), *Zeitschrift fur Tiermedizin* 1 (1897), p. 241.

39. Tessaro, "Review of the Diseases," pp. 416–22.

40. E.T. Thorne, "Brucellosis," in *Diseases of Wildlife in Wyoming*, E.T. Thorne, N. Kingston, W.R. Jolley, and R.C. Bergstrom, eds. (Cheyenne: Wyoming Game and Fish Department, 1982), pp. 54–63.

41. A.H. Corner and R. Connell, "Brucellosis in Bison, Elk, and Moose in Elk Island National Park, Alberta, Canada," *Canadian Journal of Comparative Medicine* 22 (1958), pp. 9–21.

42. Tessaro, "A Descriptive," pp. 21–37.

43. Corner, "Brucellosis in Bison," pp. 9–21; and Tessaro, "A Descriptive," pp. 213–32.

44. R. Fenstermacher and O.W. Olson, "Further Studies of Diseases Affecting Moose, III," *Cornell Veterinarian* 32 (1942), pp. 241–54; and W.L. Jellison, C.W. Fishel, and E.L. Cheatum, "Brucellosis In a Moose, *Alces americanus*," *Journal of Wildlife Management* 17 (1953), pp. 217–18.

45. L.B. Forbes, S.V. Tessaro, and W. Lees, "Experimental Study of *Brucella abortus* in Moose," unpublished.

46. Tessaro, "A Descriptive," pp. 29–33.

47. Wray, "Survival and Spread," pp. 543–50.

48. S.V. Tessaro, L.B. Forbes, and C. Turcotte, "A Survey of Brucellosis and Tuberculosis in Bison in and Around Wood Buffalo National Park, Canada," *Canadian Veterinary Journal* 31 (1990), pp. 174–80.

49. R.J. Henderson and D.M. Hill, "Subclinical *Brucella* Infection in Man," *British Medical Journal* 3 (1972), pp. 154–56.

50. D. Kaye and R.G. Petersdorf, "Brucellosis," in *Harrison's Principles of Internal Medicine*, eleventh edition, eds. E. Braunwald, K.J. Isselbacher, R.G. Petersdorf, J.D. Wilson, J.B. Martin, and A.S. Fauci, eds. (New York: McGraw-Hill Book Company, 1987), pp. 610–12.

51. T.G.S. Harkness, "*Brucella abortus* Endocarditis," *British Medical Journal* 1 (1936), p. 722; J.K. Rennie and C.J. Young, "Malignant Endocarditis Due to *Brucella abortus*," *British Medical Journal* 1 (1936), pp. 412–13; W.W. Spink, L.A. Tritud, and P. Kabler, "A Case of *Brucella* Endocarditis with Clinical, Bacteriologic, and Pathologic Findings," *American Journal of Science* 203 (1942), pp. 797–801; T.J. Quintin and M.R. Stalker, "Endocarditis Due to *Brucella abortus*," *Canadian Medical Association Journal* 55 (1946), pp. 50–52; F.D. Hart, A. Morgan, and B. Lacey, "*Brucella abortus* Endocarditis," *British Medical Journal* 1 (1951), pp. 1048–53; G.H. Grant and C.L. Stote, "Rupture of the Heart as a Result of *Brucella abortus* Endocarditis," *British Medical Journal* 1 (1953), pp. 914–16; T.M. Peery and J.M. Evans, "Brucellosis and Heart Disease. III. Chronic Valvular Heart Disease Following Nonfatal Brucellosis," *Annals of Internal Medicine* 49 (1958), pp. 568–79; T.M.

Peery and L.F. Belter, "Brucellosis and Heart Disease. II. Fatal Brucellosis: A Review of the Literature and Report of New Cases," *American Journal of Pathology* 36 (1960), pp. 673–97; J.C. Cleveland, R.J. Suchor, and J. Dague, "Destructive Aortic Valve Endocarditis from *Brucella abortus*: Survival with Emergency Aortic Valve Replacement," *Thorax* 33 (1970), 616–18; E. Pazderka and J.W. Jones, *"Brucella abortus* Endocarditis—Successful Treatment of an Infected Aortic Valve," *Archives of Internal Medicine* 142 (1982), pp. 1567–68; and L.O. Almer, "A case of Brucellosis Complicated by Endocarditis and Disseminated Intravascular Coagulation," *Acta Medica Scandinavica* 217 (1985), pp. 139–40.

52. L.A. Weed, D.C. Dahlin, D.G. Pugh, and J.C. Ivins, *"Brucella* in Tissues Removed at Surgery," *American Journal of Clinical Pathology* 22 (1952), pp. 10–21; P.J. Kelly, W.J. Martin, A. Schirger, and L.A. Weed, "Brucellosis of the Bones and Joints: Experience with Thirty-six Patients," *Journal of the American Medical Association* 174 (1960), pp. 347–53; M.M.S. Glasgow, "Brucellosis of the Spine," *British Journal of Surgery* 63 (1976), pp. 283–88; J. Torres-Rojas, R.F. Taddonio, and C.V. Sanders, "Spondylitis Caused by *Brucella abortus,*" *Southern Medical Journal* 72 (1979), pp. 1166–69; R.W. Marshall and A.J. Hall, *"Brucella* Spondylitis Presenting as Right Hypochondrial Pain," *British Medical Journal* 287 (1983), pp. 550–51; M.A. Abrahams and C.M. Tylkowski, *"Brucella* Osteomyelitis of a Closed Femur Fracture," *Clinics in Orthopaedics* 195 (1985), pp. 194–96; G.S. Alarcon, T.S. Bocanegra, E. Gotuzzo, and L.R. Espinoza, "The Arthritis of Brucellosis—A Perspective 100 Years After Bruce's Discovery," *Journal of Rheumatology* 14 (1987), pp. 1083–85; and G.L. Goodhart, J.F. Zakem, W.C. Collins, and J.D. Meyer, "Brucellosis of the Spine: Report of a Patient with Bilateral Paraspinal Abscesses," *Spine* 12 (1987), pp. 414–16.

53. A. Nelson-Jones, "Neurological Complications of Undulant Fever," Lancet 260 (1951), pp. 495–98; E. Nicols, "Meningo-encephalitis Due to Brucellosis With the Report of a Case in Which *B. abortus* was Recovered From the Cerebrospinal Fluid, and a Review of the Literature," *Annals of Internal Medicine* 35 (1951), pp. 673–93; R.W. Fincham, A.L. Sahs, and R.J. Joynt, "Protean Manifestations of Nervous System Brucellosis," *Journal of the American Medical Association* 184 (1963), pp. 269–75; C.R. Boughton, *"Brucella* meningo-encephalitis," *Medical Journal of Australia* 2 (1966), pp. 993–95; E. Bouza, "Brucellar Meningitis," *Review of Infectious Diseases* 9 (1987), pp. 810–22; K. Weissenborn, S. Weihler, and J.P. Malin, "Meningoencephalitis Owing to *Brucella abortus* Infection," *Deutsche medizinische Wochenschrift* 112 (1987), pp. 57–59; and J. Pascual, O. Combarros, J.M. Polo, and J. Berciano, "Localized CNS Brucellosis: Report of Seven Cases," *Acta Neurologica Scandinavica* 78 (1988), pp. 282–89.

54. J.S. Hewlett and A.C. Ernstene, *"Brucella abortus* Infection of the Gall Bladder Treated With Streptomycin," *Cleveland Clinic Quarterly* 14 (1947), pp. 258–63; W.W. Spink, "Histopathology of the Liver in Human Brucellosis," *Journal of Laboratory and Clinical Medicine* 34 (1949), pp. 40–58; G.M. Barrett and A.G. Rickards, "Chronic Brucellosis," *Quarterly Journal of Medicine* 22 (1953), pp. 23–42; and R.K. Williams and K. Crossley, "Acute and Chronic Hepatic Involvement of Brucellosis," *Gastroenterology* 83 (1982), pp. 455–58.

55. A.G. Isaac, "Orchitis and Epididymitis Due to Undulant Fever," *Journal of Urology* 40 (1938), pp. 201–7.

56. R.D. MacDonald, "Acute Empyema with *Brucella abortus* as the Primary Causative Agent," *Journal of Thoracic Surgery* 9 (1939), pp. 92–93.

57. C.M. Carpenter and R.A. Boak, "Isolation of *Brucella abortus* From a Human Fetus," *Journal of the American Medical Association* 96 (1931), pp. 1212–16; and C.C. Smith, I.A. Porter, and G.H. Swapp, "Mid-trimester Abortion Due to Infection with *Brucella abortus,*" *Journal of Infectious Diseases* 5 (1982), pp. 297–99.

58. W.W. Spink, *The Nature of Brucellosis* (Minneapolis: University of Minnesota

Press, 1956), pp. 145–70; and P.W. Bothwell, "Epidemiology and Prevention of Human Brucellosis," *Veterinary Record* 72 (1960), pp. 933–43.

59. W.H. Hall, "Modern Chemotherapy for Brucellosis in Humans," *Reviews of Infectious Diseases* 12 (1990), pp. 1060–99.

60. D.M. Baltzan, "Experience with Fifty-seven Brucellosis Infections in Saskatchewan," *Canadian Medical Association Journal* 36 (1937), pp. 258–62; Quintin, "Endocarditis Due to," pp. 50–52; N.V. Sanderson, R.H. Karn, W.R. LeGrow, and O.C. Raymond, "A Brucellosis Survey in Brant County, Ontario," *Canadian Journal of Public Health* 42 (1951), pp. 295–98; and E. Snell, "Brucellosis in Manitoba," *Canadian Journal of Public Health* 55 (1964), pp. 247–50.

61. Editorial, "Controlling Brucellosis," *Canadian Journal of Public Health* 41 (1950), pp. 337–38.

62. R.I. Wise, "Foodborne Diseases: Brucellosis," in *CRC Handbook of Foodborne Diseases of Biological Origin*, M. Rechcigl, ed. (Boca Raton: Chemical Rubber Company Press, 1983), pp. 317–22.

63. R.I. Wise, "Brucellosis in the United States: Past, Present, and Future," *Journal of the American Medical Association* 244 (1980), pp. 2318–22.

64. Barrett, "Chronic Brucellosis," pp. 23–42.

65. C.T. Keane, "Clinical and Laboratory Diagnosis of Human Brucellosis," *Irish Veterinary Journal* 36 (1982), pp. 155–58.

66. J.E. Davies, "Chronic Brucellosis in General Practice," *British Medical Journal* 2 (1957), pp. 1082–87; W.R. Kerr, J.D. Coughlin, D.J.H. Payne, and L. Robertson, "Chronic Brucellosis in the Practising Veterinary Surgeon—discussion," *Veterinary Record* 79 (1966), pp. 602–8; E. Williams, "A New Look at Infectious Diseases: Brucellosis," *British Medical Journal* 1 (1973), pp. 791–93; and J.L. Carpenter, E.C. Tramont, and W. Branche, "Failure of Routine Methods in the Diagnosis of Chronic Brucellosis," *Southern Medical Journal* 72 (1979), pp. 90–91.

67. Galbraith, "Milkborne infectious diseases," pp. 27–59.

68. G.G. Alton and J. Gulasekharem, "Brucellosis as a Human Health Hazard in Australia," *Australian Veterinary Journal* 50 (1974), pp. 209–15; and M.P. Flynn, "Human Clinical Bovine-type Brucellosis Not Derived from Milk," *Public Health* 97 (1983), pp. 149–57.

69. J.A. Boycott, "Undulant Fever as an Occupational Disease," *Lancet* 1 (1964), pp. 972–73; N.A. Fish, "Brucellosis," *Canadian Journal of Public Health* 55 (1964), pp. 80–83; H.R. Cayton, A.D. Osborne, and D.G.H. Sylvester, "Exposure to *Br. abortus* in Veterinary Undergraduates and Graduates," *Veterinary Record* 97 (1975), pp. 447–49; World Health Organization, *A Guide to the Diagnosis, Treatment, and Prevention of Human Brucellosis* (Geneva: World Health Organization, 1981), pp. 1–71; and B.C. Alleyne, R.R. Orford, B.A. Lacey, and F.M.M. White, "Rate of Slaughter May Increase Risk of Human Brucellosis in a Meat Packing Plant," *Journal of Occupational Medicine* 28 (1986), pp. 445–450.

MILT WRIGHT

Le Bois de Vache II:
This Chip's for You Too

Introduction

In a volume dedicated to the celebration of the North American buffalo it is important not to lose sight of the seemingly inconsequential contributions made by the species. It is difficult to believe that a serious void could exist in the voluminous literature devoted to the study of the "buffalo" (more properly termed bison), but there is one contribution of this species which has received relatively short shrift in the scholarly literature.[1] This article hopes to redress this omission, in part, by presenting archaeological data, historical accounts, ethnographic observations, and inferences derived from experimental archaeology. These various lines of evidence will be used to investigate a subject which few authors appear willing to handle (Fig.1), but which nevertheless remains an enlightening topic for discussion, that being bison chips.

For the uninitiated, bison chip is the monicker for one of the excreta of the North American Bison. It is not clear how the term chip came to be applied when referring to bison dung, but it is clear that "chips" were among the first renewable nonfossil fuel resources to be employed by mankind. This paper draws upon archaeological data from the Head-Smashed-In Buffalo Jump archaeological site (HSI), where it is thought that chips were the fuel of choice. The in-

Fig. 1. "In the Beginning...." (By permission of
Johnny Hart and Creators Syndicate, Inc.)

vestigation of the archaeological residues at HSI also provided the
impetus for a series of experimental replications using chip fueled
hearths and stone boiling technology.[2] These and other lines of evidence are employed to provide a review and critical assessment of
bison chips as a prehistoric fuel.

Historical Background

When the first European observers arrived in North America, they
were confronted by a mind boggling display of species abundance,
but the preeminent example had to have been the bison which appeared omnipresent. Account after account describes the masses of
bison, which were likened to an undulating blanket that covered the
prairie.[3] There is much less detail available regarding the aftermath
of such an event, but it seems logical that the first observers probably saw the sign of bison long in advance of confronting the creature
itself. Thus it is possible that the oft quoted gamblers lament,
"when the chips are down," may well have been coined by the first
person to view the evidence left in the wake of a passing bison herd.

Fig. 2. The Buffalo's "leavings" contribute to the
maintenance of the biome. (Archaeological Survey of
Alberta)

A brief perusal of a map of Alberta reveals a number of named features which commemorate the importance of the bison, such as Buffalo Head Hills, Buffalo Lake, and Buffalo Head Prairie. This celebration of the bison was more explicit on the early nineteenth century
maps of the province,[4] where you find the names Buffalo Dung Lake,
Bull Dung Lake, and Buffalo Chip Lake. The merits of this nomencla-
ture appear to have been lost on twentieth century map makers, who
declined to "let the chips fall where they may" when selecting place
names. Chip Lake, just west of Edmonton, may have lost the impact
of its original name, but the change was no doubt preferable to prospective European immigrants. Although we may sympathize with
the poor traveller who had to endure the hazardous footing and
fouled waterholes that remained as evidence of a passing bison
herd, such natural fertilization was undoubtedly an important component in maintaining the grasslands of North America.[5]

The grasslands were essential to the survival of the bison, and it is
fitting therefore that this animals grazing and subsequent leavings
contributed to the maintenance of this biome (Fig. 2). While potentially deadly to most prairie species, including bison, the conflagra-

tions known as prairie fires also were essential to the existence of the grasslands. Despite the barren appearance of the charred prairie stubble, this residue provided a rich nutrient supply for new growth and assisted in the grassland's constant struggle against encroaching forest and shrub parklands. It is also interesting to note that this natural phenomenon was recorded in native oral traditions, and that the Blackfoot people may derive their name from an episode where a raiding party crossed a newly burned section of prairie, with predictable consequences for their foot gear.

It is a curious fact that the bison themselves may have been unwitting accomplices to their demise in a prairie fire, for their chips appear to have contributed to the devastation. These prairie fires also may have provided the context for the discovery of chips as a potential fuel source. George Dawson, an eminent geologist and remarkable scholar, described a prairie fire in his late nineteenth century journal entries:

> After dark the Prairie fire to the S[south] began to look very threatening. Bright reflection in the sky and lurid glare along horizon.... After a time the reflection disappeared but smoke began to fill the air & the moon now risen, looked blood red through it.... Smoke sometimes suffocating & when the fire in the long grass impossible to stand near it. Dry buffalo chips once taking fire could hardly be put out & often serve to set the grass going again.[6]

Other descriptions provide a more specific statement of how it came to be understood that chips were potentially useful as a fuel.

> It is not difficult to conceive how its [chips] value probably became known. After a prairie fire, the night wind, blowing over the plain, fans them into a bright smolder, which can be seen for some time at quite a distance.[7]

The common term for bison chips in early historical accounts is "The Prairie Travellers Fuel." The French provided a more elegant sounding phrase "Le Bois de Vache," which translates into a decidedly less elegant, "the wood of the cow," when making reference to bison chips. Dedicating an academic paper to the study of bison chips[8] may seem a curious choice of topic. It also seems destined to evoke a grin or two, but there is a serious scientific side to the study of animal droppings in general, and to bison chips in particular.

Anatomy of a Chip

The expression "chip off the old block" does not apply to bison chip fuel, for chips do vary in their combustion properties. It is also true that not all dung is useful as fuel and that some dung is a better fuel in its "green state" than it is dried. In addition, dung has applications besides fuel, which is fortunate considering the global distribution and abundance of the resource. The use of animal dung is still widespread in the nonindustrialized world.[9] Such uses include mixing dung with other materials to form building blocks, broadcasting it as natural fertilizers, and a variety of dung fuel applications. While the use of dung as a fuel no longer has a global application, this may change, since gasification of fresh dung has been used to fuel experimental vehicles in North America and to power electrical generating stations for small communities in India.

In Alberta, dung (albeit nonbison) has been applied as fertilizer, and one informant indicated that dried horse dung was used as fuel during the depression.[10] More recently, and verging a little on the weird side, dung has been marketed in Alberta, and elsewhere, as a containerized novelty item (presumably to preserve freshness?) and in a variety of replica formats, including a scaled down wax version which mimics emergency roadside flares.[11] There have even been several instances of cow chips being employed as environment friendly frisbees during country fairs; however, chip tossing is unlikely to replace any of the traditional olympic pursuits. It is gratifying to report that the "state of the art" application of bison chips is found in Alberta. In a province which prides itself on research and development, it is fitting that an entrepreneur has patented (hopefully) the process of using lacquer-coated chips as a decorative surround for electronic clocks.[12] It would appear that the potential applications of dung are only surpassed by their natural abundance and variations in form.

Ethnographic and Historical Records

A review of North American historical documents and plains ethnographic accounts indicates widespread use of bison chips as fuel,[13] as a crop fertilizer,[14] as the foundation for ceremonial altars[15] and as a construction material for building drive lane cairns to facilitate bison kills at pounds and jumps.[16] There are also accounts of chips being used as a tobacco additive, as missiles and archery targets during adolescent play, as lining material for cradle boards and as tinder for igniting wood fires.[17] It seems clear that the uses of chips recorded during the historical period covered the spectrum from secular to sacred applications, but its application as a fuel appears to have been most common.

The people of the plains were quite adept at manipulating this fuel resource and could obtain sufficient heat for personal comfort and for cooking foodstuffs. The ethnographic documents state that chip fuel was used only when it was difficult to obtain wood fuel, the inference being that chip fuel was considered inferior to wood fuel. Although chip fuel was most likely to have been used on the prairie during the warmer, drier seasons of the year, it is clear that winter applications were sometimes necessary.

> Fort Qu'Appelle, 1867. True, dry buffalo dung lay almost everywhere beneath the snow, but it only made, even when heaped up like a haycock, a smouldering "smudge," on which the kettle boiled and the frying pan served its purpose; but without shelter from the cold . . . a very poor apology for a wood camp fire. Anything in the shape of a tent or lodge was considered to great an impediment on a trip performed with already heavy laden dog trains, carrying, besides the regular load, a few sticks of dry wood to make shavings necessary to start the buffalo dung to burn.[18]

Curiously, Cowie denounces the chip fire as a smouldering smudge, but in the same sentence states that it served the purpose of boiling the kettle and frying food. Additional observations on the seasonal use of chip fuel are provided below, and they offer some interesting clues to the burning characteristics of chip fuel.

> Our fireplace was in the centre of the tipi on the level ground. Five or six stones were placed around the fire; upon these we roasted meat. . . . The fireplace was surrounded by stones only when wood was scarce and buffalo chips were used for fuel, but when it was abundant the kettle was set directly on the coals and the meat was roasted on wooden spits. When we camped on the prairie, however, we could obtain no wood, and made our fire of buffalo chips.[19]

Of the many opinions offered by early chroniclers on the merits of chip fuel, only a minority could be classified as particularly glowing in nature. In some cases, the descriptions dwelt upon the limited heat and the abundance of smoke associated with the chip fire. However, these accounts need to be tempered with the knowledge that chips are not the prehistoric equivalent of "presto logs," and personal experience would indicate that first time chip users probably generated considerably more smoke than fire. While some travellers obviously lamented the scarcity of wood on the plains, others seemed quite content with the ubiquitous bison chip resource and were almost complimentary in their recounting of its performance "under fire."

The Reverend Belcourt is credited with perhaps the most eloquent description of a bison chip fire when he noted, "This [chips] when dry, produces an ardent but transient flame, sufficient for cooking out [sic] daily food; but it evokes a smell which, to the nasal organs of a stranger, is far from being agreeable."[20] A great many authors have commented on the aroma and volume of smoke associated with a chip fire, to the effect that, "Burns much like peat, producing no unpleasant effects. . . . Much less acrid than peat smoke, in my opinion, and a matter of draught."[21] The last comment is particularly telling, for it is likely that the experience of travellers employing chip fuel was in part determined by how dry the fuel was, and whether a modest draft was available. Even a neophyte prairie traveller surely must have recognized the paramount importance of selecting thoroughly dried chip fuel, but it may not always have been possible to place the chip fuel in the context of a freshening breeze. Those travellers who attempted to cook and achieve some level of comfort by virtue of igniting an indoor chip fire would seem predestined for disappointment. It is possible to use chip fuel to obtain heat for warming a shelter, but it requires some ingenuity. One traveller noted that,

> It [chips] burns in much the same manner as peat, and though making little flame, yields a very intense heat. Strips of buffalo fat thrown on at intervals during the evening add a bright blaze.[22]

Aside from the presence of a breeze, there appear to have been a variety of techniques available which served to coax heat from a smoldering chip. One author professed the opinion, presumably tongue-in-cheek, that the preparation of a steak over a chip fire obviated the need for seasonings![23] This culinary quip is perhaps indicative of the sense of humour that prevailed among prairie travellers who found themselves huddled before cheerless mounds of smoldering dung.

Early enquiries as to the means of cooking food on the plains yielded statements to the effect that,

> As a rule, there were but two ways of cooking meat, . . . boiling and roasting. If roasted, it was thoroughly cooked; but if boiled, it was only left in the water long enough to lose the red colour, say five or ten minutes. Before they got kettles from the whites, the Blackfeet often boiled meat in a green hide. A hole was dug in the ground, and the skin, flesh side up, was laid in it . . . . The meat and water having been placed in this hollow, red-hot stones were dropped in the water until it became hot and the meat was cooked.[24]

Further detail is provided by Wissler, who documents two styles of container for cooking with heated rocks.

> Boiling seems to have been the favorite Blackfoot method of preparing food and they were especially fond of soups. The preparation of such food necessitated cooking vessels of some sort. . . . Methods of boiling without pottery vessels were known . . . . This method was to boil in a fresh hide, or paunch by means of hot stones . . . heated in a fire of wood and cow chips . . . . From time to time, these [hot stones] were slid into the soup . . . . It was stated that other kinds of soup were made in such a vessel, as berry soup and common meat soup . . . . When a paunch was not at hand a fresh hide might be used in the same manner, though the usual procedure was to depress it into a hole in the ground . . . . The hide was used for boiling meat, the paunch rarely for anything but soup.[25]

The use of heated stone (stone boiling) for cooking is an ingenious way of circumventing the absence of fireproof containers, but it also provides a means for transforming thermal energy. Previous statements indicated that chip fueled fires were used with a surround of rocks, and that once these rocks had been heated the chip residue was swept away, and food was cooked directly on the rock surface. This transfer of thermal energy is not unlike stone boiling, which adds only the step of transferring the energy to the liquid, thus facil-

Fig. 3. Prehistoric roasting pit at Head-Smashed-In. (Archaeological Survey of Alberta)

Fig. 4. Profile of a boiling pit. (Archaeological Survey of Alberta)

itating the cooking of the food. The operation of sweat lodges relies on the transformation of thermal energy from the fire to the stone and finally into steam heat. In essence, stone broiling, stone boiling and sweat baths are early examples of a mechanism for thermal heat exchange. This technology not only allows for the transformation of thermal energy but may also provide the only practical means of obtaining radiant heat from chip fueled fires. As will be discussed, the necessity of employing chip fuel could well have led to the evolution of stone boiling technology.

Archaeological Record

Although there were a remarkable variety of uses to which chips were applied in the historical era, it is difficult to demonstrate such usage in the precontact period. Owing to their nature, it is the rare circumstance in which chips are preserved in an archaeological site. Therefore, the use of chips as a fuel must be inferred from the archaeological record, for the very act of burning the chip guarantees that the evidence will soon be gone with the wind. This was certainly the case at HSI in the southwest corner of Alberta, where a 6000 year old archaeological site documents the pursuit and consumption of bison by the ancestors of the Blackfoot people.

The archaeological remains from HSI made it abundantly clear that thousands of bison had been driven over the local cliffs. Equally impressive, however, was the ubiquitous evidence of fractured bison bones, thermally fractured stone cobbles and innumerable subsurface cooking features (see Figs. 3, 4) which were found over a ten hectare area. These kinds of residues were assumed to be the leavings of many episodes of bison jumps and food consumption activities.

There were no data available which addressed the question of how useful chip fuel would be in smoke-drying and roasting bison meat, if chip fuel could heat stones for placement in hide-lined boiling pits, or if chips could be used to heat the interiors of dwellings. In the absence of any detailed information that might bear on these questions, a series of experiments on the combustion of bison chips were conducted. These experiments were completed as part of the 1983 and 1984 archaeological field research at HSI, and the experimental results are discussed in more detail elsewhere.[26]

Experimental Archaeology

The objective of the experimental trials conducted at HSI was to replicate, as nearly as possible, the process by which bison meat and other remains were both consumed and converted into storable foodstuffs. Faced with the abundance of a successful kill involving several dozen bison, it was of paramount importance to process the carcasses before spoilage occurred. Undoubtedly some wastage did occur during each use of the jump, but to ensure that the proceeds of the kill continued beyond the period of immediate feasting it was important to preserve some of the meat. This preservation was probably achieved in a variety of ways, including simple drying (jerking) of the meat by hanging thin strips over smoky fires to augment the primary drying agents of wind and sun. This drying prevented spoilage of the meat by egg laying insects who could not penetrate the dried surface of the meat. We did not anticipate having any difficulty obtaining a smoky fire from chip fuel, for many of the early accounts suggested such results were easily attainable. Thus it seemed reasonable to predict that chip fueled hearths would have served admirably for smoke-drying bison meat. This jerked meat preserved well, but it was no match for the longer lasting and nutritionally superior stores of pemmican.

It seemed probable that some pemmican manufacturing occurred at Head-Smashed-In, or at least the preliminary phases of amassing the dried meat and fat stores from the bison carcass. These could then be transported to permanent camp locations for conversion into pemmican. The process of making pemmican involved pulverizing the jerked meat, mixing it with fat and berries, and then tight packing it in sewn hide bags. This near air-tight, containerized food could last for many months and, unlike jerked meat, contained a mix of protein and carbohydrates that was more nutritious and a much sought after trade commodity. Although provisioning for pemmican making may have been important, it was expected that most archaeological residues at Head-Smashed-In represented evidence of direct food consumption. This would include the cooking of meat on roasting platforms of stone, both on the surface of the ground and in earth covered pits (Fig. 3). The most impressive residues were the large, subsurface pit features which were tightly packed with bone and thermally fractured stone cobbles (Fig. 4). These appeared to conform perfectly to the large hide-lined pits referenced in the ethnographic and historical accounts and thus would have served as the main cooking facility at Head-Smashed-In. The question remained as to whether chip fuel was capable of heating the sandstone slabs preferred for platform roasting and the many tonnes of thermally altered cobbles used for boiling stone cookery at the site.

For the Head-Smashed-In experiments, it was necessary to assemble the experimental supplies of chip fuel and stone and to replicate the hearth and pit features which had been observed at Head-Smashed-In. Although constructing the pit features and gathering of the rock supplies presented no major difficulties, identifying a source and collection strategy for supplying our chip fuel requirements posed a bit of challenge.

In order to make the experiment results authentic, we elected to use only bison chips and, therefore, sought to avoid any mixed cow and bison sample assemblages. The proximity of the Waterton National Park buffalo herd provided a potentially ideal supply, and it was with great anticipation that we approached the park officials with our request. We were disappointed, however; although the majority of the park staff did appreciate the sincerity of our request, it is national park policy that nothing leaves the park unless authorized by permit. We naively offered to provide any information that might be required to facilitate obtaining such a permit. In fact, we relished the chance of having the only permit of its kind in the nation! We were informed that such a permit is not processed locally, however, and it would need to be sent to the Parks Canada Head Office for consideration. The processing time for this permit was estimated to be about six weeks, we felt this was untenable given the normal processing time for the creation of the product itself. This initial failure led us to make a series of contacts with local wild game ranchers in Pincher Creek and Del Bonita. After much explanation and a good deal of incredulous snickering, we were granted permission to have as much of the "stuff" as we liked. In retrospect, it was probably the sight of government employees loading a government truck with chips that promoted the Cheshire grins.

There are no guidelines available to the would-be experimenter about selection criteria for bison chip fuel, and this is unfortunate given the imponderable variety of shapes, sizes, and textures available. Certain variables were deemed crucial, that being dryness, size, portability, and chip integrity. While it may seem logical to go for the largest chip, such as the awesome specimen noted by McHugh[27] measuring one metre in diameter and twenty-five centi-

Fig. 5. Experimental chip-fueled hearth. Note thermocouple probe inserted in lower right corner.

metres in height, there are drawbacks inherent in such a selection. Portability and integrity are almost as important as dryness when is comes to choosing one's chips. Very large or very thin specimens tend to fragment easily and disintegrate, as do specimens which have been exposed to long periods of weathering. It was determined that chips of moderate size and firm integrity, say in the range of thirty centimetres in diameter and ten centimetres in height, proved an optimal size for stacking purposes and remained intact during transport. The process of gathering chips was found to be a labour intensive activity, but it can be accomplished using untrained persons, including the very young and the very old. Mass participation was probably the key to assembling and transporting sufficient supplies of chip fuel in the prehistoric past, but we determined that two persons could just about fill a GMC 3/4 Ton Suburban with chips after about three hours of gathering activity. Despite its impressive volume, this collection of chips failed to make much of an impression on the truck's suspension.

The prehistoric fire makers likely would have used some form of tinder and a bow drill to initiate chip combustion. We opted to sacrifice experimental archaeological rigour and employed wood shavings and matches. A small amount of fragmented chip fuel was then set atop the burning tinder. This material would soon begin to smoke and sometimes flame in the presence of a breeze. Once the initial combustion had commenced, a further eight to ten chips were loosely packed to form a mound (Fig. 5). A thermocouple probe was inserted so that the temperature sensor was located in the midst of

Table 1 Chip and wood fuel combustion temperatures in degrees celsius

Fuel Type	Exp. No.	5 Minutes	10 Minutes	15 Minutes	20 Minutes
Bison chip 1983	1	250	630	755	645
	2	500	480	525	605
	3	610	675	655	700
Bison chip 1984	1	180	358	290	368
	2	148	393	388	371
	3	230	253	241	276
	4	136	211	224	239
Spruce 1983	1	255	285	365	436
	2	547	640	597	573
	3	668	625	563	611
	4	620	635	668	661
	5	480	531	545	675
	6	293	347	410	465
Poplar 1983	1	200	230	280	375
	2	330	425	455	480
	3	402	493	588	570
	4	240	520	575	596
	5	335	475	581	630
	6	304	430	498	545
	7	617	523	509	472

the fuel pile, and temperature readings were taken at five minute intervals, over a twenty minute experimental trial (Table 1).

A brief review of these data indicates significant differences between the chip fire temperatures attained in successive years. For example, in 1983 the average chip fuel temperature attained after twenty minutes of combustion was 650 degrees Celsius, while in 1984 this value dropped by more than 50% to 313 degrees Celsius. This large discrepancy in temperature values needed to be explained, and two solutions appeared possible: measurement error and inadequacies in the fuel. The equipment used to monitor hearth temperatures was not the same in 1983 and 1984, but comparisons between wood fuel temperatures using different measurement systems revealed no significant change. This left the possibility that the

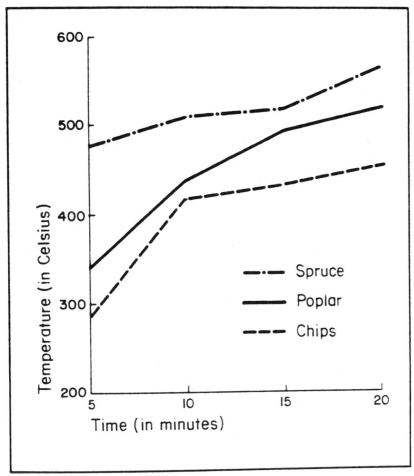

Fig. 6. Average temperature curves for the 1983 and 1984 wood and chip fires.

fuel was the culprit, and the records did indicate that we had changed our fuel supplier between 1983 and 1984. In the absence of other factors, it appears that the moisture content, or possibly the material make up of the 1984 chip fuel simply did not measure up to the quality of the 1983 chips.

Figure 6 presents averaged temperature curves for the 1983 and 1984 wood and chip fuel fires. This figure suggests that chip fuel burns cooler than wood fuel; in actual fact, the well-seasoned fuel of 1983 burned hotter than the wood fuel (see Table 1). In the course of averaging the 1983 and 1984 results, the apparently inferior quality

1984 fuel has suppressed the chip fuel temperature curve. It is interesting to note that, despite the supposedly inferior nature of the 1984 fuel, it was still possible to reach high chip fuel temperatures over the course of prolonged experiments.

As in any experimental exercise, there is always the temptation to push the materials and equipment to unprecedented levels of performance. This temptation was loosely disguised under the scientific label of "max burn" and occurred when optimal winds prevailed and the wood and chip fuel supply was plentiful. In brief, we heaped on supplies of fuel and monitored the fire until the temperature peaked, which, in the case of the 1984 chip fuel, occurred at 1003 degrees Celsius, while the 1984 spruce wood fuel reached a comparable 1040 degrees Celsius. The magnitude of the temperatures attained was impressive and caused some concern over the accuracy of our instrumentation, for it was hard to reconcile these temperature readings with the experimenter's personal impression of the respective fires. For example, the spruce wood fire which attained the 1040 degree Celsius temperature was a blazing inferno and provided plenty of radiant heat, intense light, lots of crackling sound effects, and occasional explosions of spark and ash that you come to expect from an outdoor fire. By comparison, the chip fire was a severe emotional let down, for it radiated little heat and provided none of the sensory outputs and excitement afforded by the wood fire. It appeared that the derisive historical commentaries on chip fueled fires may have been justified, for they were indeed a disappointment! Finding no fault with the accuracy of the temperature readings left us with the apparently unreconcilable facts that a 1000 degree Celsius chip fire, while hot enough to smelt a variety of metallic ores, was somehow incapable of providing sufficient heat for warming ones hands. This enigma was ultimately resolved through careful observation of the dynamics of chip combustion.

Much like any other fuel, chips burn from the exterior surface toward the interior, but this is where the similarity ends. Unlike wood fuel which is constantly in the process of shedding combusted residues, chips retain a mantle of ash and continue to burn toward their interiors. If left undisturbed, it is possible to completely burn a chip and have remaining in its place a perfect ash replica. This ash mantle serves to insulate the chip's combustion surface from other influences, which can be unfortunate should you be attempting to warm your frozen extremities! Radiant heat can be obtained from chip fires if this ash covering is removed. As an alternative, some early histor-ical accounts recommended the use of wood shavings and bison fat strips to augment the heat available from chip fires. Presumably, the radiant heat which was so obviously lacking in the chip fueled fires might also be captured through the use of a stone heat exchanger, as discussed in the ethnographic accounts.

Inference and Insight: The Case for Chip Fuel

The primary goal of archaeological inquiry is to infer what has gone on in previous times and places. These inferences can never be proven, or disproven; they do not stand as truths, but merely ap-proximations of what may have occurred. It cannot be proven that bison chips served as a fuel source during the prehistoric era, but the evidence available from historic documents and comparisons be-tween empirical observations (experimental archaeology) and the evidence found at prehistoric sites such as Head-Smashed-In seem fairly compelling. Other studies have argued the case for bison chip fuel from strictly empirical observations,[28] but some of the inferences derived from these experiments demonstrate a lack of insight into the merits of the fuel. For example, it seems unlikely that plains groups would ever have chosen to stockpile supplies of bison chips as a winter fuel store. This erroneous inference lead Holland to de-velop a scenario involving a stockpile of 1300 cubic feet of bison chips, weighing nearly six tons, assembled for purposes of heating a single dwelling over the course of one winter. Holland went to some pains to calculate the stacking volume of chips, and determined that keeping this stockpile dry would require a shelter bigger than that which it was designed to heat! Regardless of how you stack it, this proposition appears to be quite a load of chips. In all likelihood, the winter fuel requirements would have been met using the wood fuel available in the river valleys to which plains peoples retired in the winter. Even then it is highly improbable that an entire winter's wood fuel supply would have been stockpiled for subsequent con-sumption. Chips would never have stood as a wood fuel substitute, but at certain times of the year when people were mobile and focus-sing their activities on the prairie, this was likely the fuel of choice. What is remarkable are the ingenious means that prehistoric people devised to obtain radiant heat from this sometimes contrary fuel.

Conclusions

Chip fuel is probably among the most ancient, if not the most ancient form of fuel which continues to be employed by mankind. In Alberta, the use of bison chip fuel probably extends well back into the prehistoric past, possibly on a scale of several thousand years. In fact, the use of dung fuel may extend back to the first human presence in the province, at a time when the Alberta landscape was largely devoid of wood bearing plant species. [29] Shortly after the retreat of the last glacial ice mass major portions of the Alberta landscape would have been dominated by sedge and grass vegetation. This vegetation supported the plant eating animals which moved into the recently deglaciated region, and following behind them were the predators, including man. These now extinct plant eaters were of prodigious proportion and included the Mammoth, giant bison, and other large herbivores. On the assumption that the quantitative characteristics of dung are always in proportion to the species involved, there may have been a truly awesome supply of dung fuel available to these early human hunters.

Despite its humble appearance and lacklustre performance under fire, dung has never been in short supply, and its latent heat can be captured using other materials and a bit of ingenuity. Wood fuel may be a superior source of heat for most applications, but when the chips are down, and the wood fuel is exhausted a dimly glowing mound of dung may be your only reprieve from cold buffalo stew.

Acknowledgements

Several colleagues at the Archaeological Survey of Alberta provided advice and encouragement to research this important topic, all the while insisting that I was the only one qualified to undertake the task. Two anonymous reviewers are thanked for their insightful comments and scrutiny of the original text. Technical assistance in the production of this paper was provided by Martina Purdon, Karie Hardie, and Wendy Johnson. Special thanks are owed to Jack Brink who went beyond the limits of normal human endurance to obtain the dramatic, yet tasteful images of bison excreta from Waterton National Park (we hope Jack obtained the necessary permit?). Technical assistance toward the completion of the experimental studies was obtained from Don Sutherland and the Mechanical Engineering Department at the University of Alberta. The members of the Head-Smashed-In archaeological crew were seconded on various occasions to assist in the completion of rather extraordinary tasks for which thanks are extended; as promised, no names will be mentioned. Last, but not least, the bison of southern Alberta are thanked, for without them none of this would have been possible.

Milt Wright is the Northern Archaeologist with the Archaeological Survey, Provincial Museum of Alberta.

Notes
1. Milt Wright, "Le Bois de Vache: This Chip's for You." *Saskatchewan Archaeology 7* (1986), pp. 25–28.
2. See J. Brink, M. Wright, B. Dawe and D. Glaum, *Final Report of the 1983 Season at Head-Smashed-In Buffalo Jump, Alberta,* Archaeological Survey of Alberta Manuscript Series No. 1 (Edmonton, 1985), and J. Brink, M. Wright, B. Dawe and D. Glaum, *Final Report of the 1984 Season at Head-Smashed-In Buffalo Jump, Alberta, Archaeological Survey of Alberta* Manuscript Series No. 9 (Edmonton, 1986).
3. See F.G. Roe, *The North American Buffalo* (Toronto: University of Toronto Press, 1972), and T. McHugh, *The Time of the Buffalo* (New York: Alfred A. Knopf, 1972).
4. Roe, *The North American Buffalo,* p. 319.
5. D.J. Soper, "History, Range, and Home Life of the Northern Bison," *Ecological Monographs 2,* no. 4 (1941), pp. 349–412.
6. A.R. Turner, "Surveying the International Boundary, The Journal of George M. Dawson," *Saskatchewan History 21,* no. 1 (1968), pp. 1–24.
7. Roe, *The North American Buffalo,* p. 605—see note 24.
8. See Milt Wright, "Le Bois de Vache."
9. Roe, *The North American Buffalo,* p. 605.
10. Personal recollection of a resident of Fort Macleod.
11. Head-Smashed-In Buffalo Jump Interpretive Centre gift shop merchandise.
12. CBC Radio Interview from Claresholm Alberta, Fall 1989.
13. Roe, *The North American Buffalo,* pp. 605–6 and G.F. Will and H.J. Sinden, *The Mandans: A Study of Their Culture, Archaeology and Language.* Peabody Museum of American Archaeology and Ethnology Report 3, no. 4 (Harvard University, 1967), p. 117.
14. C. Wissler, *Material Culture of the Blackfoot Indians.* Anthropological Papers of the American Museum of Natural History No. 5, Pt. 1 (1910).
15. Walter McClintock, *The Blackfoot Beaver Bundle.* Southwest Museum Leaflet No. 3 (Los Angeles: Southwest Museum, 1935).
16. E. Verbicky-Todd, *Communal Buffalo Hunting Among the Plains Indians,* Archaeological Survey of Alberta Occasional Paper 24 (Edmonton: Alberta Culture and Multiculturalism, 1984), pp. 41–43.
17. McHugh, *The Time of the Buffalo.*
18. Isaac Cowie, *The Company of Adventurers: A Narrative of Seven Years in the Service of the Hudson's Bay Company During 1867–74 on the Buffalo Plains* (Toronto: William Briggs, 1913), p. 208.
19. G.L. Wilson, "The Horse and the Dog in Hidatsa Culture," *Anthropological Papers of the American Museum of Natural History 5,* Pt. 2 (1924), p. 268.
20. H.R. Schoolcraft, *Historical and Statistical Information Respecting the History, Condi-*

tion and Prospects of the Indian Tribes of the United States, 4 (Lippincott, Grambo and Company, 1856), p. 109.

21. Roe, *The North American Buffalo,* p. 606—see note 24.
22. J.A. Allen, "The American Bisons, Living and Extinct," *Memoirs of the Geological Survey of Kentucky* N.S. Shaler, Director, 1, Pt. 2 (Cambridge: University Press, 1876), p. 201.
23. McHugh, *The Time of the Buffalo,* p. 47.
24. G.B. Grinnell, *Blackfoot Lodge Tales* (London: David Nutt, 1893), p. 205.
25. Wissler, *Material Culture of the Blackfoot Indians,* pp. 26–27.
26. Brink, Wright, Dawe and Glaum, *Final Report of the 1984 Season at Head-Smashed-In Buffalo Jump,* pp. 185–88.
27. T. McHugh, "Social Behaviour of the American Buffalo (*Bison bison bison*)," *Zoologia: New York Zoological Society* 43, no. 1 (1958), p. 36.
28. T.D. Holland, "A Pilot Study of the Thermal Properties of Buffalo Chips," *Plains Anthropologist* 29, no. 104 (1984), pp. 161–66.
29. See D. Hopkins, J. Matthews, C. Schweger and S. Young, eds., *Paleoecology of Beringia* (New York: Academic Press, 1982).